MW00785461

M O T H E R

S A U C E ✦

MOTHER
SAUCE +

ITALIAN AMERICAN FAMILY RECIPES
AND THE STORY OF THE WOMEN
WHO CREATED THEM

+   +   +   LUCINDA SCALA QUINN

ARTISAN | NEW YORK

Library of Congress Cataloging-in-Publication Data

Names: Scala Quinn, Lucinda, author.
Title: Mother sauce : Italian American family
recipes and the story of the women who created
them / Lucinda Scala Quinn.
Description: New York : Artisan, [2025] |
Includes bibliographical references and index.
Identifiers: LCCN 2024027963 |
ISBN 9781648292019 (hardcover)
Subjects: LCSH: Cooking, Italian. | Cooking,
American. | LCGFT: Cookbooks.
Classification: LCC TX723 .S348 2025 |
DDC 641.5945—dc23/eng/20241009
LC record available at https://lccn.loc.gov
/2024027963

Book design by Raphael Geroni
Cover design by Becky Terhune

Published by Artisan,
an imprint of Workman Publishing,
a division of Hachette Book Group, Inc.
1290 Avenue of the Americas
New York, NY 10104
artisanbooks.com

The Artisan name and logo are registered
trademarks of Hachette Book Group, Inc.

Printed in China on responsibly sourced paper

First printing, January 2025

10 9 8 7 6 5 4 3 2 1

The grandparent is a rich mine of the Italian American imagination—mythical, real, imagined, idealized, venerated, or feared.

Start with a grandmother—those old women, sometimes illiterate or very little schooled, who had only their dreams, premonitions, and feelings to read for guidance. . . .

Feel an intense connection with the older generations and revere their iconoclasm, peculiarity, uncongeniality, and strength. In our grandparents is incorporated all of the past, all of tradition and custom, and, we imagine, some archetypal wisdom and native intelligence. We start from the people who came here.

—Helen Barolini, *The Dream Book*

AFTER WE BURY HER

How many times without complaint
Did her hands mix cold, raw meat, cheese
Eggs, parsley, breadcrumbs.
Fingers freezing, yolk oozing
Through knuckles, hours spent
Molding, mixing, browning,
Hands slippery with fat,
Washing bowls, scrubbing pans. . . .

—Dorian Cirrone, in *The Milk of Almonds*

CONTENTS

PREFACE: Aquilina's Daughters 9

INTRODUCTION: A Foodway Created by Our Italian Immigrant Grandmothers, Mothers, and Daughters 11

MAMMA KNEW: Frugal Ways to Cook in Your Own Kitchen 21

PROVISIONS TO HAVE ON HAND 27

32 Simmered on the Stovetop
SAUCY MEATS AND HEARTY SOUPS

64 Between-Meal Snacks
BREADS, PICKLES, AND TIDBITS

96 Sauced and Tossed Pasta
MACARONI DISHES FINISHED IN A SAUCEPAN

128 Layered and Baked
SAVORY OVEN-COOKED ONE-PAN MEALS

158 Cooked in a Skillet
SEARED AND SAUCED MEATS ON THE STOVETOP

182 Feasting on Fish
SEAFOOD DISHES FOR EVERY DAY AND FOR CELEBRATIONS

218 Garden and Greens
DELICIOUS SIDE DISHES
MADE FROM BELOVED
ITALIAN PRODUCE

244 Eats from the Streets
SANDWICHES AND
SWEETS INSPIRED BY
FESTIVAL FOODS

268 Sweets
TRADITIONAL PASTRIES,
CAKES, AND COOKIES

Further Reading 310

Shopping Resources 311

Acknowledgments 312

Index 314

AQUILINA'S DAUGHTERS

I am the proud great-granddaughter of a pistol-packing, beer-swigging, gambling, boss-of-her-block Italian American contessa who lived in turn-of-the-century East Rome, New York. Even before the 1906 train wreck that almost demolished the family row house, Aquilina Ferlo's life was an arduous one. She ran the family's boardinghouse and saloon, all the while often traveling back and forth to New York City's Ellis Island to retrieve other arriving southern Italian immigrant families sponsored by her husband, my great-grandfather Thomas Ferlo, who owned the businesses and worked as the baker and grocer. Aquilina was the business head of the family. By 1912, she had already made a couple of transatlantic crossings herself, the first at fifteen years old, after my great-grandparents' 1893 wedding in Aquilina's native Rogliano, Cozenza. After an overland mule-and-buggy trek through the dry southern landscape of Calabria to a small boat in the Strait of Messina headed to the port of Naples for embarkation, they finally sailed the 3,000 miles to New York City. The December 11 manifest from the ship *Kronprinz Fr. Wilheim* listed Aquilina Spadafora's occupation as "wife" (although her first name was actually written as "Angela"

there). Tommaso, a twenty-six-year-old "farmworker," was registered on the line above her, with his original surname, Ferraiuolo, still intact. Together they raised nine children to adulthood in America, while almost as many perished before or during childbirth or soon after.

Forty-five years ago, I began a journey to discover the history of the Italian women in my family. My late grandmother's sisters, all in their eighties and nineties, mostly still lived within blocks of one another in Rome, New York. During my several visits with each of them, pictures were snapped, stories transcribed, and faded photographs collected—and we cooked. Their mamma, Aquilina Spadafora Ferraiuolo, like millions of Italian women from the Mezzogiorno between 1880 and 1924, fled poverty and starvation for the promise of a better life in America. Within these pages are recipes for a foodway built on the backs of our Italian great-grandmothers, grandmothers, mothers, and daughters who made their way in the Land of Plenty. But the story often overlooks the role these women played in creating Italian American food. This book honors their memory.

INTRODUCTION

A FOODWAY CREATED BY OUR ITALIAN IMMIGRANT GRANDMOTHERS, MOTHERS, AND DAUGHTERS

In America, nonna's cooking is everyone's favorite food. Chances are that pasta and pizza were among your first beloved meals as a child. All kinds of cooks in kitchens across the nation prepare some version of spaghetti swirled into bowls with red sauce, served under fluffy clouds of finely grated cheese. Italian American cuisine is comfort food so delicious that it is embraced by eaters globally and has become a cornerstone of the authentic American food story.

Our immigrant Italian mammas fashioned a whole new foodway despite being ostracized from the mainstream society of their newly adopted country. These remarkable women in Little Italys nationwide gave birth to a cooking style that their fathers, husbands, and sons then went on to monetize outside their homes. They recognized the value of this cooking, and before long, red sauce joints arose around the country in an attempt to approximate the flavors and feelings of eating mamma's home-cooked food around an Italian family table. Its adoption by our culture transcends tasty physical nourishment. It also telegraphs the warmth of emotional wellness experienced at a multigenerational dining table rich with boisterous conversation and camaraderie. A male Italian American chef will give a nod to the memory of his grandmother's Sunday dinner, but rarely are these women actually credited as the real founders of the cooking that became known as Italian American. This is *their* story.

THE IMMIGRANT ITALIAN WOMAN

The job of an immigrant Italian wife at home was a herculean one. Although it is well documented that most male Italian immigrants worked at manual labor jobs, while others became bakers, cheesemakers, fishermen, butchers, or pushcart produce vendors, much less has been written about the women who toiled away at the equally demanding physical and psychological labor involved in domestic chores and child-rearing. They alone had to prepare the family meals through the sheer grit of necessity. Multiple mouths needed to be fed every day with little money and few other resources. Valuable imported provisions (often purchased at the expense of rent) like olive oil, salt, cheese, and prosciutto, kept hidden away under a floorboard to safeguard them, were rationed out to flavor the daily bread, macaroni, beans, greens, soups, sauces, and cheap meats.

As they were for most non-English-speaking immigrant women in the United States in those days, options for work, marriage, and overall life choices were limited by the conventions of the times. The gauzy lens of my third-generation memories and clichéd images of smiling bighearted Italian mammas, ready to selflessly feed everyone, belie a much deeper truth. At the turn of the twentieth century, the kitchen and the dining table were the only creative power centers for immigrant Italian women. The stove was their canvas, the kitchen their studio, and the family seated around the dining table their audience. This was both a gift and a never-ending burden. For most people, being able to afford a meal outside the home was impossible. But despite living in a male-dominated culture, irrevocably dependent upon on their fathers, husbands, brothers, and/or sons, Italian women in cities and towns nationwide managed to endure. They each made their own special sauce, which not only is still cherished today but also inspired a whole canon of beloved, iconic recipes. Every Italian American family has its own personal interpretations of the classics.

THE JOURNEY FROM THE MEZZOGIORNO TO AMERICA

Between 1880 and 1920, more than four million southern Italians migrated to the United States from Liguria, Abruzzo, Campania, Calabria, Apulia, Basilicata, and Sicily. Life in the Mezzogiorno (southern Italy and Sicily), ruled by Spanish Bourbons for 264 years, was under a stranglehold because of the discriminatory practices of the feudal landlords who dominated that southern economy. Land and grazing animals were loaned to peasants in exchange for crops and livestock care, but most of the produce and meat went to the overlords. Any hopes for real reform in post-unification 1871 Italy were soon dashed by the ruling policies of the north. Crippling taxes and little investment resulted in one of the greatest mass migrations in world history. Before the unification of Italy, only 25,000 refugees (most of them skilled artisans) came to the United States from northern Italy. Consequently, Italian American cooking

emerged largely from the culinary practices of the south. These recipes have descended from those impoverished immigrants who used newly available ingredients to re-create the taste memories of their ancestral homes.

The first and largest groups of immigrants were male, the so-called "birds of passage" who were either single men (many of whom eventually returned to Italy to find a wife) or husbands who left their families behind in Italy to establish a life in America, where, reputedly, the streets were "paved with gold." The majority of early emigrés came from rural regions. Some were enticed by (often-broken) promises from steamship agents or labor recruiters who supplied unskilled laborers for American owners of mines and factories. A financed voyage and job guarantee unknowingly came with high interest rates to be paid back through the garnishment of future wages. Other sons of the Mezzogiorno simply took the historic opportunity to break free of a father's control over a dead-end future. Unmarried daughters and sisters had no such path forward.

The women left behind in Italy shouldered the significant burden of keeping their families together, often safeguarding a daughter's reputation (and their own), while facing the risk of being abandoned by their husbands for other women in America. These women endured an impoverished yet familiar lifestyle in rural villages where everyone spoke the same dialect, lived and died in the same dwellings, and observed the same celebratory patron saints' days. Husbands and fathers abroad managed to keep close tabs on their families' activities back home through written messages and word-of-mouth travel reports. It wasn't uncommon for the early Italian immigrants to make multiple voyages back and forth to their hometowns in Italy.

By 1900, letters with enthusiastic reviews of life in the United States were arriving in the Mezzogiorno. Along with the prospect of a continuous stream of money from homesick relatives and friends, these lured other family members as well as further waves of the population to make the journey overseas. In addition, most prospective travelers were sponsored by family and friends already settled in America. Catholic aid organizations coordinated with parishes in Italy and the U.S. to assist immigrants, no longer just men but often families, who lacked support and aid from legitimate sponsors. Catholic hostels, missions, schools, and hospitals were created to help settle them in their new country. The Church (and its community) would continue to play a critical role in their lives beyond religious worship.

During the grueling transatlantic crossing, single women were separated from men on board. Families were crammed into tiny cubicles. The overcrowded steerage class, vermin-filled and redolent of waste, was down below next to the ship's deafening steering equipment. Passengers slept on straw mattresses with life-jacket pillows and ate dried bread and watery soups. When stormy seas subsided, they took turns outside on the tiny open deck space shared with laboring crew members in dirt-filled air from the smokestacks. The long sixty- to ninety-day voyage culminated in arrival at a crowded port of entry such as Ellis Island in New York City, which was the largest. None of the new immigrants understood English, but families had to pass a government health inspection, hoping to avoid both separation and exploitation by opportunists. Some immigrants settled in New York, while others still had weeks of further travel before reaching their destinations. Once they had been cleared by immigration, "home" usually meant family upon immigrant family crammed together in a tenement building. It didn't take long for the prevailing myth of America to be overturned. One glimpse of the human multitudes in a port city—a cacophony of noise, serious overcrowding, and the scent of filth—could be an assault on all the senses.

When these southern Italian immigrants arrived in America, they became generically "Italian," lumped together with countrymen and -women from dozens of different regions. Yet families from the same villages or provinces were able to find their own in the first newly adapted enclaves in the cities of the eastern seaboard. New York City, or, often, Philadelphia, Boston, Baltimore, or Providence, was the starting point for most. Others—either to connect with sponsors or enticed by news of jobs—headed to upstate New York, other parts of Pennsylvania, Connecticut, or Vermont. Early on, New Orleans received many Sicilians who had been lured there by the citrus trade. Other immigrants traveled west to family and jobs in Chicago, San Diego, or San Francisco. By 1910, districts of Italian immigrants escaping urban congestion had cropped up in every corner of America to farm or fish commercially, toil in the mines, or build the canals, reservoirs, highways, and railways of the growing, prosperous country. Grocers, butchers, and bakers fed the Italian laborers and their families with familiar foods. Some Italian markets dating back to 1896 still operate here today (see Shopping Resources, page 311).

MY FAMILY STORY

Every summer of my childhood, my parents undertook a twelve-hour overnight car trip to visit our Italian grandparents' house in upstate New York. The four of us kids slept side by side in the "way back" of our woodie station wagon, like linguine noodles in a box. Despite the early-morning arrival time, there would be trays of lasagna, baked ziti, pots of meatballs, and platters of cannoli waiting to greet us. We played in the greenhouse and gardens among tall vines of pole beans and fragrant tomato plants, visited Utica bakeries for tangy-sweet cups of lemon ice, and picnicked with cousins, aunts, and uncles at Lake Delta, just as the old-timers did. Little me was vaguely puzzled by the all-encompassing domestic work of my grandmother and aunts, while at the same time fascinated by the cigar-smoking, anisette-sipping great-uncles, who sat together all afternoon under a cloud of fragrant tobacco, playing cards, arguing, and laughing.

Like many Italians in this country, some of our relatives held strong to their culture, while others strove to assimilate and drop the old language in search of an Anglo-Saxon ideal. My grandmother Mary, the first educated woman of the family, disapproved of her mamma, Aquilina, with her big, boisterous, autonomous, broken-English personality. She aspired to a more genteel life of propriety and luncheons. Her old recipe box is filled with formulas for the family meatballs, minestrone, and tomato sauce, but it also includes such random recipes as one for an aspic ring and another for crab-salad–stuffed tomatoes. As a young serviceman, my father, Carmine George Scala, dropped "Carmine," unable to brook the ridicule his name brought upon him; henceforth, he always signed his name C. George Scala. He revolted against his overbearing Italian mother, marrying

our mom, the tall, blue-eyed beauty, and so-called WASP, of his dreams. Mom's stories of her first introduction to his Italian family sounded as if an alien had descended on Earth. Over time, though, the Italian aunts and sisters-in-law embraced her completely, especially Dad's sister Gina, a unique and independent teacher and single mother of four, modeled more after her unapologetic grandmother Aquilina than her very proper mother, Mary. It is ironic that my mother not only mastered her mother-in-law's Italian cooking, as expected of any good Italian wife, but transformed, streamlined, and improved on those recipes, which my brothers and our families still cook today.

For every indomitable Italian immigrant woman like Aquilina, who carried the weight of the family on her back, there was someone from the next generation like her oldest daughter, Mary—educated and desirous of liberation and change from cooking, cleaning, and doing laundry for the men and children in her life. Still, options remained limited for women. By the mid-twentieth century, cooking in the family kitchen and serving at the dinner table were still the major creative outlets for most immigrant Italian women in America, whether they liked it or not. Holidays and regular Sunday dinners were the main events over which the mammas were the maestros. No family member dared to miss Sunday dinner.

Now I've practically become *that* Italian grandmother—the one who cooks food that you can't resist, stuffs your belly at any chance, and begs for you to stay at the dinner table just a little longer—with one crucial difference. Unlike my great-grandmother, my grandmother, and her sisters, I have a choice, a choice I have had the privilege to make on my own. The independent Italian woman in America was decades in the making. Nevertheless, along the way, she sowed the seeds for the birth of an original Italian American foodway. Even if that food is not a part of your personal heritage, it is our collective one now. In America, one is likely to have had a neighbor, roommate, or friend whose multigenerational Italian family swept her up into their kitchen and dining room. Today, all around this country, we flock to Italian American restaurants when we are seeking our favorite comfort meals.

AMERICAN-MADE ITALIAN FOOD

Most Italian families who arrived in early-1900s America landed in very challenging living situations. Mamma began every morning stoking the stove to heat water for bathing herself and her children, and for cleaning the apartment or house, clothes, and kitchen sink, before a meal was ever made. With few opportunities outside the home, some women did work in factories, but most took in sewing or washing or sold two-cent squares of tomato pie from their tiny kitchens. Some women, after cooking dinner for their own families, set up a few tables in the living room to feed others to make ends meet. Those meals of home-cooked food served to paying guests were the forerunners of the true Italian American restaurant as we know it today. Soon nonna's food, recognized by husbands and sons to be in demand, was being taken to a corner store or underground rental space, places where the first Italian American trattorias began. Behind every

Patsy's, Rao's, or Carrabba's Italian American restaurant, there's a trail of mothers and grandmothers whose ingenuity made it possible.

American-made Italian cooking is a descendant of a cooking style known as "cucina povera" (the cooking of the poor), which is found in all regions of Italy. The food of peasants throughout the country—whether in the cities or the countryside, and regardless of the varied cultural influences—relied on easily available ingredients and an imaginative use of them to turn them into a desirable meal.

One hundred years ago or so, the daily diet of impoverished residents in southern Italy was based primarily on grains, beans, and limited produce. Durum wheat and chestnuts were ground into flour and mixed with water for bread or macaroni. Clever methods of breaking up and hydrating the dried leftovers repurposed them into a completely different meal. Foraged wild greens were simmered in soup with dried lentils or fava beans. Homegrown seasonal vegetables such as tomatoes, peppers, and eggplants were harvested and eaten fresh, of course, but the rest were "put up" to be consumed during the colder months. Women of the community gathered together in the fall to dry tomatoes in the sun and prepare large batches of tomato paste that were formed into small dried bricks for the larder.

Meat was eaten rarely, reserved for very special occasions. Every part of the animal was used. Slow-simmering tenderized the tough cuts and coaxed out the deep flavors. Techniques to preserve various parts of the animal produced endless varieties of sausage and salumi. Inland shepherds made pecorino cheeses from fresh grass-fed sheep's milk and aged it to various stages of ripeness for storage. Coastal southerners ate fish and seafood—especially less-desirable, inexpensive species like eel and squid. Cod, at the time teeming in local waters, was both salted and air-dried to preserve it. Many Italian sweets owe their origins to the fruits that thrived in the blistering southern Italian sun, including citrus, plums, and melons. Cooking habits developed from bare necessity in Italy became prized practices upon arrival in America.

These traditional cooking techniques and ingredients that immigrated with our ancestors blossomed into an expanded cuisine once they merged with America's lush bounty of produce. *This* was the true manifestation of the myth—rather than the streets being "paved with gold," our fields, forests, and farms were. If once a provenance of the poor, cucina povera gradually evolved into a respected and even desirable way of cooking in more modern times.

Whenever I make the food of my immigrant Italian family, I try to embody the spirit and reality of the women who were cooking at the end of the nineteenth century. They didn't follow recipes from cookbooks. And of course they didn't have modern preparation equipment like blenders or food processors or dishwashers to clean all the dirty dishes. This book steps into the shoes of a genuine nonna churning out meals every day at home. These classic recipes rely on an old-school mindset, combined with streamlined directions, using as few ingredients as possible to create a platonic ideal of modern Italian American food. Over time, some dishes have been adapted, new ingredients added and others retired, and recipe titles have changed. After all, isn't that what we have always done? Subsequent generations personalize traditions, replace outmoded ideas, and teach future cooks who, in turn, will make Italian American food their own way.

MAMMA KNEW

FRUGAL WAYS TO COOK IN YOUR OWN KITCHEN

Immigrant grandmothers, mothers, and daughters, who did all the cooking in their family kitchens, as well as canning and preserving food, plus the housecleaning, laundry, ironing, sewing, and shopping, knew a thing or two about organization. Children underfoot, small spaces, and very limited resources underpinned their everyday lives. Fortunately, nowadays men share these domestic tasks with women. But the first generations of Italian mothers and daughters were raised in twentieth-century America on fifteenth-century southern Italian customs. Even the most autonomous woman was captive to the patriarchy, albeit often the power behind the throne.

With their feet now planted tenuously on American soil, these women made the survival and well-being of their families their focus. Family and food were their essential responsibility and the well from which they derived their self-worth and power. Along the way, they employed instinctive strategies for everyday survival that you can employ in your own kitchen and that are still relevant today.

✢ Waste Nothing

Always save the tops and tails of green beans and other vegetables: Collect usually discarded trimmings and scraps of produce in a large resealable freezer bag whenever you peel and cut an onion, chop celery or zucchini, strip the leaves from parsley stems, pull off the tough outer leaves of a cabbage, or core a cauliflower or tomatoes. Keep the bag in the freezer, and when it is full, add all the bits to a pot of boiling water, reduce the heat, partially cover, and simmer for 40 minutes. Strain and season this vegetable broth and store in the refrigerator for 4 or 5 days or in the freezer for up to several months.

Modern recipes often direct us to discard rather than retain the liquids left from soaking and/or cooking nutritional ingredients. Instead, save starchy macaroni cooking liquid, bean liquor, and grain-soaking water. These are flavorful, frugal ways to enrich soups, sauces, and stews. The same goes with the hydrating liquid from dried mushrooms and sun-dried tomatoes.

Strain the liquids through a sieve and use immediately, or label and store in reusable 1-pint (475 ml) containers (2 cups are more often called for in a recipe than a whole quart/950 ml). Tightly cover these once cooled and refrigerate for a few days or freeze up to 6 months. (You can freeze smaller quantities in ice-cube trays, wrapped in plastic.) Frequently these flavorful liquids can replace chicken or beef stock in a recipe.

✧   Stretch or Swap Ingredients

Buy whole birds and cuts of meat: Lower your costs by customizing these at home (see page 168). Store chicken backs and wing tips in a resealable freezer bag until you have enough to make a rich chicken broth (page 179) for soup or stew. Debone that pork or lamb leg yourself (or have the butcher do it). Then the meat can be cut up or otherwise prepared per the recipe instructions. Bones make rich broths or can flavor a pot of beans for another meal.

Make and elevate your own breadcrumbs: Yesterday's bread heels and today's crusts can be ground together to both stretch your protein and bind ingredients. Hydrate dried breadcrumbs in milk or water to moisten, lighten, and stretch ground meat mixtures. Toast breadcrumbs in olive oil with salt and anchovy to replace expensive grated cheese and sprinkle them over macaroni. Tailor-make your own flavored breadcrumbs with fresh herbs and spices (see page 42).

Use what you have: Within these pages are recipes for success. When necessary, flip your thinking around and lead with the ingredient first. If you crave eggplant Parmesan but there's zucchini in your garden, use the zucchini instead. When spinach or Swiss chard is called for in a soup, most other leafy greens can be substituted beautifully. Dried beans, properly cooked, are interchangeable in most dishes. Grated hard cheeses, like Parmesan and Romano, can be swapped for each other. Think like the mammas who cooked at home every day by maximizing available ingredients.

✧   Flavor Every Bite

Season your food properly: Salt makes all food taste good. It also preserves and heightens flavor. Home-cooked food well seasoned with good salt is vastly more healthful than any commercially processed food. When searing meat or fish in a hot pan, pat it dry with a paper towel and salt it just before adding it to the pan. If it is salted too early, the surface of the meat will sweat and prevent it from browning. (Early salting for tenderness is an entirely different technique, not applicable to the recipes here.) Wait to season a simmering pot of soup or sauce until the end of cooking. As the simmering liquid evaporates, the flavors will concentrate and the dish could finish up too salty.

As for spiciness, many varieties of red chili peppers thrived in the sunny, arid landscapes of southern Italy whereas black pepper was an expensive luxury that most arriving cooks in America had not yet encountered. Thus, red pepper has retained a prominent place in flavoring and preserving in Italian cooking in America.

✧   Assemble a Set of Basic Kitchen Tools

You need one big pot and one big skillet. Use a large heavy oven-safe pot with a tight-fitting lid for simmering and boiling on the stovetop

or for cooking in the oven. Even if you cook for just a few people, using a pan with a large surface area, such as a 12- or 14-inch (30 or 35 cm) skillet in which all the ingredients can be cooked at once, will economize on time. Then choose a cast-iron, enameled cast-iron, carbon-steel, or stainless steel lidded frying pan to keep near the stove, ready and easy to pull out and use every day. A large pasta boiling pot, a baking sheet, a casserole dish, a cake pan, and a pie plate complete the vessel kit.

Try to develop an instinct for using your pot or pan lid to add or reduce cooking time to aid in the final texture and flavor of a dish. There's a world of options beyond just "uncovered," "covered," and "partially covered" to hasten the cooking time or slow it down, to evaporate liquid or retain it.

You also want a large cutting board, preferably one that you can lay on the counter between the sink and the stove. A sturdy colander for draining is also a must, along with prep bowls in a few sizes, measuring cups and spoons, and a cheese grater. A trio of knives—chef's, paring, and serrated (along with a sharpener)—plus a strong pair of

kitchen shears will enable you to achieve all your cutting tasks.

Keep a countertop crock filled with the essentials: One large and one small wooden cooking tool to stir, scrape, and serve. A utility cooking fork to lift and turn proteins and vegetables during prepping, breading, or frying and to transfer ingredients from a prep plate to a pan and vice versa. A pasta "spork" to stir and taste noodles for doneness. A stainless steel whisk.

Beyond that, a clean wine bottle can stand in for a rolling pin. Parchment paper comes in handy for all sorts of kitchen uses. It's hard to imagine any modern kitchen without the convenience of a blender and/or food processor, but all the jobs in this book can be done by hand.

+ Plan Your Time

Plan prepping and cooking around other at-home chores. With groceries on hand, it takes little time to chop and assemble ingredients for many recipes, but some need hours to cook, which is the time to multitask other activities. Conversely, plan on quick-cooking dishes or a meal of repurposed leftover components on days when your time at home is limited. If you take the time to properly label, date, and store basics such as chicken stock, tomato sauce, breadcrumbs, and pastry or cookie dough in your freezer in resealable bags or containers, or to store leftovers in the fridge, then organizing meals to suit your schedule will be much easier.

+ Clean Up as You Cook

It's important to tidy up as you go, no exceptions, especially when you must perform multiple tasks in the same small space. Think ahead to the next meal or chore and begin with an organized area and a clear head. Wash, dry, and put away dirty dishes, pots, and pans as you go. Leave no dirty dishes in the sink! Wipe down the counters and sink. Sweep and wash the floor. Teach your family members and others to do the same.

+ Enlist Help

Historically, the women responsible for feeding multiple mouths in a family banded together to share the work of daily cooking duties by tag-teaming their efforts. Today most modern households don't adhere to bygone roles of duty. Dads, moms, sons, and daughters, as well as roommates, generally share household duties. Teach the members of your household how to pitch in and help with shopping, meal preparation, and cleanup. Many hands make for lighter work. Start modeling this behavior for your kids when they are young. Do their future adult selves a favor!

When it comes to meals, if need be, employ the use of some convenience foods, a luxury unthinkable to our nonnas. Good-quality jarred pasta sauces, frozen ravioli, fresh pizza dough from the bakery, and store-bought antipasto ingredients can augment home cooking without supplanting it.

+ Feed Everyone

Prepare as much food as you can afford to make every time you cook. Offer everyone seconds. And be prepared for last-minute guests: Don't turn anyone away from your table. Another seat or two can always be squeezed in. There should always be enough to feed another mouth or for leftovers to save for another meal or snack. With that in mind, the serving quantities in this book refer to the number of ample servings a dish makes, not how many people I think it should serve. Also, all these recipes can be doubled (or halved).

ASPETTA

"ASHpet!" Anyone who grew up with an old-timer Italian American in their lives heard this all the time. Uttered with a sense of surprise or urgency, or to call attention to a detail, it beckons us to hang on for one more thing. Before a thought is forgotten, "Aspetta."

The pronunciation depended on one's dialect. I can imagine it came often from the lips of my grandmother and her sisters, corralling my dad, the firstborn child of his generation, whom they affectionately called "Boy." Dad said "Aspetta" to us kids a lot, usually accompanied by the finger purse: pinched fingers waved back and forth with a wrist-bending hand gesture. It rolled off his tongue to express a whole range of emotions: humor, joy, irritation, patience, lack of patience, you name it.

When you see "Aspetta" following one of the recipes on these pages, I am using it to say just one more thing before you move on—meaning there is another tidbit of information I can offer you. "Aspetta": Here's how you do it.

Read through any recipe you plan to cook before you get started. Assemble all the ingredients on your counter. Pull out the pot or pan you need. Wipe down your cutting board. Lay out your knife, cooking spoon, and measuring utensils. Prepare your ingredients before you start cooking. Wash the greens, scrub the shellfish, chop the onions, and mince the garlic. Place items that will be added at the same time together in one prep bowl or container as you work. Pull out a working platter if, for example, meat will have to be removed from a skillet while the sauce is made. Have a clean empty garbage bowl or bin ready. Heaven forbid there are dirty dishes in the sink; if there are, wash, dry, and put them away so you have space for newly used ones as you go.

Cooking is more relaxing and even fun when you can flow easily from one action to another, without having to stop and dig around to find something you need. Once the pan is fired, you should stay focused on the cooking, without having to stop and do another prep task before you can resume.

PROVISIONS to HAVE on HAND

Italian American cooking relies upon a constellation of fundamental building blocks used separately or in combination. Many recipes are made entirely from long-lasting, shelf-stable ingredients. While some meals require a trip to the grocer for fresh goods, the tried-and-true foundational ingredients, starting with olive oil and canned tomatoes, remain the same. Preparation techniques may change, cooking vessels and heat sources needed to achieve the diverse dishes we've fallen in love with may vary, but no recipe in this book requires hard-to-find components. If you're an everyday cook, it's comforting to know that you're prepared to produce a meal at a moment's notice. Improvisation requires forethought, so keep a list of your standard staples and restock the pantry and refrigerator as necessary so you don't run out.

✢ Shelf-Stable Ingredients

EXTRA VIRGIN OLIVE OIL: For daily cooking, buy extra virgin olive oil in bulk, for both value and practicality. Store it in a cool, dark place. Fill a small cruet to use daily, kept at the ready near your cooking area.

Purchase the oil from a popular purveyor that turns over their products frequently to ensure quality. There are dozens of brands to choose from, with a vast range of provenance, flavor, and price. If a bottle is simply labeled "olive oil," it means that most of the natural flavor has been treated and refined out of it to yield a dull, flavorless oil. Extra virgin olive oil is 100-percent cold-pressed, from the olives' first pressing. It is subject to strict regulations, from picking to processing and bottling. Look at the label for the bottling date, and use the oil within 2 to 3 years. A dark-colored bottle with a tightly sealed cap helps reduce degradation from light and oxygen. Depending on where you live, you might want to look at private labels from companies such as Costco that buy good-quality oils in enough volume to pass on value to the customer. Some good commercial brands to look for in the United States are California Olive Ranch Extra Virgin Olive Oil and Partanna Sicilian Extra Virgin Olive Oil. It's the single most important ingredient in this foodway. Even mamma, back in the day, with a limited budget, did not scrimp on olive oil.

CANNED TOMATOES: Whole canned tomatoes can be chopped or pureed according to the recipe and will generally retain more flavor than factory-cut or processed ones. Don't bother buying the various chopped or pureed versions available. Compare and taste brands. Buy according to flavor preference (not too acidic, although too much acidity can be offset with a pinch of sugar) and budget. Avoid succumbing to those marketing labels of a romantic pastoral Italy, which often hide oils of inferior quality. Bianco DiNapoli and Muir Glen Organic from California are solid, reliable American brands.

DRY PASTA: Keep a supply of three types in your cupboard: long strands (spaghetti, linguine, capellini), short ridged macaroni (rigatoni, penne, ziti), and small or tiny shapes (ditalini, pastina, orzo) for soups or stews. Experiment with premium brands if possible, as these usually have better flavor and stand up better to cooking. DeCecco and DeMartino are good commercial choices.

BREAD AND BREADCRUMBS: I use standard crusty Italian bread. Buy two loaves at a time and immediately freeze one (cut in half) while still very fresh to have on hand. Wrap it tightly in parchment paper, plastic wrap, or foil and place in a sealed freezer bag. The texture and taste of defrosted fresh bread is way better than that of day-old bread. Store the heels and dry bread in a resealable bag in the fridge or freezer to use for homemade breadcrumbs (see page 42). Avoid preseasoned store-bought breadcrumbs. But you can use plain panko breadcrumbs, which are dry with a large surface area, to make crunchy coatings or contribute to a fluffy filling; if necessary, they can be chopped or processed to a smaller size.

BEANS AND LEGUMES, DRIED OR CANNED: Ceci beans (chickpeas), cannellini beans, and lentils, once lowly foundation ingredients of the Italian peasant diet, are superstars today. Dried beans are cheaper than canned and tastier when cooked. Soak and cook them, portion them into containers, and freeze for several months. But canned beans are a convenient backup option, especially ceci beans, which don't usually overly soften as the others often do.

SEA SALT: Coarse salt has larger crystals than table salt, which makes it easier to pinch with your fingers when seasoning food by eye. Use one brand with crystals of the same weight and size consistently for cooking, and the salt level of your food will be predictable. Cubed sea salt and large flaky salts vary in volume. I recommend Diamond Crystal kosher salt for everyday cooking and baking. Flaky Maldon sea salt is considered the gold standard for garnishing.

DRIED RED PEPPER: For years, southern Italians have grown piquant red peppers for seasoning, which became part of Italian American cooking. Commercial red pepper flakes will bring heat without much flavor. If you can find small whole Calabrian peperoncini, stock up and store them in an airtight container. When ready to use, crush or crumble them yourself for a fruity yet lightly smoky note along with heat. See Peppers, page 80.

BLACK PEPPER: Buy whole black peppercorns and grind the pepper in the moment, especially when using it for a finishing flavor. Crushed whole peppercorns enrich stocks and broths. Avoid preground commercial black pepper, with its weak, generally inferior taste.

DRIED OREGANO AND THYME: Oregano is the most beloved (and sometimes abused) herb in the Italian American recipe canon. Buy dried oregano in small quantities and always taste before using. If your dried herbs are old, replace them if you want their true flavor to come through.

BAY LEAVES: Dried bay leaves bring a beautiful undertone not just to savory soups and stews, but also to sweet recipes (think herbal-floral, vaguely eucalyptus flavor). Fresh bay plants will thrive inside the home, and they bring a lighter herbal taste to food than the dried leaves do.

ONIONS, GARLIC, AND SHALLOTS: While all three alliums have their own distinctive identities, they can replace one another in a pinch. Italian American recipes do use garlic, aka "the stinking rose," but not as much as you might imagine, if the other ingredients are thoughtfully chosen and well balanced. While mamma's belief in its ability to ward off the evil eye is doubtful, garlic does have intense health-giving properties that are now well documented. Buy U.S.–grown garlic, firm to the touch and wrapped snugly in dry, taut skins.

VINEGAR AND WINE (RED AND WHITE): Vinegar-wise, regardless of budget, choose an affordable, reputable brand, as it'll be used often. Wine-wise, cook with what you like to drink. Marsala, Italy's most famous fortified wine, from Sicily, is used in both savory and sweet recipes. All three varieties—dry, semisweet, and sweet—are rich and nutty, with varying alcohol content. For everyday use in cooking and baking, stock Cantine Florio dry Marsala, or a similar dry Marsala.

JARRED CHERRY PEPPERS: Italians in America have grown and preserved their favorite peppers for years, but restaurants and home cooks have long relied on jarred spicy cherry peppers to enliven sautéed dishes or to serve on an antipasto platter. In cooking, the brine can be used to deglaze the pan and brighten cooked dishes; see Pork Chops with Vinegar Peppers (page 180) for an easy sauté made with these peppers.

OLIVES: Although there are multitudes of Mediterranean olives available, two classic types, Gaeta (black) and Castelvetrano (green), are good all-around choices to keep on hand for both snacking and cooking.

DRIED MUSHROOMS: Italians have a love for mushrooms of all kinds, and shelf-stable dried ones are a wonderful way of getting a concentrated mushroom flavor into your food. Porcini are the most commonly available. If they are stored in an airtight container, their flavor will last almost indefinitely. Hydrate them in water, chop, and use for fillings or sauces; save the soaking liquid to enhance a broth or sauce.

ANCHOVIES: Canned or tinned anchovies bring a deep, briny undertone to many dishes without adding a fishy flavor. Many sauces, rubs, dips, and dressings benefit from just a small amount of them. Salted and oil-packed anchovies both benefit from a rinse before using. The whole preserved little fish are preferrable to anchovy paste, which can have an inferior taste. When anchovies are added to hot oil during cooking and mashed, they completely dissolve. Ortiz is a fine commercial brand of jarred anchovies.

CANNED TUNA: One of the greatest Italian fish from ancient to modern times, tuna has been seasonally harvested in southern Italy and Sicily for millennia. Before refrigeration, preservation methods were essential. Canned tuna remains a pantry staple in American food. I always stock a few cans of "solid" or "fancy" chunk tuna. Imported jars of tuna packed in olive oil are relatively expensive but have a richer flavor than canned.

ALL-PURPOSE FLOUR: All-purpose flour works well for all the breads and baked goods in this book. However, you can expand your pantry to experiment with a few specialty flours. With its higher gluten content, which results in a stronger and more elastic dough, bread flour will enhance the texture of the dough for the Prosciutto Bread (page 71) or the Tomato Pie (page 69). Double 00 flour can swap in for all-purpose for homemade pasta. It also has a higher percentage of gluten than all-purpose flour (though less than bread flour), which results in dough with less elasticity, making it easier to roll out. But neither is mandatory for good results!

YEAST: Keep yeast on hand to satisfy a craving for fresh homemade bread or pizza. Unopened dry yeast will remain active for up to 2 years. If stored in the refrigerator or freezer, it generally keeps longer than the sell-by date.

✣ **Refrigerated and Fresh Staples**

CHEESES, INCLUDING PECORINO ROMANO, PARMIGIANO-REGGIANO, RICOTTA, MOZZARELLA, AND PROVOLONE: Although when you are preparing trays of lasagna or ziti in bulk, it's tempting to use packaged pregrated cheese, there is no comparison between cheese freshly grated from a wedge and packaged

CURED MEATS, INCLUDING SALAMI (SOPPRESSATA AND CAPICOLA), PROSCIUTTO, AND MORTADELLA: Picture the days before refrigerators were common, when southern Italian peasants had to invent ways to safely preserve meat from a whole animal, and or to supplement meager supplies of fresh protein. Few ingredients embody the history of a people as salumi does. *Salumi* is the general term for cured meats preserved from the whole animal, while *salami* refers to specific aged varieties. Fast-forward to modern days, when sliced cured meats are a star of antipasto platters and Italian sandwiches. Small quantities are used to augment and season many savory dishes and to flavor a pasta sauce or stuffing. These salty pork products can sometimes be used interchangeably in a pinch.

HERBS, INCLUDING BASIL, ROSEMARY, OREGANO, AND SAGE: Plant fresh basil (an annual) every summer. It's the quintessential aromatic for fresh vegetables. Rosemary, sage, and oregano are perennials that thrive year-round in gardens and window boxes to yield year after year. Store-bought fresh herbs are expensive and rarely used up in one go. Herbs with roots attached last longer stored upright in a container with water. For others, add a damp cloth to the container to help them last a little longer. Fresh herbs also have a milder flavor than dried herbs. Adjust the amount used in a recipe when one is switched for the other.

pregrated cheese. The flavor of freshly grated is far more intense. Traditionally Pecorino cheeses (from various degrees of aging) were primarily used by southern Italians, with access to milk from local sheep. These recipes use a basic aged Pecorino with a hard, crumbly texture and rich, salty flavor. A sturdy cheese grater is a must. When the cheese is used up, the rinds (collect them in a resealable freezer bag) will lend deep flavor to soups and stews. Mild, salty, and quick-melting fresh mozzarella tastes the best, but commercial varieties will work just fine. Provolone, which has a big, complex nutty flavor, slices and melts well for sandwiches and brings power to baked pasta dishes. And it's easy to make fresh ricotta at home; see page 78. Whether homemade or store-bought, fresh ricotta spoils quickly, so use it within 3 days.

CITRUS, INCLUDING LEMONS AND ORANGES: Cooked dishes and baked goods with roots in Sicily and the rest of southern Italy rely heavily on citrus fruit for flavor and sweetening, as it has always grown there abundantly, and fresh citrus zest and juice are ubiquitous in Italian American recipes. For candied citrus rind, seek out an imported variety.

STOVETOP +

SAUCY
MEATS
and
HEARTY
SOUPS

37 Sunday Sauce

39 Meatballs in Tomato Sauce

46 Beef Braciola

49 Rigatoni with Meat Sauce (RAGÙ)

53 Bucatini with Sausage Ragù

54 Chicken Parm Meatballs

57 Italian Wedding Soup

58 Cannellini Bean Soup

60 Green Minestrone

63 Tomato Sauce (SUGO)

IN EVERY ICONIC ITALIAN AMERICAN
home kitchen, there is a pot filled with tomato sauce simmering away on the stovetop at least one day a week, often more. "Stir the sauce" is both mamma's mental reminder to herself and a shout-out to anyone heading through the kitchen. Whether you're cooking in a humble or high-end household, a small kitchenette or a large gourmet kitchen, someone will stroll up to the stove, inhale the aromas from your pot, and seed a feeling that will create warm future memories. In an instant, one whiff can trigger that memory. One single inhalation of a bubbling red sauce, and we instantly time-travel back to our Italian grandmother's kitchen.

Sunday Sauce is chock-full of meats and a couple dozen simmering meatballs, and, on special occasions, Beef Braciola. The quicker-cooking Sausage Ragù is built on crumbled and sautéed richly flavored sausage meat. Sometimes a simple dish of spaghetti twirled in a buttery smooth Tomato Sauce is all you want! For weekday meals, Cannellini Bean Soup and vegetal Green Minestrone are both sufficient in themselves when accompanied by crusty bread and a glass of wine. Along with Italian Wedding Soup, each of these is a perfect starter for a larger feast on a special occasion. Regardless of what's inside that pot, it's a vessel of nourishment—a lifeline that holds the family together and fortifies body, mind, and soul.

SUNDAY SAUCE

A tomato sauce with the thickness and consistency of gravy, flavored with a base of meat drippings, is called "gravy" in the Italian communities of New Jersey and South Philadelphia. In the densely populated Italian American communities of Boston, Chicago, Rhode Island, and San Francisco, it's just "sauce." Regardless, it's meant to feed the whole extended family abundantly on Sunday after Mass, during the so-called day of rest. Let's face it, making the sauce is not exactly restful for the cook, but it's a labor of love. It anchors a feast, large or small, meant to be consumed languorously at the table over several hours.

As a rule of thumb, plan on about 1 pound (455 g) of meat per 28-ounce (800 g) can of tomatoes, and 3 garlic cloves per pound of pasta; use a combination of bone-in and boneless beef, pork, and/or veal, depending on what you prefer or is available at the market. Less-expensive braising cuts like chuck or shank, with their marbled fat and bones, bring the most flavor to the sauce. Trim off any excess fat to prevent the sauce from being too greasy. The meatballs get dropped into the simmering gravy to cook toward the end. Sausages vary widely in saltiness and seasoning, so unless you're using a familiar source, cook them in a separate pan and then add at the end to prevent them from overpowering the final flavor. If you're a regular Sunday sauce family cook, you'll want a large Dutch oven (such as an enamel-coated cast-iron pot) and an extra-large boiling pot to accommodate up to 2 pounds (910 g) of macaroni at a time. Finally, meal preparation is much more fun, and less exhausting, if you shop a day or two in advance and prep a few things ahead on Saturday, so you can get a fresh start on cooking the food and setting your table on Sunday morning.

Makes 8 to 10 servings

1 pound (455 g) pork ribs—country-style, back ribs, or spareribs

1 pound (455 g) bone-in beef shank, chuck, or short ribs

Coarse salt and freshly ground black pepper

⅓ cup (80 ml) extra virgin olive oil

9 garlic cloves, thinly sliced

1 onion, halved lengthwise, root end left intact to hold the layers together

Three 28-ounce (800 g) cans whole tomatoes, coarsely blended or chopped

1 pound (455 g) meat mixture from Meatballs in Tomato Sauce (page 39), formed into twelve 2-inch (5 cm) meatballs

2 large sprigs fresh basil

1 pound (455 g) sweet or hot Italian sausages (optional), each poked in several spots

3 pounds (1.4 kg) macaroni, such as rigatoni, penne, fusilli, or campanelle

Grated Parmesan or Romano cheese for serving

ASPETTA ✛ *Keep a stash of reusable storage containers on hand to fill with any leftovers (pasta, sauce, and meat) and send home with your guests. Or store the leftovers in the refrigerator for 3 to 4 days or in the freezer for up to 6 months.*

Recipe continues

Generously season the pork and beef with salt and pepper. Heat a large heavy pot over medium-high heat and swirl in the olive oil. When it glistens, and working in batches, add the meat to the pot and sear on all sides until golden brown, 8 to 10 minutes. Transfer to a plate.

Pour off most of the excess fat, leaving about ¼ cup (60 ml) in the pot. Reduce the heat to medium, add the garlic and onion, and cook, stirring constantly, for a minute, being careful not to burn them. Pour in the tomatoes, then half-fill one can with water and add to the pot, scraping the brown bits off the bottom. Return the meat and any accumulated juices to the pot and simmer, partially covered, for 1½ hours.

Remove the onion halves from the pot and discard. Increase the heat to high and carefully drop in the meatballs one by one, gently stirring (so they don't break apart before they are firmly set) as you go to coat them in the sauce. Add the basil sprigs, reduce the heat to low, and simmer, partially covered, until the meatballs are cooked through, about 30 minutes.

Meanwhile, poke each sausage a couple of times with a fork or sharp knife. Place the sausages and 1 cup (240 ml) water in a large skillet and bring to a simmer over high heat. Simmer, turning to brown the sausages on all sides, until most of the water has evaporated, about 8 minutes. Pour off any excess fat and add 1 cup (240 ml) of the simmering tomato sauce to the pan; remove from the heat and cover to keep warm. (When ready to serve,

add the sausages to the bowl with the rest of the meat.)

While the sausages are cooking, bring a large pot of salted water to a rolling boil and warm a large serving bowl. Add the macaroni (1 pound at a time unless the pot is very big) to the pot and cook for 2 minutes shy of the package instructions (the pasta should be slightly soft but with a firm chew to it). Drain the noodles, transfer them to the warm bowl, and stir in some sauce to coat. Repeat with the remaining macaroni. (If cooking all 3 pounds/1.4 kg of pasta at once, drain the noodles, return them to the pot, and stir in some sauce to coat. When ready to serve, fill the warm bowl with the sauced pasta and refill as necessary.)

If serving family-style, warm another large serving bowl and fill it with the meat and sauce. If serving individually, heat the pasta bowls or plates before serving by setting them on or next to the oven, on a warm stovetop, or in a low oven. Place extra sauce and meat in a small warm bowl on a plate, with a large spoon or small ladle. Either way, place a small dish (or two) of grated cheese on the table.

MEATBALLS in TOMATO SAUCE

Descendants of Italian immigrants all have their own meatball formulas, handed down from their grandmothers and mothers, and fierce arguments over what makes the best meatball can arise. In the kitchen when my grandmother, her sisters, and sisters-in-law were cooking together, tempers flared among these strong women as they debated whether to fry the balls first before adding the tomatoes for the sauce (my preferred way) or to drop the raw meatballs into the simmering sauce to cook (my brother's preference). The great-aunts would no doubt shudder at today's meat options (only pork was used back then) and scoff at the idea of oven-frying. Pecorino Romano (more flavorful and less expensive than Parmesan) is the grated cheese of choice. And fresh parsley always, no dried herbs (but do use them if desired). For this recipe, I use hydrated bread rather than dried breadcrumbs to moisten and lighten the balls. Be careful not to overwork the meat mixture, or your meatballs may be spongy and tough.

Meatballs cooked and cooled in the sauce freeze beautifully for several months. You can also freeze rolled raw meatballs on a tray until firm, then transfer to a sealed freezer container and cook as you please at a future date.

Makes fifteen to seventeen 1½-inch (4 cm) meatballs; 4 to 6 servings

One ½-inch-thick (1.25 cm) slice white bread or 1 cup (105 g) breadcrumbs, homemade (page 42) or store-bought

¼ cup (60 ml) milk, heated until warm

1 pound (455 g) ground meat: pork, beef, veal, turkey, or chicken, or a combination

⅓ cup (35 g) grated Romano or Parmesan cheese, or a combination

1 large egg, beaten

1 large garlic clove, minced

Leaves from 3 sprigs fresh flat-leaf parsley, finely chopped (2 to 3 tablespoons)

¾ teaspoon dried herbs, such as oregano, thyme, or basil, or a combination (optional)

½ teaspoon kosher salt if using Pecorino cheese, 1 teaspoon if using Parmesan, or more to taste

½ teaspoon freshly ground black pepper

2 tablespoons extra virgin olive oil

One 28-ounce (800 g) can whole tomatoes, pulsed to a puree

Soak the bread (or breadcrumbs) in the warm milk in a small bowl, turning it over occasionally so it absorbs the liquid. Let cool to room temperature, then finely chop if using a slice of bread.

Transfer the bread to a large bowl. Add the meat, cheese, egg, garlic, parsley, dried herbs, if using, salt, and pepper and combine the mixture with your hands. Moisten your hands to make it easier to shape the meat mixture and roll it into 1½-inch (4 cm) balls; transfer them to a baking sheet as you form them.

ASPETTA + For nonstick hands: *When shaping a meat mixture into balls, periodically run cold water over your hands or dip them in a bowl of cold water, and the meat won't stick to them as you roll.*

Recipe continues

The meatballs can be covered and stored in the refrigerator for up to 24 hours before cooking. You can also freeze them on a baking sheet, then transfer to a resealable freezer bag and store for up to 6 months. Thaw and cook as directed.

Heat a large skillet over medium-high heat and swirl in the olive oil. When it glistens, add the meatballs in a single layer, leaving some room around them (cook in batches if necessary). Reduce the heat to medium and brown the meatballs on all sides, 5 to 6 minutes. Spoon out any excess oil from the pan. (If you did this in batches, return all the meatballs to the pan.)

Pour in the tomato puree and simmer, partially covered, stirring occasionally, until the meatballs are cooked through (poke the center of one to check), 25 to 30 minutes. Taste the sauce and season with salt if necessary. Remove from the heat and serve.

VARIATIONS:

SERVE THE MEATBALLS WITH PASTA: Three or four meatballs per person over spaghetti tossed with the sauce.

MAKE SANDWICHES: Serve halved meatballs inside split warm rolls topped with sliced provolone or mozzarella cheese, melted under the broiler. Or prepare Mini Meatball Sandwiches (page 76).

SIMMER THE MEATBALLS IN SOUP: Roll the meat mixture into bite-sized (¾-inch/2 cm) meatballs, drop into the simmering broth, and simmer until cooked through, 5 to 7 minutes.

LAYER MEATBALLS INTO BAKED PASTA: Roll the meat mixture into miniature meatballs (½-inch/1.25 cm) and simmer in the sauce as directed. Scatter between lasagna layers (page 133) as you assemble it, or add to Baked Ziti (page 155).

Breadcrumbs are the great unsung frugal heroes of the Italian American kitchen. Leftover bread is never wasted. When making meatballs, the meat is extended with breadcrumbs or hydrated stale bread, and the bread imparts a fluffy quality to the balls. Spiral bundles of meats like braciola are rolled up with a filling of breadcrumbs, cheese, and herbs for a textural counterpoint, as well as to "beef up" the bundles. Not only are chicken, veal, or pork cutlets dredged in breadcrumbs and fried until crispy in olive oil heavenly delicious, the thin slices of meat are made more substantial with the coating. Where would Chicken Parmesan (page 143) be without breadcrumbs? A scattering of toasted breadcrumbs on top of twirled Spaghetti with Clam Sauce (page 195) or Turkey Tetrazzini (page 117) lends that extra oomph usually gotten from grated cheese, along with a crunchy texture.

There are several ways to make your own breadcrumbs at home. Remember that lightly stale bread has texture and flavor, but stale-stale bread is only texture.

+ If you regularly buy whole loaves of bread to slice at home for everyday use, capture the ends and store them in a sealed container in the refrigerator or freezer. When a good amount has accumulated, chop or break the stale bread into 1-inch (2.5 cm) pieces. Pulse them in a food processor or blender, about 1 cup (100 g) at a time, to the desired size crumb (processing too much at one time can weigh down the bread pieces, resulting in a combination of sawdust and oversized pieces). Return the crumbs to the sealed container and store for up to 6 months in the freezer, where they will retain a bready, not stale, flavor.

+ If using a loaf of fresh bread for breadcrumbs, cut or tear it into 1-inch (2.5 cm) pieces. Leave the crust on; no recipe here requires pristine white breadcrumbs. Most fresh bread must be dried before processing it into crumbs, or it will be gummy, not "crumby." Spread the torn pieces out on a baking sheet. If time permits, leave the bread out overnight to dry. If not, place in a 225°F (100°C) oven until it is dry, about 20 minutes. Cool and proceed as directed above.

+ If using presliced grocery-store bread that comes in a plastic bag, tear or cut the bread into 1-inch (2.5 cm) pieces. For fresh breadcrumbs, pulse in a blender or food processor, 1 cup (45 g) at a time, to the desired size crumbs and use as directed in the recipe. For dried crumbs, spread the crumbs out on a baking sheet and place in a 250°F (120°C) oven until dry, about 15 minutes. Cool and use immediately, or store as directed above.

VARIATION:

CRISPY SAVORY BREADCRUMBS TO USE AS A GRATED CHEESE REPLACEMENT: Heat a large skillet over medium-high heat and swirl in some extra virgin olive oil. Add 2 minced garlic cloves and 2 anchovy fillets and stir and smash the anchovies for 30 seconds to dissolve. Add ½ teaspoon red pepper flakes and 2 cups (90 g) fresh breadcrumbs and stir constantly over medium heat until golden and fragrant, about 5 minutes.

SUNDAY DINNER MENU

The Sunday meal in an Italian American household can be as varied as the families who serve it—with a few exceptions. The meal takes place on the so-called "day of rest" and is eaten after attending Mass, usually with the extended family. As on so many other occasions, historically it was the women who did the cooking and serving while the men tended to their homemade wine and had a leisurely day off. Fortunately, there are many men these days who choose to cook and pitch in, and conversely some women for whom Sunday is a workday at a job outside of the home. As the older generation passes on, these meal rituals have waned for families, but many still enjoy a modern version of this delicious get-together. Today, most feasts include an antipasto of some sort; a saucy, meaty pasta dish; a poultry or meat roast; a couple of vegetables; some side dishes; bread; and dessert—and, of course, wine. Your menu can be as streamlined or elaborate as befitting the occasion. This sample menu is an achievable one for any given Sunday.

Antipasto Platter: Roasted Sweet Red Peppers (page 79), Marinated Mushrooms (page 88), and Caponata (page 84)

Sliced prosciutto and capicola, cubed provolone, and olives

Bread

Sunday Sauce (with meatballs and sausage) served with macaroni (page 37)

Lemony Pole Beans (page 231)

Green salad with Italian "Vinaigrette" (page 243) or Fennel and Orange Salad (page 239)

Garlic Herb Bread (page 73)

Tiramisu (page 273)

BEEF BRACIOLA

Stuffed and rolled thinly sliced and pounded beef, braciola is a recipe (like meatballs) that can vary from family to family. Our family recipe is a classic preparation I've updated by precooking the filling for deeper flavor. Potential add-ins include prosciutto, grated provolone, pine nuts, raisins, and/or blanched greens. Traditionally braciola was served in the Sunday Sauce (page 37). Or make it for the holidays. It's a smart recipe for entertaining, as everything can be prepared up to a couple of days in advance, and the flavor only improves with time.

Serve the beefy bundles over pasta with sauce, or serve as their own course: Toss macaroni in sauce for the first course and then, for the second, arrange the braciola on a plate and serve with a cooked green such as Sautéed Escarole (page 222) or Garlicky Broccoli Rabe (page 223), or with Lemony Pole Beans (page 231).

Makes 10 bundles

3 garlic cloves, minced

4 tablespoons (60 ml) extra virgin olive oil, plus more for drizzling

1½ cups (70 g) fresh breadcrumbs

½ cup (50 g) grated Parmesan cheese

¼ cup (15 g) fresh flat-leaf parsley leaves and tender stems, chopped

Kosher salt and freshly ground black pepper

½ teaspoon red pepper flakes

½ teaspoon dried thyme

10 very thin slices top-round sirloin (about 2 pounds/910 g), pounded to 4 to 6 inches (10 to 15 cm) long

1 small onion, minced

2 tablespoons red wine

One 28-ounce (800 g) can whole tomatoes, coarsely chopped, with their juices

SPECIAL EQUIPMENT

Ten 14-inch (35 cm) pieces kitchen string

ASPETTA + *Always keep parchment paper at hand. For a job like this, line your cutting board or countertop with a large piece and lay the meat on top of it. The paper can then be lifted up at the edges and turned as you move from piece to piece. The workspace stays clean and raw-meat free. After the bundles are made and are browning in the pan, just roll up the paper, crumbs and all, for easy cleanup.*

Heat 2 teaspoons of the garlic in 1 tablespoon of the olive oil in a small skillet over medium heat until it sizzles but does not brown, about 30 seconds. Stir in the breadcrumbs, remove from the heat, and transfer to a bowl to cool.

Add the Parmesan cheese, parsley, ½ teaspoon salt, ¼ teaspoon black pepper, the red pepper flakes, and thyme to the crumb mixture and stir to mix.

Lay the slices of meat out on a clean work surface. Sprinkle each slice with salt and black pepper. Spread a scant ¼ cup (120 g) of the filling over each slice, leaving a ¼-inch (0.65 cm) border all around, and drizzle with olive oil. Roll each piece up lengthwise from the wider end to the narrower end and secure with a piece of string tied around the center of the roll.

Heat a heavy-bottomed skillet over high heat and swirl in the remaining 3 tablespoons olive oil. When the oil glistens, add the meat bundles. (Do not crowd the pan, or the meat will steam instead of brown; work in batches

if necessary.) Brown the rolls, turning once, for 2 to 3 minutes per side. Transfer the braciola to a plate and tent with foil to keep warm.

Reduce the heat under the pan to medium, stir in the onion and the remaining garlic, and cook, stirring, for 1 minute. Pour in the wine, stirring to deglaze the pan and loosening the brown bits on the bottom. Add the tomatoes and bring to a boil. Return the beef to the pan, reduce the heat, and simmer, partially covered, for 1 hour, or until the beef is tender enough to easily cut through.

Remove the bundles from the pan one at a time, snip off the string, and return to the pan. Serve.

RIGATONI with MEAT SAUCE (RAGÙ)

It's impossible to decode the origins of this sauce in America. Impoverished southern Italian newcomers in the late 1800s were used to eating meat only on feast days, if at all. But their arrival intersected with the advent of meat grinders and the availability of affordable ground meat. Meat consumption among these immigrants increased dramatically, and meat naturally found its way into red sauce as a mash-up of traditional Italian meat sauces: ragù Bolognese and Neapolitan ragù (which has many similarities to "gravy," the sauce name popularized in some northeastern cities). Eventually spaghetti and meat sauce entered the all-American dinner rotation. This is the version of the sauce I've cooked since my kids were little.

Makes 1½ quarts (715 g) sauce;
4 to 6 servings

2 tablespoons extra virgin olive oil

1 medium-small onion, finely diced (1 cup/ 100 g)

1 carrot, peeled and finely diced (½ cup/ 64 g)

1 celery stalk, peeled and finely diced (½ cup/64 g)

Kosher salt

2 garlic cloves, minced

½ teaspoon red pepper flakes

1 pound (455 g) ground beef or pork, or a combination

1 tablespoon tomato paste (optional)

½ cup (120 ml) red or white wine

One 28-ounce (800 g) can whole tomatoes, pulsed in a blender

⅓ cup (80 ml) cream or milk

2 tablespoons unsalted butter

1 pound (455 g) macaroni, such as rigatoni or ziti

Grated Parmesan or Romano cheese for serving

Freshly ground black pepper

Heat a large saucepan over medium-low heat and swirl in the olive oil. Add the onions, carrots, and celery, season with 1 teaspoon salt, and sauté over low heat, stirring occasionally, until the vegetables are lightly caramelized, 10 to 12 minutes.

Add the garlic, red pepper flakes, and meat, increase the heat to medium-high, and cook, stirring and smashing the meat until it is lightly browned and any clumps are separated, 10 to 15 minutes.

If using tomato paste, clear a space in the center of the pan, add the tomato paste, and stir for a minute. Add the wine to deglaze the pan, stirring to loosen the browned bits on the bottom, and cook until the wine is almost evaporated, about 2 minutes. Add the tomatoes and stir in the cream, then reduce the heat and simmer gently until the sauce has reduced and thickened, about 40 minutes. Stir in the butter and season to taste with salt.

Recipe continues

Meanwhile, bring a large pot of water to a boil. Salt it generously and add the pasta. Cook for 2 minutes shy of the package instructions; the pasta should be slightly soft but still with a firm chew to it.

Drain the noodles, transfer to a serving bowl, and toss with a ladleful of sauce to coat them. Serve the pasta in bowls, with the remaining sauce, grated cheese, and freshly ground pepper on top.

ASPETTA + Pasta and sauce pairings: *Italian American cooks are more flexible about sauce and noodle pairings than Italian cooks, who follow regional traditions and the belief that certain pasta shapes are best suited to certain styles of sauce. Larger macaroni shapes with curves and hollows match with "meatier" thick and hearty sauces. Lighter, delicate noodles are best with thinner oil- or cream-based sauces. Yet for this dish and the following recipe (or any sauce, for that matter), I will happily use whatever noodle is in the cabinet, or what might suit me most at the time.*

BUCATINI with SAUSAGE RAGÙ

For a twist on your typical meat sauce, start with seasoned sausage meat squeezed from its casings—a shortcut to deep flavor. Rosemary adds a hint of fresh herby/pineyness to the rich sauce. I like to make enough to eat right away with an extra quart to freeze for later. Always keep a frozen thaw-and-heat sauce in your freezer, which can be reheated in the time it takes to cook the pasta.

Makes 2 quarts (950 g) sauce; 4 to 6 servings

2 tablespoons olive oil

1 pound (455 g) sweet Italian sausages, removed from casings

1 pound (455 g) spicy Italian sausages, removed from casings

1 small onion, finely chopped

1 medium carrot, finely chopped

2 garlic cloves, minced

1 tablespoon tomato paste

Two 28-ounce (800 g) cans whole tomatoes

One 6-inch (15 cm) sprig fresh rosemary

1 pound (455 g) long pasta, such as bucatini or spaghetti

Grated Parmesan or Romano cheese for serving

Freshly ground black pepper

Heat the oil in a 4- to 5-quart (3.8 to 4.7 L) saucepan over medium-high heat until it shimmers. Add the sausage and brown the meat, breaking it up into small pieces, until just cooked through, about 5 minutes.

Add the onions, carrots, garlic, and tomato paste and cook, stirring occasionally, until the vegetables begin to soften, about 3 minutes. Stir in the tomatoes and rosemary, breaking up the tomatoes with the side of the spoon or with scissors, and bring to a boil. Reduce the heat, partially cover, and simmer, stirring occasionally, until the sauce thickens and reduces slightly, about 30 minutes.

Meanwhile, bring a large pot of water to a boil. Salt it generously and add the pasta. Cook for 2 minutes shy of the package instructions; the noodles should be slightly soft but still with a firm chew to them.

Drain the noodles, transfer to a serving bowl, and toss with a ladleful of sauce to coat them. Serve the pasta in bowls with the remaining sauce, grated cheese, and freshly ground pepper on top.

CHICKEN PARM MEATBALLS

On one of those time-challenged days, looking for a way to easily capture the satisfying yumminess of chicken Parmesan, I devised this simple meatball recipe to heap on top of spaghetti or to layer into hero rolls, top with sliced mozzarella, and melt under the broiler. The secret to the recipe's success is using chicken thighs, which have more texture than breasts, and sun-dried tomatoes, which combine with the Parmesan and garlic to achieve an authentic flavor.

Serve the meatballs in individual bowls with Garlic Herb Bread (page 73) or spoon them over pasta.

Makes twelve 1½-inch (4 cm) meatballs

1 pound (455 g) boneless, skinless chicken thighs, cut into small pieces (see Aspetta)

3 garlic cloves, roughly chopped

1 ounce (28 g) sun-dried tomatoes, soaked in warm water to soften, drained, and roughly chopped, or oil-packed sun-dried tomatoes, drained

1 large egg, beaten

½ cup (50 g) dried coarse breadcrumbs

½ cup (50 g) plus 2 tablespoons grated Parmesan cheese

1 tablespoon chopped fresh flat-leaf parsley

½ teaspoon kosher salt, plus more if needed

¼ teaspoon red pepper flakes

¼ cup (25 g) dried fine breadcrumbs

2 tablespoons extra virgin olive oil

3 cups (675 g) Tomato Sauce (page 63)

Combine the chicken, garlic, and sun-dried tomatoes in a food processor and pulse to a coarse texture (like ground meat). Transfer to a large bowl.

Add the egg, coarse breadcrumbs, grated cheese, parsley, salt, and red pepper to the chicken mixture and combine with your hands. Moisten your hands with water to keep the chicken mixture from sticking and roll it into twelve 1½-inch (4 cm) balls. Roll the balls in the fine breadcrumbs and transfer them to a baking sheet.

Heat a large skillet over medium-high heat and swirl in the oil. When it glistens, add the meatballs in a single layer, leaving room around them (cook in batches if necessary). Reduce the heat to medium and brown the meatballs on all sides, 5 to 6 minutes. Spoon out any excess oil from the pan. (If you cooked them in batches, return all the meatballs to the pan.)

Pour in the tomato sauce and simmer, partially covered, stirring occasionally, until an instant-read thermometer poked into the center of a meatball reads 160°F (72°C), 20 to 25 minutes. Taste the sauce and season with salt if necessary. Remove from the heat.

ASPETTA + *It's much easier to slice or chop raw meat or chicken if it is very cold. Partially freeze it to firm it up beforehand.*

ITALIAN WEDDING SOUP

This soup actually has nothing to do with weddings! The reference seems to be a bastardized translation from Neapolitan Italian that originally meant to "wed" together lesser cuts of meat with wild greens in a minestra designed to nourish a group affordably. In a nod to its humble origins, when it was frequently made with offal, I've used sausage meat for the meatballs rather than ground pork, which also brings big flavor to the soup.

Makes 4 quarts (3.8 L);
6 to 8 servings

1 pound (455 g) meatball mixture from Meatballs in Tomato Sauce (page 39), made with sweet Italian sausage instead of ground meat

3 quarts (3 L) chicken broth, homemade (page 179) or store-bought

1 pound (455 g) escarole, trimmed and coarsely chopped

2 large eggs

3 tablespoons grated Parmesan cheese, plus more for serving

1½ teaspoons kosher salt, or to taste

¼ teaspoon freshly ground black pepper, plus more for serving

1 cup (230 g) small macaroni, such as ditalini, pastina, or orzo, cooked and drained

Moisten your hands and roll the meatball mixture into ½-inch (1.25 cm) balls, placing them on a platter or baking sheet; you should have 24 to 30 mini meatballs. (*The meatballs can be made ahead and refrigerated for up to 2 days.*)

Bring the chicken broth to a rolling boil in a large pot over high heat. Carefully drop the meatballs into the broth and gently stir to distribute them. Add the escarole, reduce the heat, and simmer until the meatballs are cooked through, about 10 minutes.

Whisk together the eggs and cheese in small bowl and swirl into the soup. Taste the broth to determine saltiness, then stir in salt to taste and the pepper. Stir in the cooked macaroni to heat through.

Serve the soup in bowls with 4 to 6 meatballs in each, topped with grated cheese and black pepper.

CANNELLINI BEAN SOUP

White beans were a traditional staple of the Italian table for rich and poor alike. They are high in protein and calcium, are easy to grow and store, and have a nutty-earthy flavor when cooked. The immigrant Italian home cooks in America used them as a bedrock ingredient to feed large groups. When animal or fish proteins are too expensive or unavailable, dried beans offer nutrition and bulk. You can use the beans not only in soups but also in stews or salads, for purees, for Greens and Beans (page 228), and to stretch meat dishes.

Whether you soak the beans overnight or quick-soak them, don't discard that enriched liquid. Rinse the dried beans before you soak them, and then use the soaking liquid for cooking them. Beans begin to soften as they cook, simultaneously absorbing water and releasing nutrients, and their starches will thicken the liquid.

Makes
4 quarts (4 kg);
6 to 8 servings
~~~~~~~~~~~~~~

1 pound (455 g) dried cannellini beans

4 quarts (3.8 L) water

3 tablespoons extra virgin olive oil, plus more for drizzling

1 large onion, chopped (2 cups/200 g)

3 garlic cloves, minced

2 to 3 carrots, halved lengthwise and sliced (1¼ cups/170 g)

2 celery stalks, peeled and chopped (1¼ cups/170 g)

1 tablespoon kosher salt, or more to taste

1 ripe or canned tomato, chopped (½ cup/85 g)

¼ cup (15 g) fresh flat-leaf parsley leaves and tender stems, chopped

¼ cup (15 g) fresh basil leaves

A Parmesan or Romano cheese rind (optional)

Grated Parmesan cheese for serving

Freshly ground black pepper

Rinse the beans well, place them in a large pot, and add the water. Bring to a boil over high heat, cover, and turn off the heat. Let soak for 1 hour.

Drain the beans in a large colander or sieve set over a large bowl or pot; reserve the soaking liquid.

Combine the olive oil, onions, and garlic in a large heavy-bottomed pot and stir over medium heat until the garlic begins to sizzle, about 1 minute. Add the carrots, celery, and 1 teaspoon of the salt and cook, stirring, until the vegetables begin to caramelize, 8 to 10 minutes.

Stir in the tomatoes, parsley, and basil and cook for 5 minutes. Add the drained beans and cheese rind, if using. Measure the bean soaking liquid, add enough water to make a total of 2½ quarts (2.4 L), and add that liquid to the beans. Bring to a boil, then reduce the heat and simmer, partially covered, until the beans are tender and creamy, 1½ to

2½ hours, depending on the age/freshness of the dried beans, adding the remaining 2 teaspoons salt halfway through the cooking. Start tasting the beans for doneness after an hour, and add water as necessary to achieve the desired consistency; the soup should be thick. Remove from the heat.

Serve as is, or, for a creamier consistency, puree 2 cups (520 g) of the soup in a blender and return it to the pot. Add more salt if needed. Garnish each bowl with a drizzle of olive oil, a sprinkle of cheese, and some black pepper. The soup is delicious day-of but almost even better the next day for an excellent make-ahead meal.

ASPETTA + Salt warning: *For soups that cook a long time, wait until the end to add most of the salt to prevent oversalting—not because the beans will toughen with salt (which is an endlessly disputed old wives' tale), but because as the liquid reduces and concentrates over time, a soup that has been generously seasoned at the start of cooking can become too salty.*

GREEN MINESTRONE

My grandmother's minestrone soup is different from the homogenized tomato-red version. She used peas, beans, new potatoes, and herbs from her garden and topped the whole thing with a freshly pestled herb pesto. Whether they had just a tiny tenement plot or a backyard garden, most of the Italians who came to America in the great migration grew at least a few tomato or pepper plants and herbs, both for eating fresh in season and also to put up for winter. For this soup, mix and match your vegetables depending on what is in your own garden or at the farmers' market. If you collect the cheese rinds from grating cheese, store them airtight in the fridge or freezer, and they will offer wonderful depth of flavor to vegetarian soups like this one. Preceded by a small antipasti plate of sliced meat and cheese and served with some crusty bread, a bowl of this minestrone makes a satisfying meal.

Makes
4 quarts (3.8 L);
6 to 8 servings

FOR THE SOUP

4 tablespoons (60 ml) extra virgin olive oil

12 ounces (340 g) green beans, ends trimmed and cut into 1-inch (2.5 cm) pieces

1 onion, chopped

3 garlic cloves, sliced

1 teaspoon kosher salt, or more to taste

1 small cabbage (1½ pounds/700 g), cored and thinly sliced

1 large or 3 small potatoes, peeled if desired, and diced

A Parmesan or Romano cheese rind (optional)

1½ cups (260 g) cooked chickpeas or cannellini beans

1½ cups (250 g) green peas

½ teaspoon freshly ground black pepper

8 ounces (225 g) small macaroni or broken spaghetti, cooked and drained

FOR THE PESTO (MAKES ⅓ CUP/70 G)

1 garlic clove

½ teaspoon kosher salt

3 tablespoons grated Parmesan or Romano cheese

2 tablespoons pine nuts or almonds

5 tablespoons (12 g) chopped fresh herb: basil, sage, or flat-leaf parsley, or a combination

3 to 4 tablespoons olive oil

Set a large pot over medium-high heat and swirl in 2 tablespoons of the olive oil. Add the green beans, onions, garlic, and salt and cook, stirring, until the green beans soften and the onions begin to turn golden, 4 to 5 minutes.

Add the remaining 2 tablespoons olive oil and stir in the cabbage and potatoes. Add enough water to cover the vegetables by an inch (2.5 cm), then add the cheese rind, if using. Bring to a boil, cover, reduce the heat to low, and simmer until the potatoes are tender, 10 to 15 minutes.

Uncover the pot and stir in the chickpeas, peas, more salt to taste if necessary, and the pepper. Simmer until the peas are tender, about 5 more minutes. Stir in the noodles, adding more water if needed for a soupy consistency.

Recipe continues

Meanwhile, make the pesto: Using a mortar and pestle or a food processor, mash or pulse the garlic and salt together. Blend in the cheese and nuts. Mix in the herbs. Blending with the pestle, or with the food processor running, slowly pour in the olive oil until the pesto reaches your desired consistency. Transfer the pesto to a small bowl (cover with a little more olive oil to prevent browning if not serving immediately).

To serve, ladle the soup into warm bowls and drizzle some pesto over the top of each. (Store any leftover soup in labeled reusable containers in the fridge for up to 4 days or in the freezer up to 6 months.)

ASPETTA ✛ Freshly made pesto can be frozen: *Put it in a freezer-safe container and cover it with a thin layer of olive oil. Seal, date, and freeze. The layer of olive oil helps preserve the green color. You can also freeze small amounts in an ice-cube tray. Once they are frozen, transfer the pesto cubes to a freezer bag and seal it. They will keep for up to 6 months, and you can just pull out cubes as needed. If you have a lot of basil in your garden, prepare a large batch of pesto with the fragrant fresh-picked leaves at the end of the growing season to have on hand for the cold months.*

TOMATO SAUCE (SUGO)

This is my everyday, ride-or-die, last-meal red sauce. You might be surprised to see that it doesn't include onions or dried herbs. Over the years, I've learned to appreciate a clean basic tomato flavor with as few ingredients as possible to achieve the central casting tomato sauce of my dreams. This unadulterated style of sauce works well as a component of other recipes, like the Chicken Parm Meatballs (page 54).

The recipe makes just the right quantity of sauce for a pound (455 g) of pasta.

Makes 3 cups (675 g)

1½ tablespoons extra virgin olive oil

2 garlic cloves, minced

¼ teaspoon red pepper flakes

One 28-ounce (800 g) can whole tomatoes, lightly pulsed in a blender (see Aspetta)

½ teaspoon kosher salt

1 sprig fresh basil (optional)

1 tablespoon unsalted butter

1 pound (455 g) spaghetti

Grated Parmesan or Romano cheese for serving

Freshly ground black pepper

Heat a medium saucepan over medium heat and swirl in the olive oil. Add the garlic and pepper flakes and stir constantly for about 30 seconds, just long enough to release the garlic's fragrance and transform it slightly from its raw state; don't let it cook to golden.

Raise the heat to high and stir in the tomatoes and salt. Bring to a boil, then reduce the heat and simmer, uncovered, for 30 minutes. In the last 5 minutes of cooking, add the basil sprig, if using, then remove it before serving. Swirl in the butter.

Meanwhile, bring a large pot of water to a boil. Salt it generously and add the spaghetti. Cook until 2 minutes shy of the package instructions; the spaghetti should be slightly soft but still with a firm chew to it.

Drain the spaghetti, add it to the sauce, and toss to coat. Serve swirled into a bowl with grated cheese and freshly ground pepper on top.

ASPETTA + *To break down tomatoes, pulse the whole canned tomatoes right in the can with a stick blender. Or squeeze them with your hands to break them up as you add them to the pan. Kitchen shears can also be used to snip them into small pieces once they have been added to the pan.*

SNACKS ✦ ✦ ✦

BREADS,
PICKLES,
and
TIDBITS

69 Tomato Pie

71 Prosciutto
    Bread

76 Mini Meatball
    Sandwiches

78 Fresh Ricotta

79 Roasted
    Sweet Red
    Peppers

82 Marinated
    Stuffed Hot
    Red Cherry
    Peppers

83 Hot Red
    Cherry Peppers
    in Brine

84 Caponata

87 Giardiniera

88 Marinated
    Mushrooms

89 Roasted
    Chestnuts

90 Italian Tuna
    Dip

92 Mussels
    Oreganata

93 Clams Casino

MEALTIMES ARE ALWAYS THE MAIN EVENT,

but while the Sunday sauce bubbles away on the stovetop, or before the soup is served, or just to accompany a glass of wine, Italian American families routinely offer guests an antipasti platter of salumi, vegetables, and cheeses, along with a few personal touches. A snack can be any little savory bite that rouses an appetite, satisfies a craving, or portends the feast to come. Ask an Italian if they're hungry during the liminal space after lunch and before dinner, or soon after dessert but before midnight, and they won't say no. You might not get a definitive answer, but you can bet they're thinking, Yes! My mom called it the "betwixt and between" time. And when you have an array of delicious options like the ones in this chapter, you can always find room for a snack.

Antipasti were once reserved for holidays and celebrations, but the passing years have diversified their possibilities. Think of it as an entirely personal platter of little bites, to be enjoyed before a meal (not "pre-pasta," as the name might suggest). Offer something as simple as a few olives and a chunk of Parmesan cheese, or prepare a selection as elaborate as you can muster for the circumstances.

Serve warm squares of Tomato Pie fresh out of the oven for a casual bite or arrange room-temperature strips on a large platter with a few other nibbles, for an afternoon/pre-dinner snack. The tangy flavors of Hot Red Cherry Peppers in Brine, Caponata, and Marinated Mushrooms awaken a cheese board or add a mouthwatering element to sandwiches or pasta. Mussels Oreganata and Clams Casino cook in their own little serving shells for a savory starter. The uniquely delicious Mini Meatball Sandwiches created in our family can be made ahead and frozen to have on hand for quick snacks or appetizers. And try homemade Fresh Ricotta, which is a cinch to prepare and a delicious butter alternative smeared on thick slabs of bread.

TOMATO PIE

As the many regional American Italian versions of this pie are all slightly different, I'm throwing into the ring my personal favorite, which is stripped down to the essential stars of the show: crust and tomato sauce (with an optional dusting of grated cheese). Found under various names including Church Pie, Granny Pie, Red Pie, and Rhode Island Red Strips, it was originally sold from nonna's home kitchen before becoming an Italian bakery staple—until the advent of pizza parlors. While pizza joints now exist in almost every corner of the globe, New Haven, Connecticut, is what some in this country consider "the pizza capital of the world." Anchored by the original Frank Pepe's, which was founded in 1925, it begot a whole slew of similar pizzerias. New Haven pizza is notable for its Naples-inspired pies.

Makes one
11-by-17-inch
(28 by 43 cm) pie;
12 servings

FOR THE DOUGH

5 cups (625 g), all-purpose or bread flour, plus more for kneading

1 tablespoon kosher salt

2¼ teaspoons (7 g) active dry yeast (from a ¼-ounce packet)

2 teaspoons sugar

2 cups (475 ml) water

2 tablespoons extra virgin olive oil

FOR THE SAUCE

3 tablespoons extra virgin olive oil

2 garlic cloves, minced

2 tablespoons tomato paste

One 28-ounce (800 g) can whole tomatoes

1 teaspoon kosher salt

1 teaspoon sugar

1 teaspoon dried oregano (optional)

½ teaspoon dried thyme (optional)

½ teaspoon red pepper flakes (optional)

Olive oil for brushing

½ cup (50 g) grated Romano cheese (optional), plus more for serving

MAKE THE DOUGH: In a large bowl, or the bowl of a stand mixer, whisk together the flour, salt, yeast, and sugar. Add the water and olive oil and stir to combine the wet and dry ingredients.

Knead by hand, or fit the mixer with the dough hook and knead on low speed, until the dough is soft and smooth, about 5 minutes (a few more minutes if kneading by hand). Turn the dough out and shape it into a tight ball. The dough will be sticky but workable. Dust flour on your hands and the work surface as needed. Use a bench scraper to assist you. Transfer the dough to a large oiled bowl and turn to coat with oil.

Cover the dough tightly and set aside to rise in a warm spot until almost doubled, 3 to 4 hours.

Meanwhile, make the sauce: Combine the olive oil and garlic in a medium pot and stir constantly over medium-high heat until the garlic begins to sizzle, about 1 minute. Add the tomato paste and cook, stirring, for 1 to 2 minutes to smooth the harsh taste of the paste. Add the tomatoes, with their juices, the salt, sugar, and oregano, thyme, and/or pepper flakes, if using, and bring to a simmer, then reduce the heat to medium-low and simmer for about 5 minutes, smashing the tomatoes with the side of a spoon as they begin to soften.

Partially cover the pot and cook, continuing to smash the tomatoes occasionally as they cook, until they have broken down to a smooth but slightly chunky texture, about 30 minutes total. Remove from the heat and let cool. (*The sauce can be made ahead and refrigerated for up to 5 days.*)

An hour to an hour and a half before baking the pie, oil an 11-by-17-inch (28 by 43 cm) rimmed baking sheet. On a clean work surface, using a rolling pin, roll the dough out to a rectangle approximately the size of the pan. Fit the dough into the pan, pressing it into the corners (a small straight-sided juice glass can help with fitting the dough into the corners). Brush the surface with olive oil.

Cover the dough and let it rise until puffy (it should leave a fingerprint behind when pressed), at least 60 minutes, and up to 90 minutes.

Position a rack in the top third of the oven. Preheat the oven to 500°F (260°C).

Press your fingers into the dough to create dimples. Spread a thin layer of the sauce evenly over the entire surface of the dough (extra sauce can be served on the side or reserved). Sprinkle with the cheese, if using. Bake until the crust is golden brown and cooked through, 15 to 20 minutes. Remove from the oven and let cool completely. (*The pie can be wrapped tightly in plastic wrap and frozen for up to 6 weeks.*)

Cut the pie into squares or rectangles and serve with extra grated cheese to sprinkle on top.

ASPETTA ✛ Make-ahead refrigerator dough: *This dough comes together in minutes, but the longer the rise, the better the taste and texture. Slow-risen dough has a tangier flavor developed during the longer fermentation process. A long rise also divides up the labor: If I'm going to serve this pie on Saturday or Sunday, for example, the dough is the last thing I make on Friday afternoon, giving it a 24- to 48-hour rise in the refrigerator. But fear not, a standard 3-hour rise, followed by a second shorter rise in the pan, will still yield a delicious pie.*

VARIATIONS:

Forgo the sauce and squeeze 2 cups (455 g) canned whole tomatoes over the dough to break them up. Sprinkle with kosher salt.

For a more basic sauce, use 2 cups (450 g) Tomato Sauce (page 63) or any other favorite sauce.

PROSCIUTTO BREAD

Prosciutto bread, aka lard bread, aka Brooklyn street bread, grew out of the Italian communities clustered around New York City, New Jersey, and Philadelphia. It traces its roots back to the cucina povera of southern Italian peasants, which made use of the leftovers after the butchering of a pig. The lard was rendered down and used for cooking, and the crispy little leftover bits were folded into the bread known as *pane con ciccioli* (meaning crisped fatty pork). As its preparation evolved in the New World, the name of the bread changed according to the local dialect—for example, it became "cigola bread" in North Jersey. But the more appealing name prosciutto bread has stuck to this day. This was originally a Christmas or Easter treat, but one friend remembers it on her grandmother's table at every Sunday dinner as a part of her antipasto spread. A handful of regional bakeries still consistently churn out dozens of loaves every day, and thousands on holidays.

Makes two 12-inch (30 cm) round loaves

- 5 cups (625 g) all-purpose or bread flour, plus more for dusting
- 1 tablespoon kosher salt
- 2¼ teaspoons (7 g) active dry yeast (from a ¼-ounce packet)
- 2 teaspoons sugar
- 2 cups (475 ml) water
- 2 tablespoons extra virgin olive oil, plus more for brushing
- 6 to 8 ounces (175 to 225 g) prosciutto in one piece (or a combination of salamis), cut into ¼-inch (0.65 cm) cubes (1½ cups cubed)
- 1½ teaspoons freshly ground black pepper
- 5 ounces (140 g) provolone cheese, grated (optional)

In a large bowl, or the bowl of a stand mixture, whisk together the flour, salt, yeast, and sugar. Add the water and olive oil and stir to combine the wet and dry ingredients.

Knead by hand, or fit the mixer with the dough hook and knead on low speed for 5 minutes (a few more minutes if working by hand). Add the prosciutto, pepper, and cheese, if using, and continue to knead to incorporate the add-ins, about 2 minutes. The dough will be sticky but workable. Dust flour on your hands and the work surface as needed. Use a bench scraper to assist you.

Turn the dough out and form it into a tight ball (gathering up any loose meat and cheese). Transfer it to a large oiled bowl and turn to coat with oil. Cover tightly and let rise at warm room temperature until almost doubled in size (it should leave a fingerprint behind when pressed), 3 to 4 hours.

Line 2 large baking sheets with parchment paper. Divide the dough into 2 pieces. Roll one piece out into a 24-inch-long (61 cm) rope, twisting the "rope" as you go, and form it into a circular wreath shape; pinch the ends together to seal.

Recipe continues

Transfer to one of the lined baking sheets and repeat with the second piece of dough, transferring it to the second lined baking sheet.

Lightly cover the dough and let rise in a warm place until one-third larger in size (it will leave a fingerprint behind when pressed), 60 to 90 minutes.

Position a rack in the center of the oven and preheat the oven to 500°F (260°C). Place a pan of water on a lower oven rack. (If your oven cannot accommodate both baking sheets on a single rack, position racks in the top and middle of the oven and set the pan on the bottom of the oven.)

Bake until the breads are golden brown and cooked through, 15 to 20 minutes. Transfer to a wire rack and let rest for at least 10 minutes before slicing and serving.

This bread is best eaten fresh on the day it is baked, but it can be wrapped tightly in plastic wrap and frozen for up to 6 months. Thaw at room temperature.

ASPETTA ✛ *In the cooler months, find a warm spot for the dough to rise, such as on top of a warm oven or near a radiator in the warmest room in the house. Or heat the oven to 200°F (90°C) for a few minutes, then turn it off and place the dough in it to rise. On a warm day, the countertop will do just fine.*

GARLIC HERB BREAD

This flavorful bread is a delicious platform for meatballs, addition to an antipasti platter, or accompaniment to a meal.

Sizzle a peeled garlic clove in some olive oil. Add some thinly sliced basil, oregano, or thyme leaves (or a combination) and remove from the heat. Slice an oblong loaf of Italian bread open lengthwise and brush on both sides with the garlic-herb oil. Broil cut side up under a hot broiler until golden brown, about 1 minute. Keep a close eye on it to avoid burning. Or, for warm bread that is soft on the inside but crunchy on the outside, close up the two halves of the loaf, wrap in parchment paper or foil, and bake in a 350°F (175°C) oven until warmed through, about 10 minutes.

Antipasti platters should be served at room temperature, so choose your ingredients accordingly. Think of different flavor combinations: tangy, briny, sweet, spicy, salty, and buttery. Combine a variety of textures—crunchy, crispy, smooth, and creamy—too. Lastly, picture the colors and shapes on the platter: red, yellow, green; round, flat, rolled, stacked, cubed, or torn, or in ramekins (for small bits and bites). Highlight seasonal offerings: When tomatoes are in season, little more than a bowl of fresh-off-the-vine cherry tomatoes, torn basil leaves, a sprinkling of crunchy salt, torn crusty bread, and olive oil for dipping is needed for a stellar antipasto. Lay out little spoons, forks, or toothpicks as needed for serving. Arrange some cocktail napkins and small plates nearby. Don't forget small discard containers for olive pits, shells, rinds, and/or stems.

For a big holiday meal, it's nice to construct a large platter with multiple offerings. Or mix and match a few different themed platters. Put together some homemade options, including a bowl of dip or a spreadable condiment such as Caponata (page 84). Invest in some good-quality ingredients from your favorite Italian market, and add a wild card like Roasted Chestnuts (page 89), dried figs, or candied citrus strips.

Here are some suggestions for themed antipasti platters:

MEAT AND CHEESE: Choose a variety of sliced and rolled salume: soppressata, capicola, prosciutto, and/or mortadella. Add some cheeses: cubed provolone, mozzarella boconcini, shards of ricotta salata, and/or a dish of freshly ground–pepper topped Fresh Ricotta (page 78). Select some condiments for a tangy counterpunch, like spicy Calabrian chili paste or Giardiniera (page 87). Add sliced Prosciutto Bread (page 71) or small squares of Tomato Pie (page 69) to round it out for an impressive prequel to Sunday dinner or a holiday meal, or for lunch all by itself.

SEAFOOD: Offer a refreshing change for fish lovers by choosing a collection of seafood offerings: imported tinned fish like sardines, anchovies, or tuna; fresh oysters on the half shell; and Italian Tuna Dip (page 90), along with caper berries, lemon wedges, and bread sticks. Include a separate platter of warm offerings: Mussels Oreganata (page 92), Clams Casino (page 93), or a mini version of Shrimp Scampi Meatballs (page 198).

VEGETABLE: Unite fresh, pickled, and cooked vegetables; feature one star like sliced crunchy, licoricey fennel stalks, along with Braised Fennel (page 236) to smooth on toasts or garlic bread. Add Roasted Sweet Red Peppers (page 79), Marinated Mushrooms (page 88), and torn bread, olive oil, and flaky salt.

If you've prepared the antipasti ahead and refrigerated them, let the platters come to room temperature (about 30 minutes) before serving. If you serve antipasti often, stock your cupboard with relishes, tinned fish, olives, caper berries, nuts, and crackers or toasts. Freeze a couple types of cured sliced meats (well wrapped). If you are prepared to improvise an impressive offering at a moment's notice, there is always a way to present an artfully arranged platter of appetite-arousing nibbles.

MINI MEATBALL SANDWICHES

Few of our family recipes elicit such emotion as these coveted little morsels. When I was growing up, my mom baked bags of these meatballs in advance to freeze and reheat for holiday gatherings. So I regarded these as Rose's meatball sandwiches, until my father corrected me. "Those are your grandmother's sandwiches!" But at a recent Italian family gathering, a second cousin said that the sandwiches, which I'd demonstrated publicly on TV, belonged to great-aunt Valentine, my grandmother's sister, and then cousin Lisa piped up, "Yes, those are my nana's!" Cousin Mary Joy insisted that they were originally called Birdies! Birdies, balls, squares, or snacks, such is the generational way with delicious original recipes like this.

Makes sixty 1½-inch (4 cm) squares

1 loaf (450 g; about 30 slices) very thin sliced soft white bread, such as Pepperidge Farm

1 pound (455 g) ground pork, or a combination of pork and beef

¼ cup (25 g) grated Romano cheese

¼ cup (25 g) grated Parmesan cheese

¼ cup (15 g) fresh flat-leaf parsley leaves and tender stems, finely chopped

2 teaspoons extra virgin olive oil

1 large egg

1 garlic clove, minced

½ teaspoon dried oregano

½ teaspoon dried thyme

½ teaspoon kosher salt

Freshly ground black pepper

8 tablespoons (1 stick/115 g) unsalted butter, at room temperature

Preheat the oven to 350°F (175°C).

Process the end slices of the loaf of bread to fine crumbs in a food processor or blender, about ½ cup (28 g). Transfer to a large bowl, add the meat, cheeses, parsley, olive oil, egg, garlic, oregano, thyme, salt, and pepper, and mix well with your hands to combine.

Moisten your hands with cold water and roll the meat mixture into 1-inch (2.5 cm) balls; reserve on a baking sheet. Line another baking sheet with parchment or a silicone mat.

Lay 2 slices of the bread on a clean work surface. Butter one side of each slice. Place 4 meatballs on one slice of buttered bread, top with a second slice, buttered side down, and press firmly together. Use a serrated knife to cut off the crusts. (Reserve the crusts and bake separately for a "cook's treat.") Repeat with the remaining bread and filling. Cut each sandwich into 4 squares and transfer to the lined baking sheet. (This process can be done assembly-line style, lining up slices of buttered bread and assembling multiple sandwiches at a time.)

Bake until the sandwiches are golden brown, 15 to 20 minutes. Transfer to a rack pan and let cool slightly. Serve warm.

ASPETTA + Do-ahead: *There is no flavor lost by making these in advance and freezing them, and the gain is immeasurable, as you can dip into your freezer and reheat a handful, or trays, of these morsels whenever needed, especially during the busy holiday time. Bake the sandwiches and let cool completely, then freeze on the baking sheet. Once frozen, collect them into a resealable bag or freezer-safe container and freeze until needed. Defrost at room temperature on a baking sheet and heat in a 250°F (120°C) oven until warmed through and lightly crispy on the outside, 10 to 15 minutes.*

FRESH RICOTTA

Fresh ricotta drizzled with extra virgin olive oil and sprinkled with flaky Maldon salt and freshly ground black pepper is an exciting butter replacement to spread on bread, and it's an unexpected touch on a snack platter with roasted peppers, sliced meats, and other nibbles. Ricotta is the easiest cheese to make at home; it only requires about an hour from beginning to end. Personalize it with stir-ins like herbs and spices. It is quite perishable, but it will stay fresh in the refrigerator for 2 to 3 days.

Ricotta was originally made from sheep's milk, more easily accessible from shepherds in the Mezzogiorno than cow's milk, which accounts for its ubiquitous historical usage in Italian American recipes.

Makes 1 cup (227 g)

4 cups (950 ml) whole milk

½ teaspoon kosher salt

2 tablespoons fresh lemon juice

Line a small colander with cheesecloth (a paper towel will work in a pinch) and set it over a bowl. Combine the milk and salt in a small saucepan and bring to a boil over high heat. Add the lemon juice, lower the heat, and stir until the curds coagulate and separate from the whey, 1 to 2 minutes.

Pour the curd mixture into the strainer and set aside until most of the liquid has drained away, about 1 hour. Cover and refrigerate for up to 3 days if not using right away.

ASPETTA + Don't discard the drained liquid (whey): *It is loaded with enzymes that will tenderize meat, and it can add flavor (substitute it for the water called for) to baking recipes or pasta sauces.*

ROASTED SWEET RED PEPPERS

Roasted peppers are the basis of so many easy recipes. Fold into scrambled eggs, layer into your favorite sandwich, fry with sausages, add to an antipasto platter—or just eat straight out of the jar, on top of Garlic Herb Bread (page 73). When peppers are in season, stock up and prepare your own supply of shelf-stable jars.

Makes 1½ pints (690 g)

4 large sweet red peppers
(1 pound/455 g)

¾ teaspoon kosher salt

Extra virgin olive oil for drizzling

A handful of fresh herbs, such as
basil, oregano, and flat-leaf
parsley

Wash and dry the peppers and roast over the flame of a gas burner on high or a hot fire in a grill: Start with the peppers stem side down; if using a grill, cover it. As each side of the peppers chars, turn the peppers, until the entire surface is blistered, black, and charred, 10 to 15 minutes, depending on the size of the peppers.

Place the peppers in a plastic bag or a covered bowl and let stand for at least 15 minutes.

When the peppers are cool enough to handle, peel the charred skin off using your fingers and thumbs or a paring knife. Working over a bowl to catch the juices, cut out and discard the cores, seeds, and ribs.

To serve the peppers immediately, tear or cut them into strips and arrange on a serving platter, along with the accumulated juices. Sprinkle on the salt and drizzle with some olive oil. Scatter the fresh herbs on top. Or place the cooled peppers in a clean container and drizzle olive oil over them. Store in the refrigerator for up to 2 weeks.

VARIATION:

For softer, saucier peppers, sauté peeled strips in olive oil over medium heat for 5 to 7 minutes with a couple of peeled, smashed garlic cloves and kosher salt.

The variety of peppers we see in Italian American food is straightforward but can still be confusing. Both dried and fresh peppers followed the Italians from the Mezzogiorno to America and are still widely used today in classic dishes. In southern Italy, peppers (and other produce) grew year around. Most early immigrants here settled in the Northeast, where the growing season was limited; therefore, ways of preserving fresh peppers became an important autumn activity, along with canning tomatoes. Women banded together in assembly-line groups to preserve these for the cold months. By 1915, simultaneous with the early Italian immigrants' arrival in the United States, the commercial canning and preserved food industry was taking off.

There are multiple ways to use these peppers, depending on their preparation:

FRESH: Roasted Sweet Red Peppers (page 79), peeled and torn into strips, make an affordable staple ingredient. Add pepper strips to salads, toss with cooked pasta, or layer onto pizza. You can sauté them with potatoes or some sausages, or fry them with onions and eggs for a classic "ethnic" lunchbox sandwich. In American public school cafeterias between the 1930s and '50s, though, a wrapped egg-and-pepper sandwich, oil leaking out of the brown bag, didn't exactly help a young Italian immigrant child fit in—their mammas unaware of the stigma the lunch might attach to their child. A few New York City delis still have this old-fashioned sandwich on the menu.

PICKLED: Not to be confused with jarred roasted red peppers, homemade pickled peppers, or hot cherry peppers, have a spicy-sweet flavor and can be a secret weapon in your arsenal. If you grow these peppers, or purchase a quantity, you can preserve them at home—see Hot Red Cherry Peppers in Brine, page 83. The peppers can be stuffed with provolone (see Marinated Stuffed Hot Red Cherry Peppers, page 82) or with tuna and breadcrumbs. Feature them on an antipasto tray; slice for salads, sandwiches, and pizza; or pair with pan-fried meats, such as pork or veal chops.

DRIED: Southern Italians have long used dried red chili peppers rather the more expensive black pepper, and that has carried through into Italian American food. These are added to many recipes at the beginning of cooking, when the olive oil and onions or garlic are sautéing for a red sauce, braised greens, or a soup base. The crushed red pepper flakes in a supermarket spice jar are a generic combination of the seeds, skin, and veins of any of a variety of dried peppers. Like other spices, these lose their pungency over time.

SPECIALTY: Dried whole Calabrian chilies from southern Italy positively ooze with flavor and spice, which is only achieved by weeks of drying in the blazing sun. A bloodred color, they are often seen in local markets strung into necklaces or in small cellophane packages. Along with oregano and anchovies, these are the imported specialty items to invest in for your pantry. Bring back some from your next trip to Italy, implore a friend

to pick some up for you, or order them from one of the many online specialty markets (see Shopping Resources, page 311). To use, crush just before cooking as directed in recipes that call for crushed red pepper flakes. They will bring a richer, deeper flavor to your cooking than the commercial variety.

CALABRIAN CHILI PASTE: This ace-in-the-hole condiment, which is made from crushed dried chili peppers, is available at Italian markets. The flavor is fruity, smoky, salty, and spicy. If you are a serious spice lover, this will become a versatile condiment that will add serious heat and a unique taste to your food.

MARINATED STUFFED HOT RED CHERRY PEPPERS

When fresh cherry peppers are abundant, these are a savory, tangy addition to your appetizer selection. The peppers can be stuffed and marinated in advance and baked before serving. Serve slightly warm with bread or as part of an antipasto platter.

Makes 14 stuffed peppers

14 fresh hot red cherry peppers, tops sliced off (reserve the tops), cored, and seeded

4 ounces (115 g) provolone cheese, cut into ¼-inch (0.65 cm) cubes

14 small sprigs fresh marjoram or oregano

¼ cup (60 ml) extra virgin olive oil

2 tablespoons red wine vinegar

2 teaspoons kosher salt

1 garlic clove, minced

Stuff each pepper with a few cubes of cheese and a sprig of marjoram or oregano. Stand the stuffed peppers up in a baking pan and arrange the reserved tops around them.

Whisk the oil, vinegar, salt, and garlic together in a small bowl. Pour the mixture over the peppers. Let marinate at room temperature for up to 1 hour.

Preheat the oven to 400°F (200°C).

Place the tops on the peppers. Bake until the cheese has melted and the peppers are tender, 14 to 20 minutes. Serve warm.

HOT RED CHERRY PEPPERS in BRINE

These peppers are the ones you see on your supermarket shelf, packed in a syrupy brine and used to top pizzas or salads or to stuff with cheese for an antipasto platter. But if you preserve them at home, they will have a fresher and brighter taste. The pickling solution adds a wonderful punch when used to deglaze a pan of browned pork chops, brighten a sauce, or perk up a cheese dip. Tailor these to your own taste by adding bay leaves, lemon zest, peppercorns, or basil to the jar with the peppers before pouring in the liquid.

If you want to grow your own cherry peppers, look for seeds imported from Italy, which will produce plants that blossom and then fruit into spicy round peppers. They should be grown in good sun but can also thrive as a potted plant indoors. Every fall, I pickle as many as I can harvest (or buy at a farmers' market). To achieve shelf stability, follow the processing instructions below, and the jars will keep in the cupboard, unopened, for up to a year; once opened, they should be stored in the refrigerator. Alternatively, you can skip the processing; once cooled, the jars will keep in the refrigerator for 2 months.

Makes 1 quart (910 g)

1 pound (455 g) hot red cherry peppers, stems removed

3 garlic cloves, quartered

1¾ cups (415 ml) best-quality white wine vinegar, at least 5% acidity

½ cup (120 ml) water

⅓ cup (65 g) sugar

1 tablespoon kosher salt

VARIATION:

PICKLED SWEET JIMMY NARDELLO PEPPERS: Toss together one sliced onion and 8 to 10 sliced Jimmy Nardello peppers. Place in two 1-pint (475 ml) or one 1-quart (950 ml) jar and proceed as directed.

Thoroughly wash and dry the peppers. Place in two 1-pint (475 ml) jars with tight-fitting lids, layering the garlic pieces among the peppers.

Combine the vinegar, water, sugar, and salt in a small nonreactive saucepan and bring to a boil, then reduce the heat and simmer until the sugar and salt are dissolved, about 3 minutes. Carefully pour the liquid over the peppers to cover by 1 inch (2.5 cm). Top the jars with the lids and rings and screw on tightly.

Bring a large pot of water, deep enough to cover the jars, to a rolling boil. Carefully submerge the sealed jars in the boiling water and boil for 15 minutes. Carefully remove the jars, turn them upside down on the counter, and let cool completely before storing.

The peppers will be ready to eat after 1 week. Once they've been opened, store the jars in the refrigerator for up to 3 months.

CAPONATA

Caponata, which originated in Sicily, is a multifaceted eggplant preparation used as a salad, relish, side dish, sandwich spread, or component of an antipasto platter, always served at room temperature. This recipe departs from the convention of using pan-fried cubed eggplant. Instead, the eggplant is thinly sliced and oven-fried, which cuts down considerably on the amount of oil needed and adds an interesting textural dimension. The golden disks of eggplant are folded into a tomato mixture toward the end of cooking to combine with the other cooked ingredients. Once it's made, it's best to give it a couple of hours for all the flavors to meld together into a tangy-salty-sweet balance. Taste and adjust the seasoning before storing; a touch more of salt, sugar, or vinegar may be needed to balance the flavor.

Makes 1 quart (910 g)

- 1 pound (455 g) thin-necked eggplant, sliced very thin
- Kosher salt
- 3 tablespoons extra virgin olive oil, plus more for sautéing
- 2 celery stalks (115 g), peeled and cut into ½-inch (1.25 cm) cubes
- 1 small red onion (125 g), halved and thinly sliced
- ¼ teaspoon red pepper flakes
- 2 garlic cloves
- 7 ounces (200 g) ripe tomatoes, chopped, or 2 cups (455 g) canned tomatoes, chopped
- ¾ cup (180 ml) water
- ¼ cup (65 g) green olives, pitted and sliced
- 2 tablespoons capers, rinsed well
- 2 tablespoons red wine vinegar
- 1½ teaspoons sugar
- Leaves from 3 fresh basil or oregano sprigs

Garden-fresh eggplant needs no salting. But if you are using supermarket eggplant, arrange the slices on a towel-lined baking sheet (the slices can overlap). Salt generously on both sides. Cover with another towel, weight with another baking sheet, and let sit for 1 hour; change the towels as they become saturated.

Preheat the oven to 450°F (230°C).

Squeeze out any remaining liquid from the eggplant and transfer the eggplant slices to a large baking sheet. Toss with the olive oil and spread the slices out (they can overlap). Roast until golden brown, about 20 minutes. Remove from the oven.

Meanwhile, heat a large skillet over high heat and swirl in enough olive oil to cover the bottom of the pan. When it glistens, add the celery, onions, red pepper flakes, and a pinch of salt and cook, stirring, until the celery and onions are soft and lightly golden, about 7 minutes; add the garlic in the last 2 minutes. Add the tomatoes, water, olives, capers, vinegar, and sugar and cook, scraping up the browned bits on the bottom of the pan, until the tomatoes begin to break down, about 7 minutes.

Fold in the eggplant and basil and stir to combine, then cook, stirring once or twice, until the eggplant is heated through, 3 to 4 minutes. Add a little more water if the mixture becomes too dry. Remove from the heat and let cool completely. (*The caponata can be refrigerated in a tightly sealed jar for up to 2 weeks.*)

ASPETTA ✛ To preserve the caponata so it is shelf-stable: *Fill two
sterilized 1-pint (475 ml) jars with the hot caponata to within ¼ inch
(0.65 cm) of the tops. Top the jars with the silicone gasket rings and
screw the rings on tightly. Bring a large pot of water, deep enough to
cover the jars, to a rolling boil. Carefully submerge the jars in the boiling
water and boil for 15 minutes. Carefully remove the jars, turn upside
down, and let cool completely before storing.*

GIARDINIERA

The Italian relish called giardiniera is a combination of pickled vegetables. It's perfect in a small jar set out on an antipasto platter or layered into sandwiches. It's omnipresent on supermarket shelves in America, but it's easy to make at home. No respectable Chicago Beef (page 257) sandwich would be served without giardiniera.

Makes 2 quarts (2 kg)

2½ cups (590 ml) white wine vinegar

2½ cups (590 ml) water

2 tablespoons kosher salt

2 tablespoons sugar

1 bay leaf

3 whole cloves

1 teaspoon celery seeds

2 celery stalks, peeled and sliced on the bias into 1-inch (2.5 cm) pieces

2 medium carrots, peeled and sliced on the bias into ½-inch (1.25 cm) pieces

½ small head cauliflower, separated into small florets

2 serrano peppers, sliced on the bias into ½-inch (1.25 cm) pieces

2 shallots, quartered lengthwise

Combine the vinegar, water, salt, sugar, bay leaf, cloves, and celery seeds in a large nonreactive saucepan and bring to a boil over high heat. Add the celery, carrots, cauliflower, peppers, and shallots and return to a boil, then immediately turn off the heat and let cool to room temperature.

The giardiniera is ready to eat once cooled. Or transfer it to a container with a tight-fitting lid and store in the refrigerator for up to 2 weeks.

ASPETTA ✛ To preserve the giardiniera so it is shelf-stable: *Fill two (sterilized) 1-quart (950 ml) or four 1-pint (475 ml) jars with the giardiniera to within ¼ inch (0.65 cm) of the tops. Top the jars with the sealing attachment and screw the rings on tightly. Bring a large pot of water, deep enough to cover the jars, to a rolling boil. Carefully submerge the jars in the boiling water and boil for 15 minutes. Carefully remove the jars, turn upside down, and let cool completely before storing.*

MARINATED MUSHROOMS

Prepare these mushrooms ahead and refrigerate to have on hand for a quick tangy bite, the base for a pasta sauce, or as part of an antipasto spread.

Makes 1 pint (500 g)

1 pound (455 g) cremini mushrooms, washed and trimmed

Kosher salt

1½ cups (360 ml) white wine vinegar

¾ cup (180 ml) water

2 garlic cloves, smashed and peeled

Zest of 1 lemon, removed in strips with a vegetable peeler

2 sprigs fresh thyme

¾ to 1 cup (180 to 240 ml) extra virgin olive oil, or as needed

Leave small mushrooms whole and cut larger ones in half or quarters so that they are all a uniform size. Spread the mushrooms in a single layer on a towel-lined baking sheet and salt generously on both sides. Cover with another towel, weight with another baking sheet, and let sit for 1 hour; change the towels as they become saturated.

Combine the mushrooms, vinegar, and water in a medium nonreactive pot, bring to a boil over high heat, and boil for 5 minutes. Drain the mushrooms, transfer to a clean towel, and let dry completely.

Place the mushrooms in a clean 1-pint (475 ml) jar with the garlic, lemon zest, and thyme. Pour in enough olive oil to cover and let cool completely. The mushrooms are ready to eat once cooled, or they can be refrigerated, tightly sealed, for up to 2 weeks.

ASPETTA ✛ To preserve the mushrooms so they are shelf-stable: *Fill a sterilized 1-pint (475 ml) jar with the mushrooms to within ¼ inch (0.65 cm) of the top. Top the jar with the sealing attachment and screw the ring on tightly. Bring a large pot of water, deep enough to cover the jar, to a rolling boil. Carefully submerge the jar in the boiling water and boil for 15 minutes. Carefully remove the jar, turn upside down, and let cool completely before storing. Once opened, store the mushrooms in the refrigerator for up to 1 month.*

ROASTED CHESTNUTS

Roasted chestnuts seem sort of old-fashioned now, which must mean they are ripe for revival. They were very important to my dad, a holdover from his childhood. Every Christmas I was his helper, snipping an X in the rounded side of each chestnut so they wouldn't explode while roasting. On Thanksgiving, he made his very own pork stuffing, which included chestnuts and raisins, to be stuffed under the skin in the turkey neck pocket while the rest of the bird contained regular bread stuffing. My first visit to New York City with my dad is etched in my memory, with the smoky scent of chestnuts roasting over a flame in a pushcart on a frosty, crowded Fifth Avenue. Chestnuts were omnipresent in the cucina povera of southern Italy, as the nuts were also ground into an inexpensive flour for bread and pasta dough.

Makes about 18 chestnuts

8 ounces (230 g) chestnuts in the shell

Coarse salt

Prepare a fire in an outdoor grill or preheat the oven to 425°F (220°C). If you will be using the oven, set a wire rack on a baking sheet.

Using kitchen shears or a paring knife, cut an X in the round side of each chestnut. Arrange them on the grill pan or lay out on the prepared baking sheet. Grill or roast until the skins split open at the X, revealing the nutmeat, 20 to 25 minutes.

Remove the chestnuts from the heat and dust with coarse salt. Serve (in the shell) in a bowl or on a platter, with a shell discard bowl on the side. Store any leftover chestnuts in the refrigerator in an airtight container for up to 4 days.

ITALIAN TUNA DIP

My grandmother served this dip with celery sticks and crackers as an appetizer before dinner on meatless Friday nights. It also makes a great addition to a fish-centric antipasto platter. The texture is like a smooth tuna salad, made without mayonnaise and flavored with Italian seasonings. You can use your favorite canned tuna or splurge on imported olive oil packed–tuna from Sicily. The dip/spread will keep in the refrigerator for a couple of days.

Makes 1 cup (226 g)

One 7-ounce (200 g) can tuna, preferably packed in olive oil, drained

3 tablespoons fresh lemon juice (2 small lemons)

2 tablespoons extra virgin olive oil

¾ cup (75 g) finely chopped onion

¾ cup (45 g) fresh flat-leaf parsley leaves and tender stems, finely chopped

1 small garlic clove, minced

1 tablespoon capers, rinsed and drained

½ teaspoon kosher salt

¼ teaspoon freshly ground black pepper

Fresh vegetables, such as celery, fennel, carrots, and/or cucumbers, peeled if necessary and sliced, for serving

Crackers and baguette slices, for serving

Place the tuna in a blender or food processor and pulse to break it up. Add the lemon juice and olive oil and blend on low speed until it begins to smooth out but is still a little chunky, about 1 minute. Add the onion, parsley, garlic, capers, salt, and pepper and pulse until everything is thoroughly combined and the mixture is smooth.

Transfer the dip to a small bowl and serve with fresh vegetables, crackers, and baguette slices.

MUSSELS OREGANATA

Serve these mussels as a hot antipasto or as a part of a Seven Fishes Christmas Eve feast (see page 190). The shellfish can be cleaned and the recipe prepared in advance and chilled or even frozen, then cooked right before serving. Use fresh oregano or dried oregano that is still pungent and flavorful. Get in the habit of tasting your previously opened spices in the cabinet before cooking to make sure they haven't been there too long, especially when they will be the main ingredient in a dish!

Makes 12 or 28 mussels on the half shell

15 large or 30 small mussels (1½ pounds/698 g), cleaned (see Aspetta, opposite)

½ cup (120 ml) white wine

1 cup (105 g) dried breadcrumbs

3 tablespoons grated Parmesan or Romano cheese

3 garlic cloves, minced

1 fresh hot red pepper, such as Calabrian, Fresno, or serrano, halved, seeded, and minced (2 tablespoons)

¼ cup (15 g) minced fresh flat-leaf parsley

1 tablespoon dried oregano or 2 tablespoons minced fresh oregano

2 tablespoons fresh lemon juice

1 tablespoon extra virgin olive oil, plus more for drizzling

Kosher salt if desired

Lemon wedges for serving

Combine the mussels and wine in a large pot with a tight-fitting lid. Cover and steam over high heat until the shells open, 6 to 8 minutes; transfer them to a baking sheet as they open. Some may take longer than others; discard any that don't open.

Remove the pot from the heat and strain the broth through a cheesecloth-lined colander into a bowl; reserve. Pull off and discard one half of each shell and leave the meat in the other half shell.

Combine the breadcrumbs, cheese, garlic, red pepper, parsley, oregano, lemon juice, and ½ cup (120 ml) of the strained cooking liquid in a large bowl. Let the mixture stand for 5 to 7 minutes to hydrate the breadcrumbs, then stir in the olive oil. Taste for salt (some seafood is saltier than others) and season if desired.

Preheat the broiler. Lay the mussels in their shells on a baking sheet or in a roasting pan. Spoon the stuffing over the mussels. Drizzle a little olive oil and some of the remaining cooking broth over each one. Broil until the stuffing is golden and bubbling, 3 to 5 minutes; keep a close eye on the mussels to avoid burning the topping. Serve warm, with lemon wedges for squeezing over top.

VARIATION:

Clams can be swapped for the mussels: if they are large, chop the meat after steaming them; smaller ones can be left whole.

CLAMS CASINO

Clams Casino are in the lockbox of my taste memories because they were the special-occasion appetizer my family would order at restaurants in the 1960s and '70s. Back then, the shells were overstuffed with too many garlic powder–infused breadcrumbs. This update, with fewer breadcrumbs and a lot more parsley and lemon zest, lets the clam flavor shine through, for a much fresher taste.

Makes 24 clams on the half shell

24 clams, preferably littlenecks, cleaned (see Aspetta)

¼ cup (25 g) dried breadcrumbs

¼ cup (15 g) chopped fresh flat-leaf parsley

2 strips bacon or 2 slices pancetta, cooked and crumbled

3 garlic cloves, minced

Grated zest and juice of 1 lemon

½ teaspoon red pepper flakes

Kosher salt

Extra virgin olive oil for drizzling

Lemon wedges for serving

Place the clams in a large pot with a tight-fitting lid and add ¼ inch (0.65 cm) of water to the pot. Cover and steam over high heat until the clams open, about 6 minutes; transfer them to a baking sheet as they open. Some may take longer than others; discard any that don't open.

Pull off and discard one of each shell, leaving the clam attached to the other half shell (if any of the clams have fallen out during steaming, place each one in an empty shell). Arrange the clams in a single layer on a baking sheet or platter.

Preheat the broiler with the rack set at least 4 inches (10 cm) from the heating element. Combine the breadcrumbs, parsley, bacon, garlic, lemon zest and juice, red pepper, and a pinch of salt in a bowl.

Top each clam with about a teaspoon of the breadcrumb mixture and drizzle some olive oil over the top. Broil until the breadcrumb mixture is bubbling and golden brown, about 3 minutes; watch carefully, as the breadcrumbs can easily burn. Serve warm, with lemon wedges for squeezing over top.

ASPETTA ✛ How to clean bivalves: *It's important to clean bivalves thoroughly to avoid a gritty bite of seafood. Clams should be scrubbed and soaked in water to cover, changing the soaking water several times, until it stays clear. I add some cornmeal to the first batch of soaking water because the clams will open to consume it and subsequently purge any unwanted matter. For farmed mussels, such as rope mussels, a quick rinse with cold water and removal of the small "beards" (if any) are all that's necessary. Grasp the thread-like beards and give them a firm pull to remove. Wild mussels require more work—scrub the shells with an abrasive brush or sponge and pull off or trim the beards.*

TOSSED PASTA

101   Utica Riggies

102   Bucatini Puttanesca

103   Garlic and Olive Oil Spaghetti

104   Penne alla Vodka

106   Orecchiette with Broccoli Rabe and Sausage

109   Pasta alla Norma

110   Pasta e Ceci

112   Spaghetti Carbonara

113   Spaghetti Amatriciana

115   Fettuccine Alfredo with Chicken

117   Turkey Tetrazzini

119   Fried Spaghetti

120   Creamy Lemon Spaghetti

122   Basic Pasta Dough

125   Cheese and Spinach Ravioli

WHEN THE TIMING ISN'T RIGHT FOR A long-simmered sauce, there are dozens of pasta dishes you can make that are sauced and tossed together in the pan right before serving. Most of these sauces are quick to prepare and cook in a little more time than it takes to boil the noodles. A good pasta recipe balances the noodle-to-sauce ratio just right, so the pasta isn't drowned in the sauce. While you're boiling the pasta, you cook the sauce in a skillet large enough to toss everything together. Most of these pan-sauce dishes are quintessential tried-and-true Italian American favorites, but there is room for innovation too.

Always remember that cooked noodles, reserved pasta water, and just about any savory ingredients—beans, vegetables, cheeses, meats, or seafood—can be improvised into a bespoke pasta recipe. That's how most of these recipes were built: a restaurant line cook using leftover ingredients to make a meal, as in the case of Utica Riggies; mothers with few ingredients and many mouths to feed coming up with Pasta e Ceci; or a cook creating an ode to a favorite opera singer with Turkey Tetrazzini.

I always keep a couple pounds of different dried noodles in the cupboard, but don't discount how easy it is to make fresh pasta (see page 122). Just a couple of eggs and some flour are all that's needed. And after a few tries, you'll find that homemade dough is way easier and faster than you might imagine. There's no need for equipment other than a fork, some elbow grease, and a rolling pin (or clean wine bottle!). Cut the rolled-out rested dough into ribbons and boil in salted water before combining it with the sauce. A hand-cranked or electric pasta machine, or an attachment for your stand mixer, provides even more noodle shape options. Familiarize yourself with the techniques used in these recipes, find some favorite flavors and textures, and open your imagination. The foundation of Italian American cooking was built that way.

UTICA RIGGIES

The environs of Utica-Rome, New York, attracted a large population of Italian immigrants from the mid-nineteenth century into the twentieth because nearby Ellis Island was the largest port of entry, and there were work opportunities in mills, masonry, and railroads. Over the decades, generations of these immigrants came up with new recipes using their classic pantry ingredients. The Chesterfield restaurant in downtown Utica claims to have invented Riggies; no doubt a cook there used ingredients on hand to create such a memorable concoction that a nickname (from the macaroni shape, rigatoni) was coined for it.

Makes 4 to 6 servings

- 1½ pounds (680 g) boneless, skinless chicken breasts or thighs, cut onto bite-sized cubes
- Kosher salt and freshly ground black pepper
- 3 tablespoons extra virgin olive oil
- 1 sweet red pepper, cored, seeded, and cut into 1½-inch-wide (4 cm) strips
- 1 onion, chopped (1 cup/100 g)
- 4 small garlic cloves, thinly sliced
- 3 pickled cherry peppers, chopped plus ¼ cup (60 ml) of the pepper brine
- 1 cup (240 ml) white wine
- 1 cup (240 ml) heavy cream
- One 28-ounce (800 g) can whole tomatoes, pulsed to a puree
- 1 pound (455 g) rigatoni
- ½ cup (50 g) grated Romano cheese

Toss the chicken with a generous amount of salt and black pepper. Heat a large skillet over medium-high heat and swirl in the olive oil. When it glistens, add the chicken, spreading the cubes out to avoid crowding the pan, and sear until golden on all sides, about 6 minutes. Remove the chicken to a plate.

Add the pepper strips, onions, and garlic to the pan and cook, stirring constantly, until lightly golden, about 4 minutes. Return the chicken (with any juices) to the pan and add the cherry peppers, then pour in the brine and wine to deglaze the pan and cook, scraping up the brown bits from the bottom, until the liquid is slightly thickened, 2 to 3 minutes. Stir in the cream and tomatoes, reduce the heat to medium-low, and simmer for 20 minutes, or until the sauce has reduced and thickened.

Bring a large pot of water to a rolling boil. Salt the water, add the pasta, and cook for 2 minutes shy of the package instructions; the pasta should be slightly soft with a firm chew to it. Scoop out 1 cup (240 ml) of the cooking water and drain the pasta.

Add the reserved cooking water to the sauce, along with the drained pasta, and stir in the grated cheese. Cook over medium heat, stirring, for a minute or two, to coat the noodles and finish cooking them in the sauce. Serve hot.

VARIATION:

Thinly sliced sausages, browned in a skillet until cooked through, can be swapped for the chicken. Some versions of Utica Riggies also include sliced mushrooms, added to the skillet at the same time as the red peppers.

BUCATINI PUTTANESCA

Spaghetti is the classic pasta for this sauce, but because the sauce has now advanced to a general accompaniment used to top fish or chicken on many restaurant menus, the old rules are out the window. Like vodka sauce, puttanesca, originating on the southern coast of Naples, is a late-twentieth-century addition to the Italian American red sauce collection. The name itself is rooted in the Italian term "puttana," meaning lady of the night (one of the few employment options for women back then). While we have no real knowledge about why a "working woman" would have cooked this dish over others, the spiciness of the seasoning and the quick-cooking umami-rich pantry ingredients it calls for are as good a reason as any for anyone with limited time to make this dish.

Makes 4 to 6 servings

2 tablespoons extra virgin olive oil, plus more for drizzling

2 garlic cloves, minced

½ cup (115 g) black olives, such as Gaeta, rinsed, pitted, and thinly sliced

½ cup (115 g) green olives, such as Castelvetrano or Cerignola, rinsed, pitted, and thinly sliced

3 tablespoons capers, rinsed and drained

½ teaspoon red pepper flakes, plus more for serving

One 28-ounce (800 g) can whole tomatoes, roughly crushed in the can

1 sprig fresh basil

½ teaspoon dried oregano

1 pound (455 g) bucatini or spaghetti

Combine the olive oil and garlic in a large saucepan and cook over medium-high heat just until the garlic begins to sizzle but not brown, about 1 minute, then immediately stir in the olives, capers, and red pepper flakes. Add the tomatoes and bring to a boil, then reduce the heat and simmer for about 15 minutes, until the sauce has reduced and thickened. Add the basil and oregano and cook for 10 minutes.

Meanwhile, bring a large pot of water to a rolling boil. Generously salt the water, add the pasta, and cook for 2 minutes shy of the package instructions; the pasta should be slightly soft with a firm chew to it. Scoop out 1 cup (240 ml) of the cooking water, and drain the pasta.

Add the reserved pasta water and the pasta to the pan, stir well, and cook for a few minutes to coat the pasta in the sauce. Serve the pasta with a swirl of olive oil and more red pepper flakes on top.

GARLIC AND OLIVE OIL SPAGHETTI

Aglio e olio is the most delicious basic pasta dish. All the ingredients are likely in your pantry already, and it can be embellished easily with other on-hand ingredients (such as chopped sun-dried tomatoes or capers) or to satisfy a personal taste. A lot of cooks call this dish "Midnight Pasta," as you can make it straight out of the cupboard to satisfy a late-night craving if you have no fresh ingredients on hand. Old-timers from big Italian families remember this as a meatless Friday night staple, often with anchovies added along with the garlic. Sometimes I add a big squeeze of lemon or orange juice and scatter some minced parsley over the top of the whole thing before serving.

Makes 4 to 6 servings

1 pound (455 g) long pasta strands, such as spaghetti, bucatini, or capellini

⅓ cup (80 ml) extra virgin olive oil

3 tablespoons thinly sliced garlic (from 2 garlic cloves)

1 teaspoon kosher salt

½ teaspoon crushed red pepper

Grated Parmesan or Romano cheese for serving

Bring a large pot of water to a boil. Salt the water generously, add the pasta, and cook for 2 minutes shy of the package instructions; the noodles should be slightly soft with a firm chew to them. Scoop out 2 cups (475 ml) of the pasta water and drain the pasta.

Meanwhile, combine the oil, garlic, salt, and red pepper in a large skillet and cook over medium-high heat, stirring, until the garlic begins to color but not brown, 30 to 60 seconds. Pour in the reserved pasta water and simmer for a couple of minutes, stirring to emulsify the oil and liquid.

Add the noodles to the sauce and stir to coat, about 1 minute. Serve with grated cheese on top.

PENNE ALLA VODKA

What, if anything, does the vodka do to make this sauce so delicious? Combining that tangy-spicy tomato flavor with rich, silky heavy cream to make one luscious sauce is done through emulsification (binding liquid with fat), not unlike thickening a mustard vinaigrette by whisking in olive oil. And alcohol is a solvent that enhances the tomato flavor by releasing compounds that bind the components in the same way wine does, but it leaves no flavor behind to compete with the basic tomato-cream taste. A combination of tomato paste and whole tomatoes gives this sauce just the right sweetness.

Makes 4 to 6 servings

2 tablespoons extra virgin olive oil

2 tablespoons unsalted butter

1 small onion, minced (about 1 cup/100 g)

2 garlic cloves, thinly sliced

¼ teaspoon red pepper flakes

One 14.5-ounce (425 g) can whole tomatoes (about 2 cups)

½ cup (115 g) tomato paste

¼ cup (60 ml) vodka

¾ teaspoon kosher salt

½ cup (120 ml) heavy cream

1 pound (455 g) penne

½ cup (50 g) grated Parmesan cheese, plus more for serving

Bring a large pot of water to a rolling boil over high heat. Meanwhile, heat a large saucepan over medium heat. Swirl in the oil and add 1 tablespoon of the butter. Add the onions and cook until they begin to soften, about 3 minutes. Toss in the garlic and pepper flakes and cook, stirring constantly, until the onions begin to color, about 3 minutes more.

Stir in the tomatoes, tomato paste, vodka, and salt, reduce the heat to medium-low, and simmer for 10 minutes to reduce the sauce slightly. Stir in the cream. Use an immersion blender directly in the pan, or transfer the sauce to a stand blender, and carefully puree the sauce for a few minutes, until it is smooth; return the sauce to the pan if necessary.

Generously salt the water, add the pasta, and cook for 2 minutes shy of the package instructions; the pasta should be slightly soft with a firm chew to it. Scoop out ½ cup (120 ml) of the cooking water and drain the pasta.

Bring the sauce back to a simmer over medium heat and stir in the reserved cooking water. Swirl in the remaining tablespoon of butter and the cheese. Add the pasta and cook for a minute or so, stirring to fully coat the noodles. Serve right away, with grated cheese.

ASPETTA + *Use a large pot and plenty of water for cooking pasta. When boiling the pasta, there should be enough room for the noodles to "dance" around so they cook evenly. A good rule of thumb is to use at least 4 quarts (3.8 L) of water for every pound of pasta. "Salt the water generously" means about 2 tablespoons (yes, that much!) Diamond Crystal salt per pound of pasta. The salt will season the noodles themselves, giving the final dish, once sauced, full flavor in every bite.*

PRESERVED TOMATOES

It's difficult to imagine an ingredient other than olive oil that is more integral to the Italian American foodway than tomatoes in all their guises: fresh, canned, sun-dried, or as tomato paste or passata (pureed seeded pulp). Red sauce, in some form, has been made here since the first arrivals of Italian cooks in America.

By the mid-1880s, peasants and artisans on the northern coast of Sicily and around Naples (two areas that had long been heavily engaged in the cultivation and export of citrus) had begun to expand their labors to include the cultivation of tomatoes and processing them in new ways. Small factories produced dried cakes of tomato puree reduced to a thick, dark paste. Lightly cooked, peeled, and pulverized tomatoes were canned for sauces.

At home, any tomatoes not eaten fresh in season were preserved as conserva— a homemade paste put up to use for sauces during the winter months. This labor of love, an essential task before canned tomatoes were readily available, continued as a tradition in America for a long while. When tomatoes were in season, an important ritual developed whereby a group of women from the family or community would gather to prepare the paste. Ripe tomatoes were broken apart or chopped up, spread out on bedsheets stretched over makeshift frames, and left to dry to a paste under the hot sun on a rooftop, then scooped up and stored for later use.

A tablespoon of tomato paste added to a sauce or soup base enhances the rich bottom flavor without a dominant tomato taste. Sometimes the paste is called for unnecessarily in a long-simmering red sauce that would develop depth of flavor over time without it. But quick-cooked red sauces benefit from a deep hit of that concentrated pulp, cooked in extra virgin olive oil with the aromatics at the beginning. Different recipes require different preparations of canned tomatoes, but there is no need to have every different type of preserved tomatoes in your cupboard. Good whole canned tomatoes (see Provisions to Have on Hand, page 27) can be pureed or processed as needed (with a blender, food processor, knife, or scissors). Keep a tube of tomato paste in the refrigerator to dole out judiciously.

ORECCHIETTE with BROCCOLI RABE and SAUSAGE

In this sauce, broccoli rabe cooks together with sausage and a nontraditional splash of white wine vinegar to soften and transform its bitterness into a milder creamy, savory flavor. Orecchiette is a specialty of Puglia, in southern Italy, where many American immigrants hailed from. The pasta dough is traditionally made with semolina flour and then formed with lightning speed by expert local woman cooks using no more than a dull knife and skilled pair of hands into little cups that look like ears. Whether handmade or commercially produced, the macaroni shapes are ideal for collecting the rough-textured sauce, making for a delicious bite when eaten together with a sausage coin.

Makes 4 to 6 servings

1 pound (455 g) broccoli rabe

2 tablespoons extra virgin olive oil

1 pound (455 g) sweet Italian sausages, cut into ¾-inch (2 cm) coins

2 tablespoons white wine vinegar

2 garlic cloves, thinly sliced

¼ teaspoon red pepper flakes

1 teaspoon kosher salt

1 pound (455 g) orecchiette

2 tablespoons unsalted butter

½ cup (50 g) grated Romano cheese, plus more for serving

To prepare the broccoli rabe, trim off the ends, peel the thick bottoms, and thinly slice the bottom stalks. Cut the leaves and florets into bite-sized pieces. Float all the pieces in a large bowl of cold water, then lift out and drain; repeat until the water remains clear of grit. Drain the broccoli rabe, leaving the water clinging to the greens.

Heat a large skillet over medium-high heat and swirl in the olive oil. Add the sausage and cook, stirring, until the pink color is gone and the edges are golden, about 7 minutes. Add the broccoli rabe, vinegar, garlic, pepper flakes, and salt, scraping up the brown bits from the bottom of the pan. Cover and simmer, stirring occasionally, until the greens are tender, 12 to 15 minutes; add more water if necessary.

Meanwhile, bring a large pot of water to a rolling boil. Generously salt the water, add the pasta, and boil for 2 minutes shy of the package instructions; the pasta should be slightly soft with a firm chew to it. Scoop out 2 cups (475 ml) of the pasta water and drain the pasta.

Add the noodles to the sauce and stir in the reserved pasta water, the butter, and grated cheese and cook, stirring, for a few minutes, until the cheese melts and the sauce becomes creamy. Serve with more grated cheese at the table.

PASTA ALLA NORMA

The combination of fried and sautéed eggplant brings maximum oomph to this sauce. Its flavors pop when the two distinctly different cooking methods coalesce. The eggplant's essential taste is sealed within the fried disks with their crispy, caramelized coating, while the spongy, porous texture of the cubed eggplant allows it to absorb the flavors of the other ingredients it is cooked with. The result makes the most of the eggplant's potential.

Makes 4 to 6 servings

1 medium Italian eggplant

¾ cup (180 ml) extra virgin olive oil

1 teaspoon kosher salt

4 garlic cloves, thinly sliced

2 cups (425 g) chopped tomatoes

2 sprigs fresh basil, plus basil leaves for garnish

¼ teaspoon red pepper flakes

2 teaspoons red wine vinegar

1 pound (455 g) macaroni, such as rigatoni, penne, or radiatore

½ cup (50 g) grated Parmesan cheese

1 cup (170 g) grated ricotta salata or 1 cup (100 g) Romano cheese

Cut 15 to 20 thin slices from the narrow end of the eggplant. Cut the rest into ½-inch (1.25 cm) cubes.

Pour half the olive oil into a large skillet and heat over medium-high heat until it's glistening. Add the eggplant slices and fry, turning once, until a deep golden color on both sides, 6 to 8 minutes. Remove the slices to paper towels or a wire rack set over a baking sheet to drain. Sprinkle with ½ teaspoon of the salt on both sides.

Add the remaining olive oil to the pan and heat until glistening. Add the cubed eggplant and sauté until lightly golden and soft, about 7 minutes. Stir in the garlic and cook for a minute, without browning it.

Add the tomatoes, basil sprigs, pepper flakes, and the remaining ½ teaspoon salt and simmer for 10 minutes; add the vinegar in the last couple minutes of cooking.

Meanwhile, bring a large pot of water to a rolling boil. Generously salt the water, add the pasta, and boil until 2 minutes shy of the package instructions; the pasta should be slightly soft with a firm chew to it. Scoop out 1 cup (240 ml) of the cooking water and drain the pasta.

Stir the reserved pasta water and the Parmesan into the sauce. Add the pasta to the pan, stir well, and cook for a few minutes to coat the pasta in the sauce.

Top each serving with some of the fried eggplant, ricotta salata, and basil leaves.

PASTA e CECI

My great-aunt Sarah taught me this Friday family staple when I was visiting her in Rome, New York. Until 1966, the Catholic Church prohibited eating meat on Fridays, a restriction my family observed religiously, as did many Italian Americans. Simple meatless meals like this were common. Tender protein-rich chickpeas are cooked in garlicky olive oil, then tomatoes and broth are added to make a light tomato sauce and nestle themselves inside the little pasta shells.

Makes 4 to 6 servings

3 tablespoons extra virgin olive oil, plus more for drizzling

4 garlic cloves, minced

½ teaspoon red pepper flakes

4 cups (700 g) cooked or drained canned chickpeas (from two 15-ounce cans; see Aspetta)

4 cups (950 ml) chicken broth, homemade (page 179) or store-bought

One 28-ounce (800 g) can whole tomatoes, coarsely blended

1 teaspoon kosher salt

1 pound (455 g) small macaroni shells

Grated Romano cheese for serving

Combine the olive oil, garlic, and red pepper flakes in a large saucepan and cook over medium-high heat, stirring constantly, until the garlic begins to sizzle, about 1 minute (be careful not to burn it). Add the chickpeas and cook, stirring, until well coated in the oil mixture, about 3 minutes. Add the chicken broth, tomatoes, and salt, bring to a simmer, and simmer uncovered until the chickpeas absorb the flavors and are tender, about 20 minutes. (The sauce will be soupy, but the noodles will absorb some of the liquid.)

Meanwhile, bring a large pot of water to a rolling boil. Generously salt the water and add the macaroni and cook according to the package instructions (the pasta should be fully cooked and soft, not al dente).

Drain the noodles thoroughly and stir into the sauce. Serve in bowls, topped with grated cheese and a drizzle of olive oil.

ASPETTA + *One pound of dried beans is roughly the same price as a 15-ounce (425 g) can of cooked chickpeas. Dried chickpeas (ceci) triple in size when cooked. For this recipe, 1⅓ cups (220 g) dried chickpeas will yield 4 cups (700 g) cooked. Cooked chickpeas freeze beautifully, so it's worth your time to soak and cook a big batch, then store in 1-pint (475 ml) containers in the freezer. To use frozen chickpeas, defrost overnight in the refrigerator. Or place the container in a bowl of warm water, or in the microwave, for 5 minutes to partially thaw them, then turn the block of chickpeas into a saucepan and heat over low heat to completely defrost.*

To cook dried beans, soak them overnight in water to cover, or quick-soak them: Put the beans in a pot, cover with water, and bring to a boil. Turn off the heat, cover the pan, and let sit for 1 hour. Then boil the soaked chickpeas until tender, usually 1 to 2 hours; the exact timing depends on the age of the dried beans.

SPAGHETTI CARBONARA

This dish gained popularity in the postwar years, after the Americans and Brits had been to Italy and more immigrants began coming to the United States from Rome and its environs. Americanized carbonara veers from the classic preparation of eggs, cheese, black pepper, and guanciale to sometimes include heavy cream and bacon instead of guanciale—an affront to Roman cooks! You can use any cured pork product or grating cheese you like, but do leave out the cream. This recipe makes a respectable American cousin to its Roman forerunner.

Makes 4 to 6 servings

3 large eggs

1 cup (100 g) grated Parmesan or Romano cheese, plus more for serving

½ teaspoon freshly ground black pepper, plus more for serving

2 tablespoons extra virgin olive oil

8 ounces (225 g) guanciale, pancetta, or lightly smoked bacon, cut into ½-inch (1.25 cm) pieces

2 garlic cloves, smashed and peeled

Splash of white wine (optional)

1 pound (455 g) spaghetti

Bring a large pot of water to a rolling boil. Whisk together the eggs, cheese, and pepper in a large bowl.

Heat the olive oil in a large skillet over medium-high heat. Add the pork and garlic and cook until the meat is just crispy, 8 to 10 minutes; remove and discard the garlic cloves once they are golden. Skim off some of the fat, then splash in the wine, if using, and stir for a minute or so to reduce it. Keep warm over low heat.

Meanwhile, generously salt the water and add the spaghetti. Cook for 2 minutes shy of the package instructions; the noodles should be slightly soft with a firm chew to them. Drain and immediately add to the egg mixture, along with the guanciale (or other meat), tossing and turning to completely coat the noodles.

Serve immediately, with more cheese and black pepper on top.

ASPETTA + *The creaminess of this dish comes from cheese and the eggs, which slowly cook in the heat from the hot noodles while the cheese melts. The trick is for the noodles to be hot enough to just cook the eggs without scrambling them, or, conversely, without leaving them almost raw (which is why some Americans have resorted to cream, butter, and cream cheese as additions to or substitutes for the eggs). Drain your pasta and then immediately use tongs to quickly toss and turn the noodles in the egg mixture to cook the eggs and completely coat the noodles.*

SPAGHETTI AMATRICIANA

What's most important to the flavor of this sauce is cured pork. The dish is traditionally made with guanciale and just two other ingredients, Pecorino cheese and tomatoes. While it remains a pillar of Roman cooking, it's taken on its own identity on red-sauce menus and kitchen tables in America. We use what we have, from pancetta to bacon, with no apologies, often adding onions or garlic to the sauce. Here delicious success comes from emulsifying the pork fat with wine or water before incorporating juicy tomatoes and a kick of spice. If you're just using bacon, you'll want to add (in descending order of preference) red or yellow onion, garlic, or shallot. But if you have good-quality imported guanciale, nothing else is needed besides the tomatoes and cheese.

Makes 4 to 6 servings

8 ounces (230 g) thick-sliced guanciale, pancetta, or fatty bacon, cut into thick matchsticks

⅓ cup (85 g) sliced red or yellow onion or 2 garlic cloves, smashed and peeled

¾ cup (180 ml) white or red wine or water

One 28-ounce (800 g) can whole tomatoes

½ teaspoon red pepper flakes or crumbled dried peperoncini

1 pound (455 g) spaghetti, bucatini, or other long noodles

Kosher salt

½ cup (50 g) grated Romano cheese, plus more for serving

Place a large deep skillet over medium-low heat, add the guanciale, and stir constantly so the fat slowly renders out without burning and the pieces become golden and almost crispy, about 5 minutes. (Adjust the heat up or down as necessary.) Add the onions or garlic and cook until golden. Then, if using garlic, remove it from the pan and discard.

Carefully pour in the wine or water and shake the pan to emulsify the fat and liquid while scraping the brown bits up from the bottom. Then simmer until the mixture has reduced to a syrupy consistency, 2 to 3 minutes.

Add the tomatoes and red pepper flakes, lightly mashing the tomatoes and mixing them with the syrupy sauce. Partially cover the pan, reduce the heat to low, and simmer for about an hour (if you are pressed for time, 30 minutes will do). As the tomatoes cook and soften, continue to mash them occasionally to achieve the desired consistency.

Meanwhile, bring a large pot of water to a rolling boil. Generously salt the water, add the spaghetti, and cook for 2 minutes shy of the package instructions; the pasta should be slightly soft with a firm chew to it. Scoop out 1 cup (240 ml) of the pasta water and drain the pasta.

Recipe continues

Add the noodles to the sauce, then add the grated cheese and ½ cup (120 ml) of the reserved pasta water and quickly toss together to coat the pasta. Add more of the cooking water if a looser consistency is desired.

Serve the noodles with more grated cheese on top.

ASPETTA ✛ *Why use some of the starchy pasta water to finish a pasta dish? It serves to help marry the noodles with the sauce and emulsify the sauce to a pleasing consistency. And, as the pasta water is salted before cooking the noodles, it also adds flavor to the sauce.*

FETTUCCINE ALFREDO
with CHICKEN

The now almost ubiquitous Alfredo sauce was ushered into the American diet by the famous silent film stars Mary Pickford and Douglas Fairbanks, who fell in love with the dish on their Roman honeymoon. Once at home, they served it to guests, and its popularity spread among the influencers of the time. As the story goes, its namesake Alfredo, who owned a restaurant in Rome, apparently devised the dish for his infirm wife when she needed to gain weight. When he added it to his menu, it became an instant success. Using chicken in this version is a nod to Olive Garden. Unlike Mamma Leone's or Chef Boyardee, both small businesses originally founded by Italian Americans, Olive Garden was born in 1981 from the corporate brain trust of General Mills executives—a testament to how important the humble food of our immigrant forebears had become to the hearts and stomachs of wealthier suburbanites across the country.

Makes 4 to 6 servings

1 pound (455 g) skinless, boneless chicken breasts

Kosher salt and freshly ground white pepper

2 tablespoons unsalted butter

2 cups (475 ml) heavy cream

4 garlic cloves

¾ cup (75 g) grated Parmesan cheese, plus more for serving

1 pound (455 g) fettuccine

Cut the chicken into strips. Season with salt and white pepper.

Melt the butter in a large skillet over medium-high heat. Add the chicken and sauté until cooked through, about 8 minutes.

Meanwhile, combine the cream and garlic in a small pot, bring to a simmer, and simmer for 10 minutes. Add the garlic cream to the pan with the chicken, removing the garlic cloves. Stir in the Parmesan.

Meanwhile, bring a large pot of water to a boil. Salt the water generously, add the fettuccine, and cook for 2 minutes shy of the package instructions; the noodles should be slightly soft with a firm chew to them. Drain the pasta and transfer to a serving bowl.

Add the sauce to the noodles and stir to combine and coat the noodles. Serve with more Parmesan at the table.

TURKEY TETRAZZINI

Let's rescue this authentic Italian American creation from its 1950s Americana casserole legacy. Internationally acclaimed coloratura soprano Luisa Tetrazzini made her American debut in 1905. As with fellow Italian opera singer Enrico Caruso, it wasn't long before a dish named for her became popular. Turkey or chicken, butter, mushrooms, Parmesan cheese, and noodles are the generally agreed-upon ingredients, while the process and final presentation are subject to debate. Like so many recipes and foods introduced by Italian immigrants, Turkey Tetrazzini morphed into a classic American recipe with nary a nod to its origins. Here the day-after carcass of the Thanksgiving turkey provides both the meat and broth (you can use store-bought for both or either) needed for a gloriously creamy recipe worthy of the great Italian diva.

Makes
4 to 6 servings

1½ cups (1.1 ounces/31 g) dried mushrooms, such as portobello, porcini, or shiitake

2 tablespoons extra virgin olive oil

4 tablespoons (55 g) unsalted butter

3 shallots, thinly sliced

½ cup (120 ml) white wine

3 tablespoons all-purpose flour

4 cups (950 ml) turkey broth or chicken broth, homemade (page 179) or store-bought

1 pound (455 g) cooked turkey or chicken, shredded

¾ cup (75 g) grated Romano or Parmesan cheese

¼ cup (60 ml) heavy cream

½ teaspoon kosher salt

¼ teaspoon freshly ground black pepper

1 pound (455 g) spaghetti

¼ cup (15 g) fresh flat-leaf parsley leaves and tender stems, chopped

1½ cups (160 g) Crispy Savory Breadcrumbs (page 43)

Place the dried mushrooms in a small bowl, cover with boiling water, and let soak for 15 minutes. Lift out the mushrooms, reserving the soaking liquid, and chop the mushrooms. Strain the soaking liquid.

Heat a large skillet over medium-high heat. Swirl in the olive oil, then add the butter and shallots and cook, stirring frequently, until the shallots begin to caramelize, 3 to 4 minutes. Add the mushrooms and cook, stirring, for 3 minutes.

Pour in the wine to deglaze the pan, scraping up the brown bits on the bottom of the pan, and simmer to reduce it slightly, about 2 minutes. Whisk in the flour and cook, stirring constantly, for 1 minute. Pour in the broth and ¼ cup (60 ml) of the reserved mushroom soaking liquid. Bring to a simmer and cook, stirring, until the sauce thickens slightly, about 8 minutes. Fold in the turkey, cheese, cream, salt, and pepper and cook over low heat until the turkey is heated through and the cheese has melted, 1 to 2 minutes.

Recipe continues

Meanwhile, bring a large pot of water to a rolling boil. Generously salt the water, add the pasta, and cook according to the package directions (it should be thoroughly cooked, not al dente).

Drain the noodles and fold into the sauce, coating them completely. Transfer to a serving bowl and scatter the parsley and breadcrumbs over the top, and serve immediately.

VARIATIONS:

TETRAZZINI WITH FRESH MUSHROOMS AND PEAS: Swap the dried mushrooms for 2 cups (180 g) sliced white mushrooms. Sauté in the oil and butter until golden and softened. Increase the broth to 4¼ cups (1.0 L). Fold in 1 cup (160 g) frozen peas along with the turkey.

CLASSIC AMERICAN TURKEY TETRAZZINI CASSEROLE: Increase the broth to 6 cups (1.5 L) and the cream to ½ cup (120 ml). Transfer the whole mixture to a buttered 9-by-13-inch (23 by 33 cm) casserole dish, sprinkle on the breadcrumbs, and dot with butter. Bake in a 375°F (190°C) oven until bubbling and golden on top, 15 to 20 minutes.

FRIED SPAGHETTI

Reused and reimaging cooked pasta is an integral part of Italian American cooking. Nothing goes to waste, and the second go-round can be even better than the original! Imagine a dish that maximizes the covetable crunch that lasagna noodles get around the bubbly hot edges. The outside of this pasta "cake" crisps up to a golden crunch.

Makes one 12-inch (30 cm) cake; 4 servings

2 to 3 cups (255 to 385 g) leftover cooked spaghetti

⅓ cup (75 g) Tomato Sauce (page 63)

1 tablespoon extra virgin olive oil

Grated Parmesan cheese for serving

Toss the pasta with the tomato sauce in a large bowl to coat completely.

Heat a 12-inch (30 cm) cast-iron or nonstick skillet over medium-low heat, then swirl in the olive oil. Add the pasta in one layer to form a "cake" and cook, without moving it, until crisp and golden brown on the bottom, 10 to 15 minutes.

Turn the pasta out onto a plate, golden noodles face up, top with grated Parmesan, and cut into wedges to serve.

CREAMY LEMON SPAGHETTI

You won't find this recipe anywhere in the canon of classic Italian American pasta dishes. Instead, it honors my mother, Rose, the Canadian wife of my Italian father. Married into a large, boisterous Italian family, she gracefully managed to perfect and streamline her in-laws' Italian recipes while never, ever disclosing her distaste for red sauce and macaroni to us kids. Lemons were her passion. Visiting the lemon groves of Ravello in the Campagna region of southern Italy was one of her cherished travel memories. I spent much of my adult cooking life trying to delight her, lemon-wise, with the same passion she used to bring our Italian legacy to our childhood dinner table.

Makes 4 to 6 servings

2 lemons, preferably Meyer lemons

1 pound (455 g) spaghetti or other long noodles

1 cup (240 ml) heavy cream

1 sprig fresh basil, plus basil leaves for garnish

6 tablespoons (85 g) unsalted butter

1 teaspoon kosher salt, or more to taste

½ cup (50 g) grated Parmesan cheese, plus more for serving

Freshly ground black pepper

Use a vegetable peeler to peel the zest from the lemons in strips into a bowl and set aside. Squeeze ¼ cup (60 ml) of juice from the lemons and reserve both the rinds and the juice.

Fill a large pot with water, add the lemon rinds, and bring to a boil. Salt the water generously, add the spaghetti, and cook for 2 minutes shy of the package instructions; the noodles should be slightly soft with a firm chew to them. Scoop out 1 cup (240 ml) of the pasta water and drain the spaghetti.

Meanwhile, combine the cream, lemon zest, and basil in a saucepan large enough to hold the pasta and sauce. Bring to a simmer over medium heat and simmer for 2 to 3 minutes, pushing down on the zest with a spoon to release the oils, then remove and discard the zest and basil sprig. Slowly whisk the butter into the cream, about 1 tablespoon at a time, until fully emulsified (this is important to the final consistency of the sauce).

Add the salt to the sauce, then whisk in ½ cup (120 ml) of the reserved pasta cooking water

Add the pasta, along with the cheese and lemon juice, and toss and turn the noodles to fully coat with the sauce and melt the cheese. If necessary, season to taste with more salt and/or stir in additional pasta water to achieve the desired creaminess.

Serve the pasta immediately in warm serving bowls with more grated cheese and black pepper on top.

BASIC PASTA DOUGH

If you have no dried pasta in the cabinet, but you do have eggs in the fridge, fresh pasta can be easier to make than you think. Many pasta recipes call for a whole egg combined with extra egg yolks, which does make a more tender and colorful dough, but that can be wasteful unless you are diligent about reserving the unused egg whites for another recipe, like meringue (leftover whites can be frozen). In the spirit of frugality, this dough uses whole eggs, which still produce great results.

Makes 12 ounces (340 g)
dough, enough for
30 ravioli (page 125)
or 1 pan of lasagna
(page 133)

1½ cups plus 2 tablespoons
(225 g) all-purpose flour

3 large eggs (150 g; see Aspetta)

Dump the flour out onto a clean dry work surface, like wood, marble, or metal. Gather it into a little mountain, then make a well in the center, leaving the walls as high as possible. Add the eggs to the center of the well. Holding a fork in your dominant hand, cup your other hand gently around the outside of the flour wall, and start slowly whisking with the fork to incorporate small amounts of flour from the inside wall into the eggs. As the wall begins to narrow, hold the fork so it is more perpendicular to the work surface as your other hand continues to help hold up the sides; stop as needed to shore up the wall. If the wall falls, don't panic! Use a bench scraper to push it back together and then continue to mix. Once the mixture is thick and pudding-like (loose but holding together), use a bench scraper or spatula or your hands to push and mash in the remaining flour. (You can also use a stand mixer fitted with the dough hook to make and knead the dough; beat the eggs in the mixer bowl to combine, then slowly add the flour and mix/knead on low speed for 5 minutes.)

Now, using your hands, begin to turn/knead the dough until it comes together, then continue to knead for about 10 minutes. You'll feel the right consistency soon: soft enough to form into a ball without sticking but not too firm or dry. Don't worry if all the flour or the raggedy bits have not been incorporated at first; leave them off to the side in case more flour is needed once the dough begins to come together. It may feel too firm or loose as you begin kneading it, but it will eventually come together into a smooth ball. If the dough seems too sticky, add a little more flour; if too dry, add a few dribbles of water.

Next "pinch and push" the dough with both hands, using your dominant hand to push from the center of the ball away from you while pinching with the other hand to gather it back together. You want to end up with a soft and pliable dough that feels slightly squishy in the hand without sticking. Tap a little flour onto your hands if the dough is too sticky; conversely, dribble a little water over it if is too dry.

Cover the dough and let it rest for at least 30 minutes but no more than 2 hours at room temperature before proceeding. This allows the flour to further hydrate and the gluten to relax, making it easier to roll out the dough without shrinking. Wrapped tightly in plastic wrap, it will keep for up to 24 hours in the refrigerator or 1 month in the freezer; thaw in the fridge.

ASPETTA + *The key to success is to have the correct ratio of flour to eggs. Here each egg in the shell is 1.8 ounces (50 g). Together, the shelled raw eggs should weigh 4½ ounces (130 g). Adjust accordingly if your eggs are larger or smaller.*

USING FRESH PASTA DOUGH

Freshly made pasta dough can be rolled thin using a pasta machine or a rolling pin and cut into various sizes depending on the end use.

FOR RAVIOLI (PAGE 125): Lay rolled-out sheets of dough on a lightly floured work surface. Dollop teaspoons of filling spaced horizontally across the bottom half of the sheets. Fold the other half of the dough over, pinch to seal, and cut into the desired shapes.

FOR LASAGNA (PAGE 133): Whole dough sheets can be cooked immediately or frozen for later use. Cook for a few minutes in boiling salted water, drain, brush lightly with oil, and stack in layers separated by parchment paper or plastic wrap; keep covered until ready to assemble the lasagna.

FOR FETTUCCINE (PAGE 115): One at a time, roll up each floured dough sheet into a loose bundle and cut crosswise into ¼-inch-wide (0.65 cm) strips. Separate and toss in flour to store.

CHEESE and SPINACH RAVIOLI

Pasta stuffed with cheese and meat has been a common dish in some form since before the Italian Renaissance. In America, ravioli quickly became a popular mainstay of red sauce meals as an inexpensive yet hearty way to feed the family (although one with increased work for mamma) or was served as one course in a larger meal. In the 1930s, after canned food entered the mass market, its popularity exploded when immigrant Italian chef Ettore Boiardi pioneered canned cheese ravioli in tomato sauce—sold under an easier-to-pronounce name, Chef Boyardee. Serve the ravioli in the tomato sauce or, alternatively, in a butter and herb sauce; see the Variation below.

The filling is multi-use; you also stuff shells, cannelloni, or manicotti with it; layer it into lasagna (page 133); or dollop it around baked ziti. Any leftover filling can be frozen for up to 6 months.

**Makes thirty-two
2-by-2½-inch (5 by 6 cm)
ravioli**

8 ounces (230 g) fresh greens, such as spinach, chard, dandelion, or escarole, washed and trimmed

1 cup (250 g) ricotta cheese, homemade (page 78) or store-bought

⅓ cup (50 g) grated Parmesan or Romano cheese

1 large egg

½ teaspoon kosher salt, or more to taste

½ teaspoon freshly ground black pepper, or more to taste

Hefty pinch each of cinnamon and sugar (optional)

1 recipe Basic Pasta Dough (page 122)

1 recipe Tomato Sauce (page 63)

Steam the greens in a covered pot with a little water until tender, 5 to 8 minutes, depending on the choice of green. Drain and let cool slightly, then squeeze out as much water as possible and chop the greens (you should have about 1 cup/165 g).

Transfer to a bowl and mix in the ricotta, grated cheese, egg, salt, pepper, and cinnamon and sugar, if using. Taste for seasoning, adding more salt and/or pepper if needed. (*The filling can be made ahead and refrigerated, covered, for a day or two.*)

Cut the dough into quarters. Press each piece into a small rectangle of even thickness; work with one piece of dough at a time, keeping the remaining pieces covered. Lightly flour a baking sheet; have extra flour nearby to use sparingly for your hands and work surface. Have ready clean kitchen towels or sheets of parchment paper to separate the pasta sheets.

Be sure to read this paragraph and the following one thoroughly before proceeding. Set the rollers of a pasta machine at their widest setting and roll one piece of dough (starting from a narrower side) through the rollers. Repeat on successively higher numbers until the dough is thin but not transparent (probably 3 more rolls). Before the final roll, the dough sheet should be 12 inches (30 cm) long. Cut it in half and roll each half through the machine again on the second-thinnest setting. Each sheet should still be approximately 12 inches (30 cm) long, but this doesn't have to be exact! Arrange the sheets side by side on the floured baking sheet and cover with a towel or parchment paper. The pasta sheets can also be hung over string (like a clothesline) to rest. Repeat with the remaining pieces of dough, separating the layers as you add more sheets, for a total of 8 sheets of dough.

Lightly fold one sheet of dough lengthwise in half to make a crease (this will give you a line guide to work with), then unfold it onto a floured work surface. Drop heaping teaspoonfuls of the filling side by side across the bottom half of the dough about 2½ inches (6 cm) apart, leaving a border at each end, to create 4 ravioli. Fold the top half of the dough over and press firmly with your fingers all around the 3 unfolded edges and around the mounds of filling. Using a ravioli cutter or knife, cut the dough into rectangles approximately 3 by 2 inches (7.5 by 5 cm). (This doesn't have to be an exact process! Any scraps can be cooked separately like pasta noodles.) Place the filled ravioli on a floured baking sheet. Repeat with the dough and filling.

Bring a large pot of water to a boil and salt it generously. Rewarm the tomato sauce in a large pan. Add the ravioli to the boiling water and cook until they float to the top, 4 to 5 minutes. Lift out with a slotted spoon and add to the warm sauce.

Serve 4 to 5 ravioli per bowl, with more sauce spooned on top and some grated cheese

sprinkled on top. Any extra uncooked ravioli can be stored in an airtight container in the refrigerator for up to 2 days or in the freezer for up to 6 months.

VARIATION:

For a quick butter sauce, melt and sizzle butter with fresh sage or whatever hearty herb you have on hand (fresh thyme or oregano sprigs or a bay leaf from the cupboard) along with a few garlic cloves or slices of onion. Slide the cooked ravioli into the pan, add a little of the pasta water and a squeeze of lemon, and serve.

ASPETTA + *Since most of us don't have a large enough workspace to fill all the dough sheets at the same time, this recipe has you roll the dough one quarter at a time to fill and shape it. But if your surface is big enough, roll all the dough, then fill at the same time, completing the whole task at once.*

BAKED ✛ ✛ ✛ ✛

SAVORY
OVEN-
COOKED
ONE-PAN
MEALS

133 Lasagna with Mini Meatballs

136 Eggplant Romano Carolina

141 Eggplant Rollatini

143 Chicken Parmesan

144 Steak Pizzaiola

147 Boneless Pork Roast

149 Italian Oven Fries

151 Brother Jim's Easter Lamb

152 Savory Easter Pie

155 Baked Ziti

156 Baked Artichoke Casserole

LAYERED BAKED DISHES ARE SOME OF
the most beloved Italian American recipes. Magic ensues when different components are layered into a baking dish and slowly melded together in a hot oven, transforming them into one glorious overall flavor. Cooking this way was a practical matter in the old days, the original one-pan solution when families without their own ovens took their filled baking dishes to the town community ovens to bake.

It's hard to imagine a more iconic poster child for layered and baked Italian American dishes than Lasagna, oozing with melted cheeses, sauce, meats or vegetables, and noodles. Giant trays of Baked Ziti feature on wedding banquet hall menus all over the country. A mouthwatering chicken or eggplant Parmesan is a universal favorite.

Flavorful but tough cuts of meat will become meltingly tender during a slow roast in the oven; the fat dissolves into what becomes a mouthwatering sauce, as in Steak Pizzaiola, releasing an intoxicating trail of aromas that fills the air. Brother Jim's Easter Lamb and Italian Oven Fries are among our favorite versions of roasted garlicky meats and potatoes. The oven brings out the soft earthy taste of artichoke hearts when cooked with lemony olive oil and a crunchy breadcrumb topping in the Baked Artichoke Casserole. And the Savory Easter Pie encases a tender, savory spinach-cheese filling in a buttery, flaky crust. All of these generous dishes embody the unmistakable allure of home cooking.

LASAGNA with MINI MEATBALLS

The lasagna of my childhood was studded with mini meatballs, which made eating it a treasure hunt. A large tray of it was always ready when our family arrived at our Italian grandparents' house in upstate New York for our summer visits after the twelve-hour drive. No matter what time of day or night we got there, a table was laid out with multiple favorite family dishes, all the work of my grandmother and her sisters. For this dish, I drop the meatballs into the simmering sauce to cook, like the great-aunts from our Ferlo family did. The Scala family fried the meatballs first before layering them into the lasagna.

Well-wrapped, the unbaked lasagna will freeze nicely for up to 6 months. Bake it straight from the freezer for 1 hour, covered for the first 30 minutes.

Makes 12 servings

A double recipe of Tomato Sauce (page 63)

1 recipe meatball mixture from Meatballs in Tomato Sauce (page 39), rolled into mini meatballs (about ½ inch/1.25 cm in diameter)

1 recipe Basic Pasta Dough (page 122) or 1 pound (455 g) dried lasagna noodles

Extra virgin olive oil

1¼ cups (285 g) ricotta cheese, drained if not thick

1 pound (455 g) mozzarella, grated

1 cup (100 g) grated Parmesan cheese, plus extra for serving

2 tablespoons chopped fresh flat-leaf parsley

1 large egg

½ teaspoon kosher salt

¼ teaspoon freshly ground black pepper

Bring the tomato sauce to a boil in a large pot. One by one, stir the raw meatballs into the sauce and cook for 20 minutes. Remove from the heat and cover to keep warm.

Meanwhile, if you're using fresh pasta dough, roll it out and cut into sheets as directed on page 125.

Bring a large pot of water to a rolling boil and salt it generously (you will have to cook the noodles in batches unless you have an extra-large pot). Fill a large bowl with cold water and stir in a glug of olive oil. If using fresh pasta, add the pasta sheets a couple at a time to the boiling water and cook until al dente, 1 to 2 minutes. Carefully remove from the pot and float in the bowl of water. If using dried noodles, cook according to the package instructions and transfer to the bowl of water. Remove the noodles from the cold water and pat dry. Lay them flat on a baking sheet, separated by parchment paper or plastic wrap.

Combine the ricotta, ½ cup (225 g) of the grated mozzarella, half of the Parmesan, the parsley, egg, salt, and pepper in a medium bowl and stir together.

Preheat the oven to 350°F (175°C).

To assemble the lasagna, spread 1 cup (245 g) of the tomato sauce over the bottom of an oiled 9-by-13-inch (23 by 33 cm) baking dish. Overlap one quarter of the noodles over the sauce to cover the pan bottom. Spread a third of the cooked meatballs over the noodles and spoon over another 1 cup (225 g) sauce. Overlap another quarter of the noodles on top. Dollop all the ricotta mixture on top of the noodles and flatten it with the back of a spoon to make an even layer. Overlap another quarter of noodles on top. Spread over the second third of meatballs and 1 cup (225 g) sauce. Cover with the remaining noodles. Pour 2 cups (450 g) of the sauce to cover. Scatter the remaining meatballs on top. Scatter the remaining mozzarella over the top. Sprinkle with the remaining Parmesan cheese and drizzle with olive oil.

Bake uncovered for 40 to 45 minutes, until the lasagna is bubbling all over and lightly golden on top. Let rest for at least 20 to 30 minutes before slicing. Serve with plenty of grated cheese and the remaining tomato sauce at the table.

VARIATIONS:

The meatballs can be swapped for 1 pound (455 g) sweet Italian sausage meat, or 1 pound (455 g) ground beef and/or pork (seasoned with salt and pepper). Fry in a large skillet, breaking the sausage or ground meat into small chunks as you cook, until golden brown. Toss either one with 2 cups (450 g) Tomato Sauce before layering into the dish as directed.

The spinach and cheese filling on page 125 can be used to make a hearty vegetarian lasagna. Omit the meat and layer the filling into the lasagna as directed.

ASPETTA + Prep the lasagna in stages: *If using homemade pasta dough, you can roll out the noodles, cook them, and store in the fridge for up to 24 hours. Prepare the meatballs, which is a time-consuming task, since they are so little, and simmer them in the sauce. Make the cheese filling up to 3 days ahead and refrigerate. Don't race to get this dish done or cook it too close to dinner without time for a sufficient rest period to achieve neat edges and compact slices. If you are pressed for time, it's better to cook lasagna a day ahead, cool, and refrigerate it, then reheat at serving time. Skimping on the resting time prevents the flavors and textures from melding together, and the lasagna will fall apart as it is cut.*

EGGPLANT ROMANO CAROLINA

This dish is named for my niece Carolina, an eggplant lover, and Aquilina's great-great granddaughter. In the spirit of the evolution of classic recipes, this one takes off from eggplant Parmesan, but it's simpler and more stripped down, using just one skillet for the entire dish and finished in the oven (or, without an oven, finished on the stovetop). The casserole is thinner, therefore crispier than a traditional eggplant Parmesan, and made with less cheese and sauce, yet the result is still delicious. Fresh late-summer eggplant, which requires no pre-salting and sweating, inspired the recipe. If using mature or supermarket eggplant, you will need to presalt it (see the method below).

Makes 4 to 6 servings

2 medium Italian eggplants
(about 1½ pounds/680 g)

Kosher salt

½ cup (120 ml) olive oil

⅓ cup (35 g) dried breadcrumbs

⅓ cup (35 g) grated Romano or
Parmesan cheese

⅓ cup (75 g) thinly sliced
mozzarella or provolone cheese

A handful of torn fresh basil leaves
or oregano or thyme leaves

1½ cups (340 g) Tomato Sauce
(page 63), plus more for
serving if desired

Preheat the oven to 425°F (220°C).

Cut the eggplants lengthwise into slices about ⅓ inch (0.85 cm) thick. If using mature or supermarket eggplant, salt the slices on both sides and place in a colander to drain for at least 30 minutes, and up to several hours. Blot dry with a towel.

Heat a large ovenproof skillet over high heat and swirl in half the olive oil. When the oil is hot, add half the eggplant and fry, turning once, until golden and soft, about 12 minutes. Reduce the heat slightly if needed to prevent burning. Remove the eggplant to a rack or towel to drain. Add the remaining oil to the pan and heat until hot, then fry the second batch of eggplant and transfer to the rack. Remove the pan from the heat to cool off.

Combine the breadcrumbs and cheese and cover the bottom and the lower part of the sides of the skillet, tilting the pan, with half the mixture. Layer half of the eggplant slices in the pan and top with the mozzarella or provolone. Scatter around the herbs and drizzle on half of the tomato sauce. Repeat with the remaining eggplant, tomato sauce, breadcrumbs, and grated cheese.

Bake until the eggplant is silky soft inside and the top is golden brown, about 20 minutes. Finish the dish under the broiler for a couple of minutes if you want it extra crispy.

Serve the eggplant with a dollop of tomato sauce on the side, if desired.

ASPETTA ✛ To make this dish entirely on the stovetop: *Assemble the dish, set the pan over medium-high heat, cover, and cook for 10 minutes. Remove from the heat, invert a plate slightly larger than the skillet over the top, and turn over the pan so the eggplant slides onto the plate, then return it to the skillet, top side down. Cook for 10 minutes, or until the cheese is melted and the breadcrumbs are golden and crispy.*

The eggplant can also be roasted in a 400°F (200°C) oven: *Place the eggplant slices on a baking sheet and brush on both sides with olive oil. Roast until softened and flexible, about 20 minutes, flipping the slices halfway through.*

The mighty eggplant was a bedrock ingredient for our southern Italian forebears. Historically, eggplant eaters worldwide, especially in lands of sunshine and scarcity, have relied on this chameleon ingredient to fill the belly. We think of it as a vegetable, yet technically it's a fruit—and botanically a berry. With its texture and bulk, and spongy flesh capable of sucking up other flavors, it is often swapped in for meat because of dietary or religious restraints, frugality, or lack of availability. Modern eaters love eggplant shining solo in a side dish, antipasto, dip, or spread. The traditionally humble peasant ingredient has earned its rightful place as a pillar of international vegetarian cooking.

Countless recipes ask the cook to salt cut eggplant for 5 minutes to purge bitterness. Nowadays, though, a freshly harvested eggplant from the garden is unlikely to be bitter, and most commercial varieties have had the bitterness bred out. Thus the need to draw out bitterness has become debatable and is mostly applicable to a large mature eggplant that has sat on a shelf at the market after storage. My rule of thumb now is not to bother salting eggplant from the garden or farmers' market, but to salt grocery store eggplant. Its peak season is late summer, August through September.

Age and time spent in cold storage are the factors that produce bitterness in eggplant. Not only does it dislike out-of-season cold storage, but it also doesn't love sitting in your refrigerator or on the countertop for too long. If need be, loosely wrap eggplant in a kitchen towel and refrigerate it for a couple of days max before using.

The main virtue of salting, which will take at least 30 minutes and up to several hours, is to break down cell walls and draw out water. Also, theoretically, less oil is absorbed into a salted slice during cooking, especially frying, where a golden crust seals in the creamy eggplant texture. Conversely, the spongy, porous texture of unsalted flesh will suck up adjacent flavors it's cooked with, which can be an asset. In reality, though, the salting directions are mostly meaningless unless seasoning is the goal.

To test these illusive theories on a farm-fresh eggplant, I fried equal numbers of slices that had been salted for 1 hour and unsalted slices in the same amount of olive oil: 7 slices of each, in ¼ cup (60 ml) hot oil. In both instances, only 2 teaspoons of oil remained after 12 minutes of frying. The unsalted slices just soaked the oil up a little faster. As for the flavor-texture difference, the taste was the same for both, meaning not bitter, but the salted slices had slightly tighter and denser flesh; still, the difference was barely discernible, hardly enough to warrant an hour's wait for the home cook just trying to get dinner on the table. Next, I took a big purple mature eggplant—age unknown—from a grocery store and did the same salted and unsalted test. Bitterness was purged from the salted pieces and less oil was absorbed.

So enjoy eggplant freshly picked in the last months of summer or preserve them at that

time to enjoy for cold-weather eating. Early in the season, eggplant plants in the garden display a profusion of the most gloriously beautiful blossoms, which herald a plethora of tight-skinned purple fruit to come a couple of months later. But if you must source your eggplant from the supermarket, salt it before cooking, and the mature eggplant will taste garden-fresh.

EGGPLANT ROLLATINI

This dish, tucked inside many an Italian grandma's recipe box, is still worthy of a modern meal. The thinly sliced, filled, and rolled eggplant melts together with the cheese and savory prosciutto or ham, bubbling away in a tangy red sauce for a crave-worthy dinner at any time of year. The recipe can be prepared up to several hours in advance before baking. Be sure to allow enough time for it to cool somewhat before serving so that the liquid from the sauce, eggplant, and cheese is reabsorbed before you slice it. To make this vegetarian, omit the ham.

Makes 6 to 8 servings

2 eggplants, peeled and cut lengthwise into slices about ¼ inch (0.65 cm) thick (about 12 slices)

Kosher salt if salting the eggplant

1 to 1½ pounds (455 to 680 g) fresh mozzarella

¼ cup (60 ml) extra virgin olive oil

2 cups (455 g) ricotta cheese, drained if not thick

3 tablespoons grated Parmesan cheese, plus more for sprinkling

1 large egg white

½ teaspoon coarse salt

⅛ teaspoon freshly ground black pepper

2 to 3 cups (450 to 675 g) Tomato Sauce (page 63)

8 ounces (225 g) sliced prosciutto or ham

A loaf of Italian bread for serving

If using mature eggplant, salt the slices on both sides and place in a colander to drain for at least 30 minutes and up to several hours. Blot dry with a kitchen towel. If using fresh-picked eggplant, no need to salt it (see Eggplant, page 138).

Shred enough of the mozzarella to make ½ cup (112 g). Thinly slice the remaining cheese; you should have at least 12 slices. Set aside.

Heat a large skillet over high heat. Swirl in the olive oil until it glistens (test with a small piece of eggplant to make sure it is hot enough; it should bubble immediately). Working in batches, add the eggplant slices to the oil and fry, turning once, until they are flexible enough for rolling up, about 3 minutes per side. Drain the fried eggplant on paper towels and let cool. (The eggplant can also be roasted in a 400°F/200°C oven: Place the eggplant slices on a baking sheet and brush on both sides with olive oil. Roast until softened and flexible, about 20 minutes, flipping the slices halfway through cooking.)

Meanwhile, make the filling: Combine the ricotta, the ½ cup (112 g) shredded mozzarella, grated Parmesan cheese, egg white, salt, and pepper in a large bowl and mix well.

Preheat the oven to 400°F (200°C).

Recipe continues

Coat the bottom of a deep 9-by-13-inch (23 by 33 cm) baking dish with some of the tomato sauce.

Working in batches, fill and roll the eggplant: Spread a thin layer of the ricotta cheese mixture on each eggplant piece. Place a slice of prosciutto/ham on top of the cheese and roll up, starting from a short end; arrange the rolls in the pan as you roll them. Pour the remaining sauce over the top of the eggplant. Sprinkle some grated cheese on top. Cover the top of the rollatini with the sliced mozzarella.

Bake until the cheese is melted and bubbling, about 20 minutes. Remove from the oven and let rest for at least 10 to 15 minutes before serving.

CHICKEN PARMESAN

When the Italian immigrants arrived in America, meat was so much more readily available than it had been at home. After they became more prosperous, chicken and veal often replaced (or were added to) the eggplant in the traditional Parmesan preparation. This recipe has been in my family for years. You can make the different components ahead; prepare the chicken and sauce, and then assemble it before baking. Unbaked chicken Parm also freezes well, and it can go straight from the freezer to the oven. But if the labor of this recipe isn't for you, yet you crave those flavors, try the Chicken Parm Meatballs (page 54).

Makes 6 to 8 servings

3 pounds (1.5 kg) boneless, skinless chicken breasts

½ cup (50 g) dried breadcrumbs

¾ cup (75 g) grated Parmesan cheese

2 teaspoons kosher salt

¼ teaspoon freshly ground black pepper

2 tablespoons extra virgin olive oil, plus more as needed

1 tablespoon unsalted butter, plus more as needed

1 recipe Tomato Sauce (page 63)

1½ pounds (680 g) mozzarella cheese, thinly sliced

Line a work surface with parchment paper or plastic wrap. Lay down the chicken breasts a few at a time and, using a sharp slicing knife, cut each one horizontally in half. (I don't pound the meat thin here in order to have thicker, juicier pieces.)

Combine the breadcrumbs and ½ cup (50 g) of the Parmesan cheese in a large baking pan or dish, spreading them over the entire bottom. Lay down as many chicken breasts as will fit easily, sprinkle with salt and pepper, and turn to coat thoroughly with the breadcrumb mixture; transfer to a baking sheet. Repeat the process with the remaining pieces of chicken.

Heat a large skillet over medium-high heat. Add the olive oil and butter and swirl to coat the pan. Add only as many chicken pieces as will fit in one layer and cook, turning once, until golden brown, about 3 minutes on each side; transfer to a tray. Repeat the process with the remaining chicken, adding more oil and butter to the pan as needed.

Preheat the oven to 400°F (200°C).

Spoon enough of the tomato sauce into an oiled 9-by-13-inch (23 by 33 cm) baking dish to cover the bottom. Layer in the chicken pieces and top with the mozzarella slices. Spoon over about 1¼ cups (280 g) more sauce and sprinkle on the remaining ¼ cup (25 g) Parmesan cheese.

Bake until golden and bubbling, 30 to 35 minutes. Remove from the oven and let rest for at least 10 to 15 minutes before serving. (Any leftovers can be stored, well-wrapped, in the fridge for up to 3 days.) Serve any remaining sauce on the side.

STEAK PIZZAIOLA

Steak Pizzaiola became popular in the early 1900s as a home-cooked dish with "pizza" flavors, prepared by many Italian cooks on Thursday nights to use up the last of the tough (inexpensive) braising meat from the butcher, which tenderizes when slow-cooked in tomato sauce. It was served over macaroni to add some important protein, but you could serve it over polenta too. Meat had yet to become an everyday food for many of the impoverished southern Italian newcomers. This dish can feed many mouths, and nothing beats the aroma of it as it cooks in the oven.

Makes 6 to 8 servings

One 2½-pound (1.13 kg) bone-in beef chuck steak or one 2-pound (910 g) boneless chuck steak

1 teaspoon coarse salt

Freshly ground black pepper

2 tablespoons extra virgin olive oil

3 to 4 garlic cloves, minced (to taste)

1 teaspoon dried oregano

1 teaspoon dried thyme

½ teaspoon red pepper flakes

One 28-ounce (800 g) can whole tomatoes

1 pound (455 g) rigatoni or other big macaroni shape

Grated Parmesan or Romano cheese for serving

Preheat the oven to 325°F (175°C).

Season the meat on both sides with the salt and pepper to taste. Heat a large ovenproof skillet with a lid or a Dutch oven over high heat and swirl in the olive oil. Add the meat and brown on both sides, about 3 minutes per side. Transfer the meat to a platter.

Remove the pan from the heat (so the garlic doesn't burn from the hot skillet) and stir in the garlic, oregano, thyme, and red pepper flakes. Return the pan to medium heat and add the tomatoes, with their juices, breaking up the tomatoes with a spoon. Return the meat to the pan, spoon the sauce over it, and cover tightly. Transfer to the oven and braise for 2 hours, stirring occasionally.

Uncover the pan and cook for 30 minutes longer, or until the sauce has thickened and the meat is falling-apart tender. Remove the pan from the heat and pull the meat apart into pieces with a fork, removing the bone if using bone-in chuck.

Meanwhile, bring a large pot of water to a boil. Salt the water generously, add the macaroni, and cook until 2 minutes shy of the package instructions. The noodles should be slightly soft with a firm chew to them.

Drain the pasta, transfer to a large serving bowl, and toss with some of the meat sauce. Add the shredded meat and spoon the remaining sauce over the top. Serve with grated cheese at the table.

ASPETTA ✛ With or without bones: *A bone-in chuck steak is preferrable for this dish because the collagen surrounding the bones will melt during the low, slow cooking and add deep flavor to the sauce. However, it's sometimes difficult to find bone-in chuck at the grocery store these days. Made with a boneless steak, the dish will still be delicious, just without that extra depth of flavor.*

BONELESS PORK ROAST

This pork roast dish delivers the flavors of a classic porchetta, that beloved festival dish made with a seasoned and rolled boneless pork belly, or a whole baby pig roasted on a spit. An economical pork butt roast is more practical for home cooks and makes a satisfying alternative. To feed a larger crowd, use an 8-pound (3.5 kg) roast and double the other ingredients; a larger roast will take longer to cook. Serve as a special centerpiece after a pasta first course, or for a family dinner with greens on the side. Braised Fennel (page 236) is especially tasty with pork.

Makes 6 to 8 servings

3 tablespoons fresh rosemary and/or sage leaves, chopped, plus a few sprigs for garnish

3 tablespoons fennel seeds

5 garlic cloves, roughly chopped

2½ teaspoons kosher salt, plus more for the potatoes

1½ teaspoons freshly ground black pepper

Grated zest of 1 lemon; lemon reserved

2 tablespoons extra virgin olive oil, plus more for the potatoes

One 4-pound (1.8 kg) boneless pork butt roast

1½ pounds (680 g) potatoes or sweet potatoes, or a combination, peeled and cut into wedges

Red pepper flakes

Using a mortar and pestle or a food processor, smash or pulse together the herbs, fennel seeds, garlic, salt, pepper, and lemon zest to a coarse paste. Add the olive oil, stirring or processing to make a thick paste.

Place the pork on a baking sheet. With the tip of a sharp paring knife, score an ⅛-inch (0.3 cm) crosshatch pattern into the fat all over the roast. Rub the paste all over the pork, getting into the cracks and crevices of the meat. Using butcher's twine, tie the roast at 3-inch (7.5 cm) intervals to create an even oblong roll. (Each roast is different—don't worry if it is uneven. Just roll it into a generally uniform shape and tie it so it holds together.)

Wrap the seasoned roast tightly in plastic wrap and refrigerate overnight. Or let it stand at room temperature for at least 2 hours before cooking.

Preheat the oven to 325°F (165°C). Choose a roasting pan big enough to hold the meat with the potatoes around it. (If necessary, roast the potato wedges in a smaller pan alongside the pork.)

Put the meat fat side up in the pan and drizzle olive oil over the top. Drizzle 1 cup (240 ml) water around the meat.

Recipe continues

Roast the pork for 1 hour and check to make sure there is still some liquid, with some juices, in the bottom of the pan; if not, add more water. Roast for another 2 hours or so (for a total of about 3 hours), basting the pork with the juices a couple of times.

Meanwhile, toss the potatoes or sweet potatoes with olive oil to coat and season with salt and red pepper flakes.

Thirty minutes before the pork is done, add the potatoes to the pan, scattering them around the meat (or put the pan of seasoned potatoes in the oven). Continue to cook until the meat is done; it should register 135° to 140°F (60° to 75°C) on an instant-read thermometer.

Remove the roast from the oven and squeeze the juice of the lemon over the top. Transfer the meat to a cutting board, tent with parchment paper or foil, and let rest for 15 to 20 minutes before slicing.

At this point, the potatoes should be tender and golden brown; if not, raise the temperature to 400°F (200°C) and return the pan to the oven to caramelize the potatoes while the meat rests.

Slice the roast and serve with the potatoes, garnished with sage and rosemary sprigs.

ASPETTA ✛ Instant-read thermometers: *If you cook roasts and other cuts of meat often, it's worth investing in an instant-read thermometer. These are inexpensive and no bigger than a pocketknife. Once you start using one to determine the doneness temperature (pressing and feeling the surface of the meat as you check), it will help teach you how to intuitively gauge the correct doneness to the touch when cooking all meats. In the old days, the recommended guidelines for cooking meat (especially pork) would give you meat that was way overcooked. When this roast is cooked perfectly to the temperature given above, the center will be moist and ever so slightly pink, and the outside will be golden brown.*

ITALIAN OVEN FRIES

Few recipes in my personal arsenal exemplify the ingenuity and evolution of Italian American cooking more than this one. Oven fries are not a traditional Italian preparation, but they are one that uses all its iconic flavors: cheese, garlic, oregano, and olive oil, in what will become the oven-fried potatoes of your dreams.

Makes 6 servings

6 or 7 Russet potatoes (7 ounces/200 g each), peeled, sliced into ⅓-inch-thick (0.85 cm) French fries, and soaked in a bowl of cold water

4 tablespoons (60 ml) extra virgin olive oil

1 tablespoon dried Italian seasoning (or some combination of dried oregano, thyme, marjoram, and basil)

2 cups (200 g) grated Romano cheese

¼ cup (15 g) fresh flat-leaf parsley leaves and tender stems, finely chopped

4 tablespoons (55 g) salted butter, cut into small cubes

Coarse salt and freshly ground black pepper

Preheat the oven to 400°F (200°C), with the racks in the upper and lower thirds.

Drain the potatoes and pat dry with a towel. Spread 1 tablespoon of the olive oil over each of two rimmed baking sheets and spread the potatoes out on the sheets. Overlapping is fine.

Sprinkle the dried herbs evenly over the potatoes. Sprinkle the cheese and parsley evenly over the top. Drizzle the remaining 2 tablespoons of olive oil evenly over the cheese on both sheets. Scatter the cubed butter around the potatoes and sprinkle salt and pepper over the top.

Bake the potatoes for 45 to 50 minutes, rotating the pans after 30 minutes, until golden brown. Use a spatula to lift off the potatoes with all the crusty cheese adhered to them and serve.

BROTHER JIM'S EASTER LAMB

In an Italian American home, roast lamb is frequently the centerpiece of lunch or dinner on Easter, the second most important religious holiday after Christmas. Traditionally spring lamb and fresh herbs are featured in elaborate feasts to signify rebirth and resurrection. This decidedly modern recipe, perfected by my brother Jim, uses the typical flavorings with a boneless cut of meat; because a butterflied leg of lamb will be of uneven thickness, it allows for various degrees of doneness to accommodate different personal preferences. You can buy a whole bone-in leg, which will weigh about 6 pounds (3 kg), and have the butcher remove the bones and trim the fat, so you can reserve the bones for broth. Or buy a 4-pound (1.8 kg) butterflied lamb leg, as called for here. The lamb is best when marinated overnight, so you will need to plan ahead.

Rosemary can be swapped in for oregano, if you like. And leftovers are perfect made into sandwiches, slathered with Caponata (page 84). Serve with steamed asparagus.

Makes 8 to 10 servings

1 tablespoon extra virgin olive oil

5 garlic cloves, coarsely chopped

1 tablespoon kosher salt

A handful of fresh oregano leaves, roughly chopped, plus more for garnish

A handful of fresh mint leaves, roughly chopped, plus thinly sliced leaves for garnish

1 tablespoon honey

1 tablespoon balsamic vinegar

One 4-pound (1.8 kg) butterflied boneless leg of lamb

Freshly ground black pepper

1 lemon, cut in half, one half cut into thin slices

VARIATION:

To grill, place the lamb on the grate over medium-high heat, at least 6 inches (15 cm) from the flame. Cover the grill and check the meat for doneness after 25 to 30 minutes.

Using a mortar and pestle or a food processor, mash or process the olive oil, garlic, and salt to a paste. Add the oregano, mint, honey, and vinegar and blend into the paste. You should have about ½ cup (125 g).

Place the lamb on a clean work surface and massage all over with the herb paste. Place in a resealable container or wrap tightly in plastic wrap and refrigerate overnight.

The next day, remove the lamb from the fridge at least 1 hour before cooking.

Preheat the oven to 425°F (220°C).

Place the lamb flat on a rack set over a rimmed baking sheet or in a shallow roasting pan and massage the paste into the meat again. Grind black pepper all over the meat.

Roast for 35 to 40 minutes, until the thickest part of the meat reads 120°F (48°C) on an instant-read thermometer, for a rosy medium doneness. Remove the meat to a cutting board, tent with parchment paper or foil, and let rest for 15 to 20 minutes.

Thinly slice the meat against the grain and place on a serving platter. Squeeze the juice of the lemon half over the top. Garnish the lamb with thinly sliced mint, oregano leaves, and the lemon slices and serve.

SAVORY EASTER PIE

Torta Pasqualina is a savory, cheesy pie with a rich history. It originated in Liguria, where a small but historically important percentage of Italian immigrants emigrated from in the mid-eighteenth century (and mostly settled in San Francisco) before the mass migration from the south after unification in 1871. Tender greens are mixed with a flavorful cheese filling and baked in a buttery, crispy crust. Make it with the first fresh tender greens of the spring and serve for Easter lunch alongside a leafy green salad. The ham is optional, if you'd prefer a vegetarian version.

The dough and filling can be made in advance and the pie assembled the day before baking, and the entire pie freezes well, wrapped tightly, for a couple of months. If frozen, bake straight from the freezer and add an extra 10 minutes to the cooking time.

Makes one
9-inch (23 cm)
double-crusted
pie; 8 servings

FOR THE PASTRY
DOUGH

2 cups (250 g)
all-purpose flour

1 teaspoon kosher salt

8 ounces
(2 sticks/225 g) cold
unsalted butter, cut
into small pieces

½ cup (120 ml) ice water

FOR THE FILLING

2 pounds (910 g)
spinach, chard, or
dandelion greens,
trimmed and well
washed

3 tablespoons extra
virgin olive oil

1 onion, chopped

1 pound (455 g) ricotta
cheese, drained if
not thick

½ cup (50 g) grated
Parmesan cheese

2 large eggs, beaten

1½ teaspoons coarse
salt

½ teaspoon freshly
ground black pepper

8 ounces (225 g) ham,
cut into ¼-inch
(0.65 cm) cubes
(optional)

1 egg, beaten, for egg
wash

MAKE THE DOUGH: Combine the flour and salt in a large bowl or the bowl of a food processor. Add the butter and cut in or pulse until the mixture resembles coarse meal. Pour in the water and mix just until the dough comes together in a ball.

Turn the dough out onto a piece of plastic wrap and lift the edges toward the middle to press the dough together. Cut the dough in half. Form each piece into a disk, wrap well in plastic wrap, and refrigerate for at least 15 minutes. (*The dough can be made up to 1 day in advance and refrigerated; remove it from the fridge 15 minutes before rolling it out. Or freeze for up to 3 months; thaw overnight in the refrigerator.*)

MAKE THE FILLING: Place the spinach, chard, or dandelion leaves in a large pot, with the water still clinging to the leaves. Cover and cook over medium-high heat, stirring occasionally, until the greens are wilted, 4 to 5 minutes. Drain and let cool, then squeeze

the greens dry and chop them. You should have 2 to 3 cups (200 to 400 g).

Heat a medium skillet over high heat and swirl in the olive oil. Add the onions and cook, stirring, until translucent, 3 to 4 minutes. Remove from the heat and let cool.

Combine the ricotta and Parmesan cheeses, eggs, salt, and pepper in a large bowl and stir together. Stir in the spinach, onion, and ham, if using, until well combined. Cover and refrigerate until chilled, 15 to 20 minutes.

Preheat the oven to 375°F (190°C).

On a well-floured surface, roll out one disk of dough to a round about 11 inches (28 cm) in diameter and fit it into a 9-inch (23 cm) pie plate. Trim the edges of the dough flush with the edges of the pie plate. Pile the filling into the dough-lined pie plate.

Roll out the second disk of dough to a round about 11 inches (28 cm) in diameter. Lay it over the filling. Trim the edges of the top crust so it overhangs the bottom crust by ¾ inch (2 cm). Tuck the edges of the top crust under the bottom and roll it under itself all around. Pinch the edges together to seal, then crimp the edges with your fingers or a fork.

Brush the egg wash evenly over the top of the pie. Make a few slits in the top to allow steam to escape during baking. Bake the pie for 45 to 50 minutes, until golden brown.

Remove the pie from the oven and let rest for 15 minutes before cutting and serving. Store any leftovers, wrapped tightly in plastic wrap, in the fridge for up to 2 days.

VARIATIONS:

Some cooks make this pie using puff pastry or even bread dough. For puff pastry, thaw 2 sheets of dough slowly in the refrigerator. Roll each sheet out to an 11-inch (28 cm) square and trim to a round. Proceed as directed above.

Or, to make the pie with bread dough, use the pizza dough recipe on page 69, or use about 22 ounces (625 g) store-bought dough. Divide the dough in half. Roll each piece out to an 11-inch (28 cm) round. Fit one piece into a pizza pan or pie plate. Place the second piece over the filling, stretching it if necessary to cover the filling, and pinch/crimp the edges to seal. Proceed as directed above, but bake the pie in a 350°F (175°C) oven for 25 to 30 minutes.

BAKED ZITI

When baked ziti traveled with immigrants from southern Italy to America, it retained its role as a classic wedding meal starter. In Italian, the word "ziti" is short for maccheroni di ziti. Ziti was often referred to as macaroni of the brides because it was traditionally served at weddings. For decades, every large Italian American family gathering, from baptisms to confirmations to weddings and funerals, has been likely to have trays of baked ziti as part of the feast. The various components can be made ahead and then assembled before baking, or the whole dish can be refrigerated for a couple of days before baking, a boon to the cook preparing multiple celebratory dishes for one big meal. These days, baked ziti is almost but not quite as Americanized as lasagna.

Makes 6 to 8 servings

1 pound (455 g) ziti or other short macaroni

4 cups (900 g) Tomato Sauce (page 63)

1¼ cups (285 g) ricotta cheese, drained if not thick

1 pound (455 g) mozzarella, grated

1 cup (100 g) finely grated Parmesan cheese

2 tablespoons chopped fresh flat-leaf parsley

1 large egg

1 teaspoon kosher salt

¼ teaspoon freshly ground black pepper

VARIATION:

For a meaty version of this dish, layer in 1 pound (455 g) sausage meat, broken into small chunks and fried until golden brown. Any other tomato sauce you like can be swapped in here.

Preheat the oven to 375°F (175°C).

Bring a large pot of water to a rolling boil. Salt the water generously, add the pasta, and cook for 2 minutes shy of the package instructions; the pasta should be slightly soft with a firm chew to it. Scoop out 1 cup (240 ml) of the pasta water, drain the pasta, and transfer to a large bowl.

Add 1 cup (225 g) of the tomato sauce and the reserved pasta water to the pasta and toss well.

Combine the ricotta, 8 ounces (225 g) of the mozzarella, ½ cup (50 g) of the Parmesan, the parsley, egg, salt, and pepper in a bowl and stir together.

Spread 1 cup (225 g) of the tomato sauce over the bottom of a 13-by-9-inch (33 by 23 cm) baking dish. Spread one-third of the noodles over the sauce and dollop with half of the ricotta mixture. Repeat with another one-third of the noodles and the remaining ricotta. Top with the remaining noodles, sauce, and mozzarella and the remaining ½ cup (50 g) Parmesan.

Bake the ziti until golden brown on top and bubbling, about 35 minutes. Turn on the oven broiler and broil for 5 minutes, until lightly golden and crispy on top. Remove from the oven and let rest for 15 minutes before serving.

BAKED ARTICHOKE CASSEROLE

My mom adapted this from her Italian mother-in-law's whole steamed artichoke recipe (see page 232) to make a dish that easily feeds a crowd. It uses the same flavors but eliminates the prep work required for whole artichokes and capitalizes on that mid-twentieth-century game-changer—frozen food—in the form of a package of frozen artichoke hearts. As in many ethnic families who have added their personal flavor to the standard Thanksgiving meal fare, this is my family's "Italian" staple side dish and the first leftover scavenged the next day.

Makes 6 to 8 servings

1½ cups (160 g) fresh breadcrumbs (page 42)

¼ cup (15 g) chopped fresh flat-leaf parsley

¼ cup (25 g) grated Parmesan cheese

¼ cup (25 g) grated Romano cheese

1 tablespoon dried Italian seasoning (or some combination of dried thyme, oregano, marjoram, and basil)

½ teaspoon kosher salt

Freshly ground black pepper

⅔ cup (160 ml) extra virgin olive oil, plus more for the baking dish

¼ cup (60 ml) fresh lemon juice (from 2 lemons)

2 garlic cloves, minced

Three 9-ounce (255 g) packages frozen artichoke hearts, thawed and drained

Preheat the oven to 325°F (165°C).

Combine the breadcrumbs, parsley, cheeses, dried herbs, salt, and pepper in a medium bowl. Whisk together the olive oil, lemon juice, and garlic in a small bowl.

Rub the inside of a 13-by-9-inch (33 by 23 cm) baking dish with olive oil. Lay the artichoke hearts side by side in the dish. Distribute the crumb topping evenly over the artichokes, pushing it down in between them. Tap the dish on the counter to allow the crumbs to sink down into the cracks. Drizzle the olive oil dressing all over the crumb topping.

Cover the dish with foil and bake for 30 minutes. Increase the temperature to 375°F (190°C), remove the foil, and bake for 10 to 15 minutes, or until the crumb topping is golden brown. Remove from the oven and serve warm.

SKILLET +++

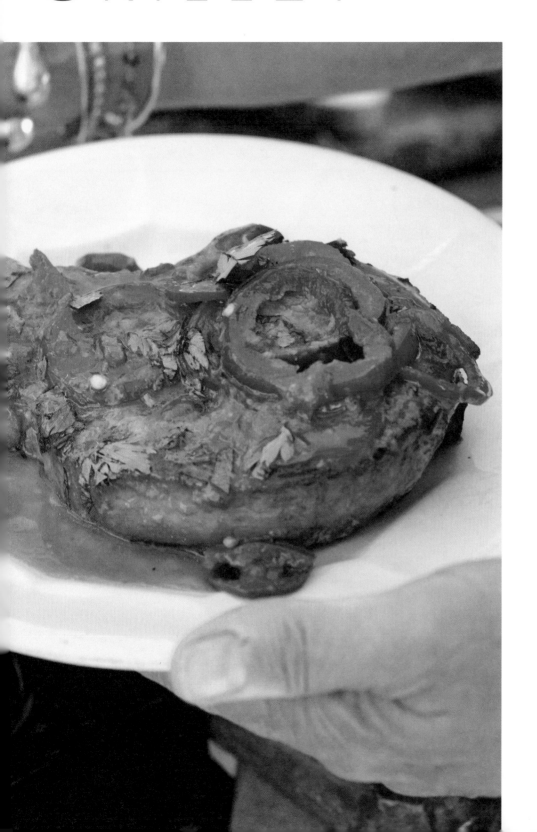

SEARED
and
SAUCED
MEATS
on the
STOVETOP

162 Chicken Marsala

165 Chicken Oreganata

166 Chicken Cacciatore

169 Chicken Francese

171 Chicken Vesuvio

173 Chicken Scarpariello

176 Turkey Piccata

178 Veal Birdies

180 Pork Chops with Vinegar
Peppers

MEALS COOKED IN A SKILLET ON THE

stovetop are as important to the Italian repertoire as the oven-baked and pot-simmered dishes. Indeed, an Italian woman who was traveling to America often tucked a beloved pan from home in her trunk. Today every home cook has a favorite sauté pan in her kitchen. Tender cuts of meat quickly seared in a hot frying pan leave behind enough caramelized bits on the bottom to become the foundation of a sauce. Pouring in a flavorful liquid and stirring dislodges the brown bits on the bottom of the pan to "deglaze" it, and then simmering concentrates the mixture.

Thinly sliced tender cuts of meat are interchangeable proteins for most skillet meals. Where once veal and pork scallopini might have been more common choices, now boneless chicken and turkey breasts are more popular. The Marsala, piccata, and oreganata preparations in this chapter cook in a flash, with each sauce imparting its own complement to the tender meat. A delicate cheesy egg coating enrobes boneless chicken breasts in Chicken Francese. Pork Chops with Vinegar Peppers is a few-ingredient dinner full of flavor. Layered crispy potatoes combined with the sauciness of Chicken Vesuvio makes a crave-worthy recipe to repeat. Seared and simmered bone-in chicken parts make the beloved country-style dish Chicken Cacciatore.

A sturdy stainless steel or low-sided enameled cast-iron skillet will do most jobs. Two pans, one small (6-inch/15 cm) and one large (12- to 14-inch/30 to 35 cm), will cover all your bases. Choose a pan (or pans) with an oven-safe handle for more flexibility.

CHICKEN MARSALA

Marsala's rich, nutty, and slightly smoky-sweet flavor has a depth to it that makes it a wonderful counterpoint for caramelized well-seasoned mushrooms and meats. Marsala has been produced in Sicily and shipped internationally since 1773, with a dip in popularity in the second half of the twentieth century, when a glut of mediocre low-quality producers flooded the market. Like many other Italian spirits, it was once considered medicinal, and therefore legal (and affordable) during Prohibition, which accounts for its ubiquitous use in Italian American savory and sweet dishes at that time. If you also love Tiramisu (page 273) or zabaglione, you'll want to keep a basic bottle of Fine (lightly aged) Marsala in your cupboard.

Serve the chicken with linguine tossed with butter or roasted potatoes to sop up the sauce. Sautéed Escarole (page 222) makes a great accompaniment.

Makes 4 to 6 servings

2 pounds (910 g) boneless, skinless chicken breasts

Kosher salt and freshly ground black pepper

½ cup (65 g) all-purpose flour

¼ cup (60 ml) extra virgin olive oil, plus more as needed

10 ounces (283 g) cremini or button mushrooms, thinly sliced

⅓ cup (170 g) sliced shallots

¾ cup (180 ml) dry Marsala wine

½ cup (120 ml) chicken broth, homemade (page 179) or store-bought

2 tablespoons unsalted butter

1 tablespoon fresh lemon juice

2 tablespoons chopped fresh flat-leaf parsley

VARIATION:

The chicken can easily be swapped for turkey, veal, or pork.

Slice each chicken breast horizontally in half. Place each piece between two pieces of parchment paper or plastic wrap and pound to a ¼- to ½-inch (0.65 to 1.25 cm) thickness. Sprinkle each piece with salt and pepper on both sides. Spread the flour on a shallow plate, lightly dredge each piece of chicken in the flour, and transfer to a different plate.

Heat a large skillet over high heat and swirl in the olive oil until it glistens. Working in batches, place the pieces of chicken in the pan, leaving space between them, and cook until lightly browned, 2 to 3 minutes per side. Transfer the cooked chicken to a warmed plate near the stovetop and set aside while you cook the rest of it; add a little more olive oil to the pan after each batch. Loosely cover the chicken to keep it warm.

Add the mushrooms to the pan, sprinkle with salt, and cook for 4 minutes. Add the shallots and cook, stirring, for 2 minutes (add more oil if the pan is too dry). Pour in the Marsala, scraping up the brown bits from the bottom of the pan. Add the chicken broth and simmer for about 3 minutes to reduce the liquid. Reduce the heat to medium and swirl in the butter, then add the lemon juice.

Return the chicken to the pan and turn to coat with the sauce and heat through. Serve on warm plates, with the parsley scattered on top.

CHICKEN OREGANATA

If there is one herb that's been mishandled in modern Italian American dishes, it's oregano, which is added to practically every red-sauce recipe with little regard to its actual suitability. Too much dried oregano will add an acrid bitterness to a dish. But when used appropriately, the fragrant herb can be a star. Often, though, an opened jar of dried oregano languishes in our cupboards for too long, losing flavor. Taste yours before using it and replace it if necessary, which is easiest done if you keep an unopened container in reserve. This recipe comes together in the time it takes to boil pasta, which makes a delicious accompaniment to swirl in the savory sauce.

Makes 4 servings

- 1½ pounds (680 g) boneless, skinless chicken breasts or thighs, cut into 2-inch (5 cm) cubes
- Kosher salt and freshly ground black pepper
- 2 tablespoons extra virgin olive oil
- 3 garlic cloves, minced
- 1 tablespoon dried oregano
- ½ cup (120 ml) white wine
- ½ cup (120 ml) chicken broth, homemade (page 179) or store-bought
- 1 tablespoon fresh lemon juice
- 2 tablespoons unsalted butter

Pat dry the chicken pieces and generously salt and pepper them (do this just before cooking so they don't sweat out liquid because of the salt).

Heat a large skillet over high heat and swirl in the olive oil until it glistens. Working in batches if necessary, add the chicken to the pan in a single layer and cook, without moving the pieces, until they begin to brown, then cook, stirring, until golden on all sides, about 3 minutes.

Reduce the heat to medium-low and return all the chicken to the pan if you cooked it in batches. Add the garlic and oregano and cook, stirring, for 1 minute. Increase the heat to high and pour in the wine to deglaze the pan, scraping up the browned bits on the bottom, about 2 minutes. Add the chicken broth and cook, stirring, until it reduces slightly to a glaze, about 2 minutes. Swirl in the lemon juice and then add the butter, stirring to emulsify the sauce and coat the chicken.

Serve on warm plates with cooked noodles or crusty bread to sop up the sauce.

CHICKEN CACCIATORE

It is likely that rabbit or other wild game was in the cooking pot for the original Italian cacciatore, meaning "hunter," along with other foraged ingredients like mushrooms and herbs. Today the recipe has morphed into one of those ubiquitous rustic Italian American dishes made with chicken, aromatics, and tomatoes, though recipes may vary depending on the cook. This simple version has been served at our family table for years, made with whatever ingredients are on hand. Swap red wine for the white, oregano for the rosemary, or fresh tomatoes for canned, and use whatever salty pork product you have. The sauce is as delicious as your favorite tomato gravy, so serve the chicken with macaroni on the side.

Makes 4 to 6 servings

One 3- to 4-pound (1.4 to 1.8 kg) chicken, cut into serving pieces; reserve the back, neck, and wing tips for chicken broth (page 179)

Kosher salt and freshly ground black pepper

¼ cup (60 ml) extra virgin olive oil

2 ounces (60 g) pancetta in one piece or 2 strips bacon, chopped

1 onion, chopped

3 garlic cloves, minced

1 tablespoon chopped fresh rosemary or oregano

12 ounces (340 g) cremini or white button mushrooms, sliced

¾ cup (180 ml) white wine

1 cup (240 ml) chicken broth, homemade (page 179) or store-bought

One 28-ounce (800 g) can whole tomatoes, chopped, with their juices, or 1¾ cups (370 g) chopped ripe tomatoes

Place the chicken on a clean work surface and season generously with salt and pepper.

Heat a large deep skillet or brazier pan over medium-high heat and swirl in the oil. When it shimmers, working in batches to avoid crowding the pan, add the chicken, skin side down, and brown on both sides, 3 to 4 minutes per side. Don't move the parts at first; it takes a couple of minutes to sear the chicken so it doesn't stick. Transfer the cooked chicken to a plate.

Reduce the heat slightly, add the pancetta or bacon, onions, garlic, and rosemary or oregano, and cook, scraping up the brown bits, until the fat starts to render, about 3 minutes. Add the mushrooms and cook until softened and golden, about 4 minutes.

Return the browned chicken, along with the accumulated juices, to the pan. Raise the heat to high and add the wine, stirring to deglaze the pan, then simmer until most of the wine has evaporated, about 2 minutes. Add the broth and tomatoes, with their juices, reduce the heat to low, partially cover the pan, and simmer, stirring occasionally, until the chicken is cooked through and tender, 35 to 40 minutes; remove the lid during the last few minutes of cooking to let the sauce thicken slightly.

Season the sauce to taste and serve.

AN EASY WAY TO BUTCHER A CHICKEN

Not only is butchering your own chicken more cost effective than buying parts, it also allows you to control the size of the parts and to reserve the back and wing tips for broth. Reserve these in a resealable freezer bag until you've accumulated enough to make broth (see page 179).

1. Using kitchen shears, cut down along both sides of the backbone to remove it (there's a spot on either side of the bone where the sharp point of the shears will slide through easily).
2. With a sharp, sturdy medium-thin-bladed knife (such as a boning knife), remove the wings from the breasts by cutting through the center of the joint between the drumette and breast (find the separation point, which is closer to the breast, with the knife).
3. Separate the drumsticks from the thighs and then the thighs from the breasts.
4. Cut down through the breastbone and cartilage to separate the breast into two pieces (shears can be easier than a knife for this).

CHICKEN FRANCESE

Eggs and cheese combine in this dish to create a delicate savory coating for chicken breasts, adding a tasty, porous layer that will absorb the saucy lemon-wine butter. Serve this over capellini pasta, the sauce pooled around it, as one might find it in an Italian American restaurant, with a simple steamed green vegetable alongside.

Makes 4 servings

2 large eggs

½ cup (50 g) grated Parmesan cheese

2 tablespoons all-purpose flour

1½ pounds (680 g) boneless, skinless chicken breasts (about 4)

Kosher salt and freshly ground black pepper

¼ cup (60 ml) extra virgin olive oil

1 tablespoon capers, rinsed

1 cup (240 ml) white wine

2 tablespoons unsalted butter

Grated zest and juice of 1 lemon

Chopped fresh flat-leaf parsley for garnish (optional)

Beat the eggs in a shallow dish and whisk in the cheese. Spread the flour on a plate. Lay the chicken breasts side by side on a clean work surface and season on both sides with salt and pepper. Add the chicken to the flour and turn to lightly coat on both sides, then dip each piece in the egg mixture, turning to fully coat both sides, and return to the plate.

Heat a large skillet over high heat and swirl in the olive oil. When it glistens, add the chicken pieces in a single layer, without crowding (cook in batches if necessary), and cook, turning once, until cooked through and a light golden color, 2 to 3 minutes per side. Transfer to a warm plate.

Add the capers to the pan, pour in the wine, and swirl it around the pan. Let it bubble away to cook off the alcohol and reduce its volume in half. Add the butter and swirl the pan until it melts. Stir in the lemon zest and juice. Return the chicken to the pan and turn the pieces to coat in the sauce. Remove the pan from the heat.

Serve the chicken on warm plates, topped with parsley.

CHICKEN VESUVIO

This dish is a delicious combination of textures, with crispy golden potatoes doused just before serving in the tangy garlic-oregano-flavored chicken juices and studded with creamy green peas. The only fact *not* disputed about the origins of this recipe is that it was invented and popularized in Chicago's Italian community, which, by 1920, had the third largest ethnic Italian population in the nation behind New York City and Philadelphia. Next to Chicago's signature sandwich, Chicago Beef (page 257), Chicken Vesuvio, named for the famous volcano outside Naples, is the Windy City's most popular Italian American restaurant menu choice

Makes 4 to 6 servings

1 pound 6 ounces (625 g) Russet potatoes, peeled and cut lengthwise into 8 wedges each

¼ cup (60 ml) olive oil

Kosher salt

1 tablespoon plus 1 teaspoon dried oregano

One 3½-pound (1.6 kg) chicken, cut into serving pieces; reserve the back for broth (page 179)

Freshly ground black pepper

4 garlic cloves, sliced

1 cup (240 ml) white wine

1½ cups (360 ml) chicken broth, homemade (page 179) or store-bought

1 cup (160 g) frozen peas

Juice of 1 lemon

Preheat the oven to 425°F (220°C).

Place the potato wedges on a baking sheet and toss with 2 tablespoons of the olive oil, 1 teaspoon salt, and 1 teaspoon of the oregano. Spread the potatoes out on the baking sheet.

Bake the potatoes for 30 to 35 minutes, until golden.

Meanwhile, pat the chicken parts dry and season generously with salt and pepper. Heat a large skillet over high heat and swirl in 2 tablespoons of the olive oil until it glistens. Working in batches to avoid crowding the pan, add the chicken, skin side down. You should hear an immediate sizzle when the chicken hits the pan. Don't move the pieces at first; it takes a couple of minutes to sear the chicken so it doesn't stick. Cook, turning to brown the chicken on all sides; this will take about 10 minutes. Transfer the chicken to a plate as it is browned.

Return all the chicken to the pan, make a little space in the pan, add the garlic and the remaining 1 tablespoon oregano, and cook, stirring, for 30 seconds. Pour in the wine to deglaze and cook, scraping up the brown bits from the bottom of the pan, for 2 to 3 minutes.

Recipe continues

Stir in the chicken broth, partially cover the pan, reduce the heat to medium-low, and cook until the chicken is cooked through, about 20 minutes. Stir in the peas and lemon juice in the last 5 minutes of cooking.

To serve family-style, place the chicken parts side by side on a large warm platter, top with the potatoes, and pour the sauce over. Alternatively, arrange the chicken pieces on individual plates, top with the potato wedges, and pour the sauce over at the table.

ASPETTA + If you don't want to turn on the oven: *Here the potatoes are oven-roasted while the chicken is skillet-cooked on the stovetop to save time, but the whole process can be done on the stovetop by browning the potatoes in one skillet and the chicken in another at the same time.*

CHICKEN SCARPARIELLO

While Chicken Cacciatore (page 166) belongs to the hunter, scarpariello is the shoemaker's style of preparing chicken. But any other details about the recipe's origins end there. Did the Neapolitan shoemaker "cobble" together ingredients on hand for dinner, or did the bones protruding from the chicken pieces resemble his shoemaking nails? No doubt it was the shoemaker's wife or mother who cooked the meal anyway! Even though this dish has become an Italian American standard, one is hard-pressed to determine the definitive cooking method. What is agreed upon is that the dish contains chicken, sausage, and peppers in a tangy-sweet sauce. Sometimes potatoes and/or mushrooms are added, and lemon may be swapped in for the vinegar. Nontraditionally, I love it serving with polenta for another one-plate American mash-up of disparate regional recipes that would not appear in Italy.

This technique of acidulating herbs, garlic, and sugar with red wine vinegar prior to cooking delivers just the right saucy balance with the meat. Use a whole bird cut into parts, and each one chopped in half again, which lets each small piece bathe in the sauce. Most butchers will happily cut up the chicken for you; otherwise, use a sharp knife or cleaver to do it at home (see An Easy Way to Butcher a Chicken, page 168). This is an excellent meal to make a day ahead, refrigerate, and gently reheat in the sauce, as the flavors deepen with time.

Makes 6 to 8 servings

1 cup (240 ml) red wine vinegar

5 garlic cloves, minced

2 tablespoons chopped fresh sage

2 teaspoons sugar

3 to 4 pounds (1.4 to 1.8 kg) bone-in, skin-on chicken pieces, each part cut in half

Kosher salt and freshly ground black pepper

¼ cup (60 ml) extra virgin olive oil

1 pound (455 g) sweet Italian sausages, cut into 1-inch (2.5 cm) pieces

1 onion, quartered lengthwise and sliced crosswise

1 sweet red pepper, cored, seeded, quartered lengthwise, and sliced crosswise into 1-inch-wide (2.5 cm) strips

8 ounces (225 g) white button or cremini mushrooms, sliced

2 tablespoons Calabrian chili paste or 1 teaspoon red pepper flakes

½ cup (120 ml) chicken broth, homemade (page 179) or store-bought

Recipe continues

At least 15 minutes and up to 2 hours before cooking, whisk together the vinegar, garlic, sage, and sugar in a small bowl; set aside to macerate.

Thoroughly season the chicken pieces with salt and pepper. Heat a 14-inch (35 cm) skillet (or two smaller skillets) over high heat and swirl in the olive oil. When the oil glistens, place the chicken in the skillet(s), skin side down, leaving space around the pieces (work in batches if necessary to avoid crowding the chicken). You should hear an immediate sizzle when the chicken pieces hit the pan. Don't move them; it takes a couple of minutes to sear the chicken enough so it will release from the pan. Brown the chicken on all sides, 8 to 10 minutes per batch. Transfer the chicken to a plate.

Add the sausage to the pan and cook until golden brown, about 2 minutes. Add the onion, red pepper, and mushrooms, stir to combine, reduce the heat to medium, and cook until the vegetables are softened and lightly golden, about 6 minutes. Stir in the chili paste or red pepper flakes.

Return the chicken pieces to the pan, increase the heat to high, and pour in the vinegar mixture. Swirl the pan and stir as the vinegar mixture reduces to a simmering glaze, 2 to 3 minutes. Stir in the chicken broth and simmer, uncovered, until the chicken is cooked through and the sauce is slightly reduced, 15 to 20 minutes. Remove from the heat and serve.

TURKEY PICCATA

Piccata refers to a luscious lemon sauce that is used to coat seared thinly sliced cuts of meat, especially veal, with its subtle taste and delicate texture. The popularity of veal has waned in the United States, but to the newly arrived Italians in 1900s America, it signaled the prosperity of a new life; here turkey cutlets make an ideal alternative to veal. In this dish, quick and easy meets elegant and fancy, a perfect combination for a special meal. The lemon slices, which soften in the pan, aren't just for garnish. They are served on top of the meat, so you can press the slices down with your fork as you eat to release more juice. This recipe goes quickly, so it's best to have every other part of the meal prepared and organized (including warmed) before you begin cooking the piccata.

Makes 4 servings

1½ pounds (680 g) boneless, skinless turkey breasts, cut into thin slices (8 or 9) and pounded flat

Kosher salt and freshly ground white pepper

¼ cup (60 g) all-purpose flour

2 tablespoons olive oil

2 tablespoons unsalted butter

¼ cup (60 ml) white wine

2 lemons, one juiced, one thinly sliced

Lay the turkey slices side by side on a clean work surface. Season on both sides with salt and white pepper. Spread the flour on a shallow plate, add the turkey, and turn to lightly coat each piece, shaking off the excess, and transfer to another plate.

Heat a large skillet over medium-high heat and swirl in the olive oil and butter. When the oil glistens and the butter has melted, add the turkey slices and turn the heat to high. Cook, turning once, until the turkey is golden on both sides, 1 to 2 minutes per side. Pour in the wine, swirl it around the pan for 20 seconds, and turn the turkey slices over. Add the lemon juice and slices and swirl the pan to emulsify the sauce and coat the meat.

Serve immediately, sprinkled with salt and pepper and the lemon slices on top of the meat.

VEAL BIRDIES

Italians have long prized the meat of very young animals, so as the Italian Americans prospered in this country, veal and lamb served as markers of a richer way of life. My old Italian family recipe box contains no less than five different veal rollatini recipes. Unlike long-simmering Beef Braciola (page 46), tender veal scallopini bundles don't need much cooking time. The nutty tasting Marsala wine sauce beautifully complements the flavors of the sage and mushrooms. Serve these with Sautéed Escarole (page 222) or Garlicky Broccoli Rabe (page 223).

Makes 4 to 6 servings

2 garlic cloves, minced

2 tablespoons minced fresh sage

6 slices boneless veal (about 1 pound/455 g), pounded flat

Kosher salt and freshly ground black pepper

6 thin slices prosciutto (about 3 ounces/60 g)

1 cup (85 g) grated provolone cheese (about 3 ounces)

3 tablespoons extra virgin olive oil

1 tablespoon unsalted butter

10 ounces (285 g) cremini or white button mushrooms, thinly sliced

¾ cup (180 ml) dry Marsala wine

¾ cup (180 ml) chicken broth, homemade (opposite) or store-bought, or beef stock

Combine the garlic and sage in a small bowl. Lay the veal slices side by side on a clean work surface and sprinkle with salt and pepper. Scatter the garlic and sage mixture evenly over the veal. Lay a piece of prosciutto on each slice and sprinkle the cheese evenly over the top. Firmly roll each piece up, starting from the narrow end, into a bundle and secure it with a toothpick. Lightly salt the outside of the bundles and place on a plate.

Heat a large skillet over high heat and swirl in the olive oil. When it glistens, add the veal bundles to the skillet, seam side up, leaving room around them. Cook until golden on the bottom, about 2 minutes, then carefully turn the veal and brown for another minute or so. Remove the veal to a warm plate and set it near the stovetop.

Add the butter and mushrooms to the pan and cook, stirring to coat the mushrooms with the oil and butter, and cook until the edges of the mushrooms begin to turn golden and the mixture smells nutty, about 3 minutes. Return the veal parcels to the pan, seam side up.

Whisk together the wine and broth in a bowl and pour into the pan to deglaze, scraping up the brown bits, then simmer for a few minutes. Reduce the heat to medium, cover, and simmer until the veal is cooked through, turning the bundles over halfway through, 9 or 10 minutes. Remove from the heat.

Remove the toothpicks and arrange the veal on plates. Spoon the mushrooms and sauce over the top and serve.

CHICKEN BROTH

A cup of strong chicken broth is one of the most powerful kitchen cures there is, but good chicken broth is also a very versatile ingredient. It's easy to make homemade broth. Buy about 3 pounds (1.4 kg) chicken backs, drumsticks, and/or wings—any chicken parts that are mostly bone (not breasts, unless the meat has been removed for another use). The carcass from a whole cooked bird can be used too if you've used the meat for salad or soup. Whenever you have random chicken parts, say a neck that comes inside a whole bird, add them to a resealable plastic bag and store in your freezer until you're ready to make broth. You can also swap the chicken out for turkey.

To make the broth, start by infusing the liquid. Dump all the parts into a pot and add a cut-up onion, some peeled garlic cloves, a carrot, celery stalk, bay leaf, and a handful of parsley. (Or whatever you have on hand.) Add water to cover (if you happen to have a box of store-bought chicken broth, add that too for more flavor). Bring the liquid to a boil, then reduce the heat and simmer for 1 hour.

Drain the broth in a sieve set over a bowl, discard the solids, and return the liquid to the pot. Bring to a boil over high heat, reduce the heat to low, and simmer for about 30 minutes, until the broth is reduced by half. You should have about 1 quart (950 ml); this is liquid gold! Season with salt to taste.

Pour the broth into storage containers, cover, and let cool, then refrigerate for 2 to 3 days. You can also freeze some of the broth in smaller containers to pull out as needed for sauces or soups.

PORK CHOPS
with VINEGAR PEPPERS

Spicy pickled cherry peppers bring such a big punch to this dish that few other ingredients are needed to create a full-flavored quick meal. Here 1-inch-thick (2.5 cm) pork chops are served one to a person, but they can be sliced and sauced before serving to accommodate more eaters. To stretch the meal further, serve with pasta or polenta, with butter and grated cheese, on the same plates so the tangy sauce can seep into it.

Makes 4 servings

4 pork loin chops, 1 inch (2.5 cm) thick (about 2 pounds/910 g)

Kosher salt and freshly ground black pepper

3 tablespoons olive oil

4 garlic clove, minced

One 12-ounce (355 ml) jar cherry peppers in brine, drained, ½ cup (120 ml) of the liquid reserved, and sliced (or buy pre-sliced)

1 cup (240 ml) white wine or chicken broth, homemade (page 179) or store-bought

2 tablespoons unsalted butter

Lay the pork chops side by side on a clean work surface. Make vertical slits in the fat around the chops so they will lay flat when cooking. Season on both sides with salt and pepper.

Heat a large skillet over medium-high heat and swirl in the olive oil. When the oil glistens, add the chops to the pan and cook, without moving them for the first few minutes, and then turning once, until browned on both sides, 8 to 10 minutes. Remove the chops to a warm platter.

Add the garlic and peppers to the pan and cook, stirring and scraping up the brown bits on the bottom, for about 1½ minutes. Pour in the wine or broth and the reserved ½ cup (120 ml) pepper brine, increase the heat to high, and cook, stirring occasionally, until the liquid has reduced and is syrupy, about 3 minutes. Swirl in the butter.

Return the chops and their accumulated juices to the pan and cook, turning once, until the meat registers about 140°F (75°C) on an instant-read thermometer, 10 to 15 minutes more. The meat should have still have a very slight give to the touch and not be firm. Remove from the heat.

Transfer the chops to a warm platter and spoon over the sauce and peppers.

ASPETTA + Brining liquid: *Don't discard it! When you have brining liquid left over from jars of cherry peppers or other preserved vegetables, add cut-up fresh vegetables, such as carrots, celery, or cauliflower, to the brine left in the jar and let them quick-pickle in the fridge for at least a day or two or up to 3 weeks. Serve the tangy vegetables as part of an antipasti platter.*

on FISH ✦ ✦ ✦

SEAFOOD
DISHES
for
EVERY DAY
and for
CELEBRATIONS

186 Seven Fishes Seafood Stew
(CIOPPINO)

193 Lobster Fra Diavolo

195 Spaghetti with Clam Sauce

198 Shrimp Scampi Meatballs
with Pasta

201 Shrimp Francese

202 Shrimp Rice Balls (ARANCINI)

205 Seafood-Stuffed Shells

209 Haddock Italiano

211 Poached Fish Fillets (ACQUA PAZZA)

212 Tuna or Swordfish Kebabs with
Salsa Verde

215 Stuffed Squid in Tomato Sauce

MOST ITALIANS WHO IMMIGRATED TO

America in the mass migration between 1880 and 1920 came from and then settled in coastal towns, villages, and cities. Thus fish and seafood were a familiar part of the diet and a staple of Friday night meatless dinners. Most neighborhoods had fish vendors who pushed their carts from door to door or set up stalls on market day. Even today, the favorite fishmongers in Italian enclaves have lines of home cooks at Christmastime who are shopping for multiple varieties of sea creatures for their Christmas Eve feasts. Much of the fish and seafood that is prohibitively pricey today, like Dungeness crab, was plentiful and inexpensive in coastal communities like San Francisco's North Beach, where Cioppino originated. Calamari was so inexpensive that cooks with little money would grind it for "meatball meat" and use it to fill the creatures' natural pouches, as for Stuffed Squid in Tomato Sauce. The Sicilian tuna trade is millennia old, with dozens of preparations like grilled fresh kebabs doused in salsa verde. The idea for Shrimp Scampi Meatballs tumbling off a lemony mound of spaghetti presented itself to me in a dream, and it tastes just as good as I'd imagined.

SEVEN FISHES SEAFOOD STEW (CIOPPINO)

Cioppino, a spicy tomato-based fish and shellfish stew, is likely San Francisco's most famous dish from its Italian American history. By the mid-nineteenth century, well before the mass migration onset of 1870, North Beach was home to northern Italian gold seekers, agriculturalists, and artists. By 1880, though, the region's economy was dominated by Sicilian and other southern Italian fishermen and oystermen who plied their trade alongside the Ligurians from farther north aboard small boats and large fleets in San Francisco Bay and the deep-sea Pacific beyond. Filbert Street Wharf, the original Fisherman's Wharf, was then known as Italy Harbor. When fishermen returned home with extra seafood from the day's commercial catch, their wives cooked it with tomato sauce in simmering pots over open fires on Telegraph Hill. Crabs and squid were especially plentiful and cheap.

Nowadays this brothy dish is celebratory one, chock-full of seafood. It comes together quickly just before serving if the seafood has been cleaned and the spicy-rich tomato broth has been made in advance. Then all that's left is a 10-minute simmer to finish. Part of the fun of eating cioppino is the surprise that every bite brings, with so many different textures and tastes from the sea. This dish is an excellent addition to the Christmas Eve Feast of the Seven Fishes (see page 190), or it may even be the feast itself if served with macaroni and sourdough bread.

Makes 6 to 8 servings

Two 1-pound (455 g) live lobsters

About ½ cup (120 ml) extra virgin olive oil

2 shallots, minced

1 cup (120 g) finely chopped onion

9 garlic cloves, minced

2 anchovies

2 preserved Calabrian chilies, minced, or 1 tablespoon Calabrian chili paste or 2 teaspoons red pepper flakes

2 tablespoons tomato paste

¾ cup (180 ml) white or red wine

4 cups (950 ml) canned whole tomatoes (from about one and half 28-ounce/800 g cans), finely chopped or pureed

8 fresh basil leaves

1 pound (455 g) ridged penne pasta

12 cockles, Manila clams, or small little necks, cleaned (see Aspetta, page 93)

12 small mussels, cleaned (see Aspetta, page 93)

1 teaspoon dried oregano or 1 sprig fresh oregano

8 ounces (230 g) monkfish or other firm-fleshed white fish fillet, cut into 2-inch (5 cm) chunks

8 ounces (230 g) sea or bay scallops (cut sea scallops in half if using)

8 ounces (230 g) rock shrimp or small shelled shrimp

About 5 ounces (140 g) cleaned squid, bodies cut into thin rings, tentacles cut into bite-sized pieces

Kosher salt

Warmed sourdough bread for serving

Recipe continues

Pour 1 inch (2.5 cm) of water into a large pot with a tight-fitting lid and bring it to a boil. Add the lobsters, cover, and steam for 13 minutes. Remove the cooked lobsters and let cool slightly, until you can handle them.

Strain the broth through a cheesecloth or kitchen towel–lined sieve set over a bowl and reserve it. Remove the lobster meat from the tails, claws, and knuckles; reserve all the shells. Let the meat cool, then cover and refrigerate.

Heat a medium pot over high heat and swirl in 3 tablespoons of the olive oil. Add the shallots and the reserved lobster shells, stirring to coat them in oil, and cook until the shallots are translucent, about 3 minutes. Add the lobster broth and enough water to cover, bring to a simmer, and simmer for an hour or two (the longer, the better, for deeper flavor).

Strain the lobster broth through a cheesecloth- or kitchen towel–lined sieve into another pot and discard the solids. Simmer the broth to reduce it to 4 cups (950 ml). (*This can be done up to 1 day in advance; store the broth in a sealed container in the fridge.*)

Heat a large pot over medium-high heat and swirl in ⅓ cup (80 ml) olive oil. Add the onions and cook slowly until lightly golden, 6 to 8 minutes; add the garlic in the last 2 minutes. Stir in the anchovies, chilies (or chili paste or flakes), and tomato paste and cook, mashing the anchovies into a paste as they cook and scraping the bottom of the pot, a couple of minutes.

Add the wine, stirring to deglaze the pot. Add the tomatoes, the reserved lobster broth, and the basil and bring to a boil, then reduce the heat to low and simmer until the sauce is slightly reduced, about 30 minutes. (*The brothy sauce can be made up to a day in advance, covered once cool, and refrigerated. Return the sauce to a clean pot and bring to a simmer when ready to serve.*)

Meanwhile, about 20 minutes before cooking, remove all the raw seafood from the refrigerator and place on a platter to bring to room temperature. Cut the lobster meat into large bite-sized pieces (leave small claws whole).

Bring a large pot of water to a boil. Salt the water generously, add the penne, and cook until 2 minutes shy of the package instructions; the pasta should be slightly soft but with a firm chew to it. Drain the noodles, transfer to a bowl, toss with a little olive oil, and cover to keep warm.

Submerge the clams, mussels, and oregano in the simmering tomato sauce. After 3 minutes, add the monkfish and cook for 5 minutes. Carefully fold in the scallops, rock shrimp, and cooked lobster and simmer for 2 minutes. Add the squid and stir gently for about 1 minute. Turn off the heat and season the sauce to taste with salt. It should be slightly spicy; add more chili if necessary.

To serve, divide the penne among warmed serving bowls and ladle the stew over the top, including some of each type of fish/seafood in each portion. Drizzle with olive oil and serve immediately, with warm bread.

ASPETTA ✦ Use local ingredients for this dish
if possible: *Choose shellfish and seafood from
waters close to you. On the East Coast, lobsters are
more affordable and available than the original
Dungeness crab but deliver similar satisfaction. This
recipe combines seven different types of shellfish and
fish, but you should use any combination available
to you, substituting in equal weights or volume. Try
to include at least one flavor-rich crustacean such as
lobster, shrimp, or crab.*

If you want to use Dungeness crab instead of
lobster: *Replace the lobster with a 2-pound (910 g)
crab, cleaned and cut into pieces, and add to the
pot along with the clams and mussels. Replace the
homemade lobster broth with 4 cups (950 ml) fish
stock from a good seafood market.*

+ + FEAST OF THE SEVEN FISHES

The Feast of the Seven Fishes is a rich Christmas Eve meal made up of multiple seafood dishes enjoyed with the extended family to kick off the holiday. This feast is one of the most enduring nostalgia-fueled meal traditions to remain from the early arrival of southern Italians to America, made possible because many families settled in areas close to the shore. Each type of fish or seafood for the meal was prepared in a different manner: broiled, fried, stewed, or baked, or served raw. For the cook, the extensive preparation involved in the meal is as much a gift to loved ones as any presents could be.

The long-established feast has survived both assimilation into American life and the 1966 end, by the Second Vatican Council, of a centuries-old Catholic edict prohibiting the consumption of meat on Fridays. La Vigilia, as it is still called in Italy, is the predecessor of the Italian American Seven Fishes Feast. Observant Catholics would also abstain from eating meat on the eve of a feast day such as December 25. It's important to understand how intertwined feasting and religion once were. For Italian families today, Christmas Eve feasting is as essential to celebrating the holidays as attending Midnight Mass that night once was, and often still is.

There is no clear history of why the feast calls for seven fishes, but there's a multitude of possible explanations to consider. Was it a reference to the number of days it took for God to create the universe? Or to the seven sacraments: baptism, Eucharist,

confirmation, penance, anointing of the sick, matrimony, and holy orders? Or perhaps it was the seven virtues: chastity, temperance, charity, diligence, patience, kindness, and humility. Or even the seven deadly sins: pride, greed, wrath, envy, lust, gluttony, and sloth. Or is it the seven gifts of the holy spirit: wisdom, understanding, counsel, fortitude, knowledge, piety, and fear of the Lord? The number seven is mentioned hundreds of times in the Holy Bible. Yet some insist that it should be a feast of thirteen fishes, in a nod to the twelve apostles plus Christ. Others say nine fishes, for the Holy Trinity times three. Regardless, an odd number of dishes is considered to portend good luck.

Southern Italians originally broke the fast on La Vigilia with eel, which was considered symbolic. It was a rich and nutritious fish but cheap enough that even the poorest family could afford it during difficult times. Then imagine the unfathomable sea bounty available in this country to the new arrivals fleeing poverty. The great variety of inexpensive seafood permitted the tradition of a Christmas Eve feast of fish and seafood to survive and flourish. Family traditions evolve and are nurtured by successive generations. To this day, ask any Italian American to tell you about the Christmas Eve fish feast in their own family, and they will mention at least one or two dishes that must always be on the menu.

The shopping and preparation involved is significant and, as on so many other days of the year, that work traditionally fell to the women. To enjoy an updated Seven Fishes Feast meal, or to begin your own Christmas Eve ritual, start by considering the shopping, time, space, and prep tasks. Enlist other people to help. Draw up a full production schedule days in advance. Shop ahead as much as you can. Choose a few dishes that can be prepared ahead, frozen, and then baked the day of the feast. Select some other recipes to make in advance and refrigerate. Consider the temperature, texture, and flavor contrasts of the recipes you want to serve. Choose a combination of hot and cold or room-temperature offerings. Leave very few tasks to complete at the last minute.

Finally, if you're pressed for time or disinclined to prepare a multicourse meal, make the Seven Fishes Seafood Stew (page 186) and serve it with Garlic Herb Bread (page 73), and you've got yourself a modern La Vigilia dinner! With thoughtful planning and a cooking partner or two, the experience can be fun, delicious, and festive.

Here's a suggested Christmas Eve menu:

COLD

Oysters on the half shell

Preserved white anchovies with crackers *or* Seafood antipasti platter (see page 74) with Italian Tuna Dip (page 90)

HOT

Mussels Oreganata (page 92)

Clams Casino (page 93)

Shrimp Rice Balls (page 202)

MAIN COURSES (SERVE TWO)

Lobster Fra Diavolo (page 193) *or* Seafood-Stuffed Shells (page 205)

Tuna Kebabs with Salsa Verde (page 212) *or* Haddock Italiano (page 209)

DESSERT

Sherbet-Stuffed Frozen Lemons (page 291)

Tarallucci (page 296)

LOBSTER FRA DIAVOLO

All stories point to an Italian American restaurant kitchen in New York or New Jersey as the source of this recipe. The intense spicing makes it a "devilish brother," or "fra diavolo." If you're lucky enough to be near the shore with a plethora of fresh lobsters available, it's a fantastic summer dish served with garlic bread and a salad, or as a starter before a grilled fish main dish. It can also be a part of the Seven Fishes Feast. The lobsters, broth, and tomato sauce can be cooked up to a day in advance. Then finish it off just before serving, in the time it takes to cook the noodles.

Makes 4 to 6 servings

Three 1½-pound (680 g) live lobsters

4 tablespoons (60 ml) extra virgin olive oil, plus more for drizzling

2 shallots, minced

½ cup (120 ml) white wine

1 bay leaf

6 black peppercorns, crushed

4 garlic cloves, thinly sliced

2 teaspoons red pepper flakes, plus more for serving

One 28-ounce (800 g) can whole tomatoes

1½ teaspoons dried oregano

1 pound (455 g) spaghetti

2 tablespoons unsalted butter

Toasted breadcrumbs for serving (see Aspetta)

Bring 1 inch (2.5 cm) of water to a boil in an extra-large pot with a tight-fitting lid. Add the lobsters, cover, and steam for 13 minutes.

Remove the lobsters from the pot and set aside. Strain the broth through a cheesecloth- or kitchen towel–lined sieve set over a large bowl or other container and reserve. When the lobsters are cool enough to handle, remove the meat from the tails, claws, and knuckles (you should have 4 cups/1 kg meat).

Crack the lobster shells into smaller pieces. Heat a large pot over medium-high heat and swirl in 2 tablespoons of the olive oil. Add the shallots and cook, stirring, until translucent, about 2 minutes. Add the shells and stir to coat with the oil. Stir in the wine, then add the reserved lobster steaming liquid, bay leaf, peppercorns, and enough water to fully cover the shells. Bring to a simmer, and simmer, uncovered, for 45 minutes. Skim any foam from the top of the broth and strain the broth through a cheesecloth- or kitchen towel–lined sieve into a bowl; you should have 4 to 6 cups (950 ml to 1.5 L) broth. Measure out 2 cups (475 ml) of the broth for this recipe and freeze the remaining broth in a resealable container to use for another soup or a sauce recipe.

Heat a large skillet over medium-high heat and swirl in the remaining 2 tablespoons olive oil. Add the garlic and pepper flakes and stir until light golden, about 1 minute. Add the tomatoes and the reserved lobster broth, bring to a simmer, and simmer uncovered for 30 minutes, mashing the tomatoes in the pan as they soften and break down. Add the oregano and lobster meat to the sauce in the last 3 to 5 minutes of cooking, just to heat the lobster through.

Meanwhile, bring a large pot of water to a boil. Salt the water generously, add the spaghetti, and cook until 2 minutes shy of the package instructions; the pasta should be slightly soft but with a chew to it. Scoop out 1 cup (240 ml) of the pasta water and drain the pasta.

Add the pasta to the sauce along with the butter and toss and stir for 1 to 2 minutes, adding some of the reserved pasta water as necessary for the desired consistency. Serve in warm bowls, topping each with a drizzle of olive oil, some red pepper flakes, and toasted breadcrumbs.

ASPETTA ✛ Plain toasted breadcrumbs: *For some pasta dishes that are already chock-full of flavor, all you need is something with a savory crunch to top the dish and act as a cheese replacement. Heat 2 tablespoons unsalted butter or olive oil in a large skillet over medium heat. Add 1 cup (105 g) fresh breadcrumbs and cook, stirring frequently, until toasted, 5 to 8 minutes. Season with salt and pepper. These can be made a few hours ahead and left uncovered until serving.*

SPAGHETTI with CLAM SAUCE

There are white clam sauces, red clam sauces, and clam sauces in various shades in between. Regardless of how the dish is prepared, the clams should be the star, letting their sea-scented flavor shine and not masking their essence by adding too many competing seasonings. Buy the smallest clams available for this dish, unless you can dig big ones up yourself—in which case, they should be removed from their shells and chopped into a manageable bite size. Theoretically, clam essence is akin to the umami flavor found in cheese, which is the reason Italian-Italians shun the use of cheese with seafood. So, instead of heaping on grated cheese (though don't we all secretly want to do that with any pasta?), sprinkle on crispy savory breadcrumbs for a crunchy texture and boost of flavor.

Makes 4 to 6 servings

24 small clams such as littleneck, Pismo, or sweet butter, cleaned (see Aspetta)

1 pound (455 g) spaghetti or linguine

3 tablespoons extra virgin olive oil, plus more as needed

3 garlic cloves, thinly sliced

¼ teaspoon red pepper flakes

1 cup (340 g) grape or cherry tomatoes, sliced crosswise

½ cup (120 ml) white wine

2 fresh basil sprigs, plus ¼ cup (15 g) basil leaves, torn, for serving

1 recipe Crispy Savory Breadcrumbs (page 43)

Put the clams in a large pot, add 1 inch (2.5 cm) of water, and cover tightly. Steam over high heat until the shells open, 3 to 5 minutes. As the clams open, transfer them to a bowl (some will take longer than others). If any of the clams do not open eventually, discard them. Leave the clams in their shells. Strain the broth through a cheesecloth- or kitchen towel–lined sieve set over a bowl and set aside.

Bring a large pot of water to a boil. Salt the water generously, add the spaghetti, and cook until 2 minutes shy of the package instructions; the pasta should be slightly soft but with a firm chew to it. Scoop out 1 cup (240 ml) of the pasta water, drain the spaghetti, transfer to a bowl, and toss some olive oil to prevent sticking.

Meanwhile, heat a large skillet over high heat. Swirl in the olive oil, add the garlic and pepper flakes, and cook, stirring constantly, until the garlic begins to turn golden on the edges, about 1 minute. Stir in the tomatoes and cook until they just begin to break down, 3 to 4 minutes. Pour in the wine to deglaze the pan, scraping up any browned bits on the bottom, and simmer until the sauce has reduced by half, about 2 minutes. Stir in the clam broth and bring to a simmer, then fold in the clams.

Recipe continues

Add the noodles, reserved pasta water, and basil sprigs to the sauce and heat, shaking the pan and tossing the pasta, until it is fully coated with the sauce. Discard the basil sprigs and serve the pasta in bowls, topping each with a drizzle of olive oil, a handful of the toasted breadcrumbs, and some torn fresh basil leaves.

ASPETTA + Clean the clams thoroughly: *Place the clams in a bowl and cover with cold water. One at a time, lift each clam out and scrub it under the faucet, then rinse it to remove the grit and transfer to a bowl. Discard any clams with broken shells. This is nonnegotiable, as sandy clams will ruin the dish. Repeat the process until the clams are grit-free.*

SHRIMP SCAMPI MEATBALLS
with PASTA

One night I had a dream in which small pink spheres of shrimp scampi meatballs were rolling off a mound of noodles awash in lemon butter. I woke up and concocted this recipe from memory, using all the typical scampi flavors, and it was exactly as divined. You use the shells from the shrimp to make a quick stock for the sauce. (If you would rather start with peeled shrimp, omit the stock-making instructions and substitute chicken broth.) Serve the sauce spooned over angel hair pasta.

**Makes twenty-eight
1⅓-inch (3.3 cm)
meatballs; 4 servings**

12 ounces (340 g) large shrimp, peeled and deveined, shells reserved

Leaves from 3 sprigs fresh flat-leaf parsley, chopped, stems reserved

6 garlic cloves, 2 minced, 2 sliced, and 2 left whole

Kosher salt

5 black peppercorns

⅓ cup (35 g) dried breadcrumbs or panko crumbs

¾ cup (180 ml) white wine

½ teaspoon red pepper flakes

Grated zest and juice of 2 lemons (¼ cup/60 ml juice)

1 large egg

About ¼ cup (60 ml) olive oil

2 tablespoons unsalted butter

8 ounces (230 g) angel hair pasta

Combine the shrimp shells, parsley stems, whole garlic cloves, ½ teaspoon salt, and the peppercorns in a small saucepan, cover with water, and bring to a simmer, then reduce the heat slightly, partially cover, and simmer gently for 30 minutes.

Strain the broth through a cheesecloth- or kitchen towel–lined sieve set over a bowl; you should have 1 cup (240 ml) broth. Set aside.

Pulse the shrimp in a food processor until finely minced. Place the breadcrumbs in a bowl and pour in ¼ cup (60 ml) of the wine to hydrate them. Add the shrimp, minced garlic, red pepper flakes, 1 teaspoon of the lemon zest, the egg, and 1 tablespoon of the chopped parsley and stir to combine.

Use damp hands to roll the shrimp mixture into 1-inch (2.5 cm) balls and place on a platter or baking sheet; you should have 28 balls.

Heat a large skillet over medium-high heat and swirl in half the olive oil. When the oil shimmers, working in batches to avoid crowding the pan and adding more oil as needed, sauté the shrimp balls until golden-pink and slightly firm, 2 to 3 minutes. Transfer the balls to a warm plate.

Add the sliced garlic to the pan, adding more olive oil if necessary, and stir until soft and lightly golden, about 1 minute. Pour in the remaining ½ cup (120 ml) wine to deglaze, stirring to release any shrimp bits on the bottom of the pan, and cook

until it has reduced by half, about 3 minutes. Stir in the shrimp broth and lemon juice, bring to a simmer, and simmer until slightly thickened, about 2 minutes. Whisk in the butter, return the shrimp balls to the pan, and heat through.

Meanwhile, bring a large pot of water to a boil. Salt the water generously, add the angel hair, and cook until 2 minutes shy of the package instructions; the pasta should be slightly soft with a firm chew to it. Drain the noodles and toss in some olive oil. Scoop out 1 cup (240 ml) of the pasta water, drain the noodles, and toss with a little olive oil.

Add the noodles and the reserved pasta water to the sauce and meatballs and heat, stirring well, until the noodles are coated with the sauce. Serve garnished with the remaining chopped parsley.

ASPETTA + Buying shrimp: *Look for shrimp caught in the United States, but don't overlook seafood from the grocery store frozen section, as most shrimp in the market is actually frozen at sea on the boats to keep it fresh.*

SHRIMP FRANCESE

Italian Americans give the "Francese" treatment to just about anything—shrimp, chicken, meat, and vegetables—by dredging the food in flour and then coating it in beaten eggs (with optional grated Parmesan or Romano cheese) before cooking. Sauce is optional, but a white wine lemon-butter sauce is a traditional choice; see the recipe below. Given the small size of shrimp, I find it much easier to make a big frittata-style "pancake," rather than dip and cook the shrimp individually, for my shrimp Francese, and then cut it into wedges. It's delicious served hot out of the pan, with the sauce, if you like, or cut into bite-sized pieces and serve at room temperature for an appetizer or snack. Look for large frozen U.S.-caught shrimp sold in 2-pound (910 g) resealable bags (which defrost in under half an hour). That way, you can multiply the recipe as you like to suit your desired quantity.

Makes 4 servings as a main course, 8 as an appetizer

3 large eggs

⅔ cup (60 g) grated Romano or Parmesan cheese

½ teaspoon kosher salt

¼ teaspoon freshly ground black pepper

2 tablespoons all-purpose flour

12 ounces (340 g) large shrimp (about 14), peeled and deveined

2 tablespoons extra virgin olive oil

White Wine Lemon Sauce (see below; optional)

¼ cup (15 g) chopped fresh flat-leaf parsley for serving

Lemon wedges for serving

Beat together the eggs, cheese, salt, and pepper in a medium bowl. Spread the flour in a shallow dish. Pat the shrimp dry, dredge each one in flour, and transfer to a plate.

Heat a medium 10-inch (25 cm) nonstick or well-seasoned cast-iron skillet over medium-high heat and swirl in the olive oil. When the oil shimmers, gently toss the shrimp in the egg mixture. Place each shrimp into the pan, leaving space between them. Cook the shrimp until golden, 3 to 4 minutes per side. Alternatively, pour the whole mixture into the pan, spreading the shrimp evenly. Cook the "pancake" until golden on the bottom, about 3 minutes, then flip it over and cook until set, 3 to 4 minutes. (It should flip easily, but if you prefer, invert a plate slightly larger than the skillet on top of the pan and turn the pancake out onto it, cooked side up, then slide it back into the pan.)

Transfer the shrimp to a platter, or slide the pancake onto a cutting board and cut into wedges or bite-sized pieces. Serve topped with the sauce, if desired, and garnished with parsley, with lemon wedges for squeezing.

WHITE WINE LEMON SAUCE

After removing the shrimp from the pan, follow the instructions for the wine sauce for squid on page 217.

SHRIMP RICE BALLS (ARANCINI)

Arancini, rice balls, can be stuffed with just about anything. Think of them as a vehicle, the way the dough is the canvas for pizza. If you don't have shrimp, you can use other shellfish, like 1 pound (455 g) lobster or crab and use those shells to make the flavorful broth for cooking the rice.

    Serve these as a part of a Seven Fishes Christmas Eve meal (see page 190), if you like.

**Makes twenty
2-inch (5 cm) balls**

2½ tablespoons extra virgin olive oil

1 pound (455 g) large shrimp, shells and tails removed and reserved, shrimp refrigerated until needed

2 shallots, minced

6 cups (1.5 L) water

Kosher salt

2 cups (370 g) Arborio or Carnaroli rice

Pinch of saffron threads

¾ cup (75 g) finely grated Parmesan cheese

4 tablespoons (55 g) unsalted butter, at room temperature

3 large eggs

½ teaspoon paprika

¼ cup (60 g) frozen peas, thawed (optional)

4 ounces (115 g) mozzarella cheese, cut into ½-inch (1.25 cm) cubes

2 cups (210 g) dried breadcrumbs

1 cup (125 g) all-purpose flour

2 to 3 cups (475 to 720 ml) olive oil for frying

Tomato Sauce (page 63) for serving

Heat a medium pot over high heat and swirl in 2 tablespoons of the olive oil. When the oil shimmers, add the shrimp shells and shallots and cook, stirring, until the shells are fully pink, about 2 minutes. Add the water and bring to just below a boil, then reduce the heat, partially cover, and let simmer to infuse the liquid with flavor, about 20 minutes.

Strain the broth through a cheesecloth- or kitchen towel–lined sieve set over a medium saucepan, pressing against the shells to release as much liquid as possible; you will have about 4 cups (950 ml) broth. Season the broth with 1 teaspoon salt, or to taste; the rice needs a well-seasoned broth for flavor.

Bring the broth to a boil and stir in the rice and saffron, then reduce the heat to low, partially cover, and simmer, stirring occasionally (especially toward the end), until the rice is tender and the mixture is thick but still stirrable, 18 to 20 minutes (add up to 1 cup/240 ml more warm water as the rice cooks if needed). Season with more salt to taste.

Remove the rice from the heat and stir in the Parmesan and butter. Let cool, then beat one of the eggs and stir into the rice until thoroughly combined. Spread the mixture out

on a baking sheet lined with parchment paper, smoothing the top, and let cool completely.

Coarsely chop the shrimp and transfer to a bowl. Drizzle the shrimp with a little olive oil, add the paprika and a sprinkle of salt, and mix well.

Using a sharp knife, score the rice mixture into 24 sections, to ensure that the rice balls will be evenly sized. Dip your hands in cool water, scoop up a section of rice, and smooth it out a little with your other hand. Place a couple of peas, if using, a cube of mozzarella, and a small spoonful of shrimp in the center, then loosely close your hand around the rice mixture to enclose the filling and form it into a smooth ball. Transfer to a baking sheet and repeat with the remaining rice mixture, peas, if using, cheese, and shrimp. Cover and refrigerate to firm up the balls for at least 20 minutes, or up to 12 hours.

When ready to cook the arancini, beat the remaining 2 eggs together in a small bowl. Put the breadcrumbs and flour in two separate small bowls. One at a time, dip each rice ball in the flour, and then in the egg to coat, and then roll in the breadcrumbs and put it on a tray.

Pour about ¾ inch (2 cm) of oil into a heavy pot and heat until it bubbles up when a bit of the rice mixture is added; it should be about 375°F (190°C). Fry the balls in batches, without crowding, turning them over as they cook until golden brown and crispy on all sides, 5 to 8 minutes. Transfer to paper towels to drain as they are ready.

Serve hot, with tomato sauce.

ASPETTA ✢ Make ahead: *The uncooked rice balls can be refrigerated, covered, for up to 2 days or frozen in a sealed container for up to a couple of months. Thoroughly defrost overnight in the refrigerator. Let stand at room temperature for 15 minutes before frying as directed above.*

The rice balls can also be fully fried ahead of time. Let the balls cool completely, then place in a resealable plastic bag and freeze for up to a month. Defrost overnight in the refrigerator or at room temperature for a couple of hours. Reheat on a baking sheet in a preheated 350°F (175°C) oven until they are hot and the cheese is melted, about 20 minutes.

SEAFOOD-STUFFED SHELLS

Seafood-stuffed shells make a special dish for a feasting occasion, such as Christmas Eve, or the centerpiece of a dinner party. The shells can be stuffed in advance and frozen until ready to bake. They can also be stuffed earlier in the day and held in the pan in the fridge until ready to bake for dinner. Lobster is used in this recipe to take advantage of the shells for the broth. One pound (455 g) cooked crab or shrimp meat can be substituted for lobster. Replace the lobster broth with 2 cups (475 ml) fish broth procured from a good seafood market.

Makes 6 to 8 servings

Two 1-pound (455 g) lobsters

1 bay leaf

1 onion, roughly chopped

1 pound (455 g) jumbo pasta shells

3 tablespoons extra virgin olive oil, plus more as needed

2 leeks, halved lengthwise, cut crosswise into thin slices, thoroughly washed of grit, and dried

1 cup (230 g) frozen baby peas, thawed

1 orange

6 tablespoons (85 g) unsalted butter

6 tablespoons (80 g) all-purpose flour

½ cup (120 ml) heavy cream

¾ teaspoon kosher salt

½ teaspoon red pepper flakes

¾ cup (90 g) Crispy Savory Breadcrumbs (page 43)

⅓ cup (20 g) chopped fresh flat-leaf parsley

Bring 1 inch (2.5 cm) of water to a rolling boil in a large pot with a tight-fitting lid. Add the lobsters, quickly cover the pot, and steam until the shells have completely turned red-orange, 13 to 15 minutes. Remove the lobsters from the pot and let cool enough to handle. (Set the empty pot aside.)

When they are cool enough to handle, crack the lobsters and remove the lobster meat from the shells and place it in a bowl; reserve the shells. Let the lobster meat cool completely, then cover and refrigerate.

Put the lobster shells, bay leaf, and onions in the pot, cover with water, partially cover the pot, and bring to a boil, then reduce the heat and simmer for a couple of hours to infuse the broth. Add water, if needed, to keep the shells submerged. Remove from the heat.

Strain the broth through a cheesecloth- or kitchen towel–lined sieve set over a bowl and let cool. Reserve 2 cups (475 ml) for this recipe; transfer the remaining broth to a lidded container and refrigerate (*The broth can be prepared in advance and refrigerated for up to 2 days or frozen for up to 6 months.*)

Meanwhile, bring a large pot of water to a boil. Salt the water generously, add the pasta shells, and cook until 2 minutes shy of the package instructions; the shells should be slightly soft but with a chew to them. Drain the shells, toss with olive oil to coat, and let cool.

Recipe continues

Heat a medium skillet over medium heat and swirl in the olive oil. Add the leeks and cook until soft, 5 to 6 minutes. Remove from the heat and let cool.

Chop the lobster meat into bite-sized pieces and place in a bowl. Mix in the cooled leeks and the peas.

Grate 1 tablespoon zest from the orange. Halve it and squeeze ¼ cup (60 ml) juice into a small bowl.

Melt the butter in a large saucepan over medium heat. When it is bubbling, whisk in the flour and cook, whisking constantly, for 1 minute. Whisk in the 2 cups (475 ml) reserved lobster broth and cook, whisking constantly, until the mixture bubbles and thickens, 3 to 5 minutes. Remove from the heat, stir in the cream, orange zest, juice, salt, and red pepper flakes and let cool.

Preheat the oven to 325°F (165°C).

Stir 1 cup (240 ml) of the sauce into the lobster and leek mixture. Spread another 1 cup (240 ml) of the sauce over the bottom of a 9-by-13-inch (23 by 33 cm) baking dish.

Fill each shell with a tablespoon of the lobster mixture and arrange in the baking dish. (Any remaining filling can be stored in a resealable bag, frozen, and reserved for future use for up to 6 months.) Spoon the remaining sauce over the shells and sprinkle the breadcrumbs over the top. Drizzle with olive oil and bake, uncovered, until the shells are bubbling and golden brown, about 30 minutes. (You may need to set the oven to broil for a few minutes at the end; if you do, keep an eye on it to avoid burning.)

Remove the shells from the oven and let cool for 5 to 10 minutes before serving with the parsley scattered on top.

HADDOCK ITALIANO

This recipe breaks the cardinal rule throughout much of Italy that you never, ever pair cheese with fish, because it's thought to overwhelm its delicate taste. But here a lightly cheesy and toasty breadcrumb mixture makes a perfect combination with haddock, a thick, flaky white fish that is still plentiful and affordable in eastern U.S. waters. Any similar-textured fish like flounder or cod can be subbed in.

Makes 4 servings

One 1-pound (455 g) haddock or other mild, flaky white fish fillet, cut into 4 pieces

Kosher salt and freshly ground black pepper

2 tablespoons Dijon mustard

2 teaspoons extra virgin olive oil, plus more for the baking dish

1 lemon

½ cup (50 g) coarse fresh breadcrumbs (page 42) or panko crumbs

¼ cup (15 g) chopped fresh flat-leaf parsley

2 tablespoons grated Parmesan cheese

1 garlic clove, minced

2 teaspoons unsalted butter

Preheat the oven to 425°F (220°C).

Season the fish on both sides with salt and pepper and place in an oiled baking dish.

Whisk together the mustard and 1 teaspoon of the olive oil in a small bowl. Spread a layer of the mustard mixture over each piece of fish.

Grate the zest from half the lemon. Cut the lemon in half and juice one half. Cut the other half into 4 wedges for serving.

Combine the breadcrumbs, parsley, cheese, lemon zest, garlic, and the remaining 1 teaspoon olive oil in a bowl and mix well. Pile some of the breadcrumb mixture onto each piece of fish and press it down gently. Drizzle ½ teaspoon of the lemon juice over each one. Dot the tops with the butter.

Bake the fish until golden brown on top and just cooked through, 6 to 8 minutes, depending on the thickness of the fish. The fish should feel slightly firm when pressed with your finger.

Serve the fish with the lemon wedges.

POACHED FISH FILLETS
(ACQUA PAZZA)

We all need a quickie fish recipe in our meal rotation. The genesis of this dish for "crazy water" fish seems to have come from coastal Neapolitan fishermen who would cook themselves a meal from the catch of the day, right there on the boats, by steaming or poaching the fish in seawater and some of whatever jug of wine might be around. As is typical of these ancient recipes, it has morphed into various styles over the years, united by the cooking method and personalized with different herbs and liquids. Since most of our fish isn't coming directly from the sea to our pan these days, bringing the fish to room temperature before cooking will allow for more even heating and a more consistent texture by taking the chill off.

Makes 4 servings

Four 4-ounce (115 g) white fish fillets, such as bass, snapper, or cod

Kosher salt

¼ cup (60 ml) extra virgin olive oil

4 garlic cloves, thinly sliced

¼ teaspoon red pepper flakes

½ cup (120 ml) white wine

1 pound (455 g) ripe tomatoes, chopped, or one 14.5-ounce (412 g) can whole tomatoes, drained and chopped

1 tablespoon fresh oregano leaves or sliced basil leaves or 2 teaspoons dried oregano or basil

1½ cups (360 ml) water

Crostini (see Aspetta) for serving

ASPETTA ✛ Homemade crostini: *Take 4 hefty slices of country bread and toast them. Rub a peeled clove of garlic over each toast and drizzle with olive oil and salt. Serve warm or at room temperature.*

About 20 minutes before cooking, remove the fish from the refrigerator and let it come to room temperature. Then thoroughly pat each fillet dry with paper towels. If the fish has skin, carefully score the skin lightly with a sharp knife (so the fillets don't curl too much during cooking); do not pierce the flesh.

Choose a skillet that will hold the fish comfortably, with a little room between the fillets. Heat the pan over very high heat and swirl in the olive oil. Add the garlic and red pepper and stir until they begin to turn lightly golden, about 2 minutes. Pour in the wine, stirring to deglaze the pan, and cook until reduced by half, 1 to 2 minutes. Add the tomatoes, herbs, water, and 1 teaspoon salt and bring to a simmer, then reduce the heat to medium-high and simmer for 15 minutes to reduce the sauce.

Salt the fish and add it to the pan, skin side down. Reduce the heat to medium-low and spoon some sauce over the fish to cover, repeating this a couple of times, and then gently poach the fish (at just below the boiling point), uncovered, until cooked through, 3 to 5 minutes, depending on the thickness of the pieces.

Remove the fish to shallow bowls and spoon some sauce over each portion. Serve with crostini at the sides of the bowls.

TUNA or SWORDFISH KEBABS with SALSA VERDE

Many Sicilian families in the United States have a version of this sauce in their family archives. Seaside communities like San Diego, California, attracted arriving immigrants skilled in the deep-water swordfish and tuna fishing trade practiced for millennia back home. Salsa verde is a green sauce made with fresh herbs, capers, and garlic that is traditionally mashed together with a mortar and pestle, but a sharp knife or a food processor is today's tool of choice. For this recipe, you want a firm-fleshed fish that will stand up to the hot grill without flaking apart when cooked; tuna and swordfish are both good choices. Drizzle the fish with some of the salsa verde just before serving and pass a small bowl of the remaining sauce at the table.

These kebabs are even delicious at room temperature, which makes them an excellent choice for a summer cookout. Conversely, you might want to consider this dish an excellent addition to the Christmas Eve feast, as most of the preparation can be done in advance.

**Makes
6 to 8 servings**

2 lemons

4 garlic cloves, 2 roughly chopped, 2 smashed

2 tablespoons capers, rinsed and roughly chopped

Kosher salt

1 cup (60 g) fresh mint leaves, finely chopped

¼ cup (15 g) finely chopped fresh flat-leaf parsley

½ cup (120 ml) extra virgin olive oil, plus more as needed

1 tablespoon red wine vinegar

1 tablespoon dried oregano

½ teaspoon freshly ground black pepper

2 pounds (910 g) tuna steak or swordfish, cut into 2-inch (5 cm) square chunks

3 small zucchini, sliced into ½-inch-thick (1.25 cm) coins

1 large red onion, cut into 2-inch (5 cm) pieces, layers separated

Grate the zest from one of the lemons. Juice both lemons to get ¼ cup (60 ml) juice.

Using a mortar and pestle, food processor, or sharp knife, mash or chop the chopped garlic, capers, and ½ teaspoon salt; transfer to a small bowl. Stir in the mint, parsley, ¼ cup (60 ml) of the olive oil, 2 tablespoons of the lemon juice, and the vinegar, mixing well. Drizzle some olive oil over the top (to prevent oxidation, which would dull the bright green color of the sauce) and set aside, or cover and refrigerate for up to 2 days.

Whisk together the lemon zest and remaining juice, the remaining 2 tablespoons olive oil, the smashed garlic, oregano, ½ teaspoon salt, and black pepper in a large baking dish. Add the fish and zucchini to the dish, turning to coat, and marinate for 20 to 30 minutes at room temperature.

Recipe continues

If using wooden skewers, soak them in water for 20 minutes so they don't burn during cooking.

Thread the fish chunks, zucchini, and onion pieces alternately onto the drained wooden skewers or metal ones and return to the baking dish. (*The skewers can be assembled up to 8 hours in advance and refrigerated.*)

Prepare a hot fire on an outdoor grill or turn on the broiler. Lift the skewers out of the marinade and lay them directly on the grill grate or in the broiling pan. Grill or broil, turning once, until the fish is just cooked through and the vegetables are caramelized and hot, 3 to 4 minutes per side.

Transfer the skewers to a serving platter. Drizzle a little salsa verde over each skewer and spoon the rest into a small bowl to serve at the table.

VARIATION:

The salsa can also be used for both a marinade and a sauce for shrimp.

STUFFED SQUID
in TOMATO SAUCE

Squid's mild flavor marries well with many ingredients, but you need to take care in cooking it to ensure a tender result. Either cook it fast over high heat (as in grilling or flash-frying) or simmer it slowly in sauce (but no longer than 30 minutes). Squid is much more affordable than many other seafood choices, and it freezes well; you can freeze the stuffed squid, wrapped well, once assembled, and then cook them in the sauce before serving. Or serve the stuffed parcels whole or sliced into bite-sized pieces. You can also serve the squid with a white wine sauce; see the Variation below.

Makes 6 servings

1 cup (105 g) dried breadcrumbs

½ cup (120 ml) water

1 pound (455 g) cleaned small squid, 4 to 5 inches (10 to 13 cm) long, tentacles separated from bodies and finely chopped

2 tablespoons chopped fresh flat-leaf parsley

1 tablespoon minced fresh oregano or 2 teaspoons dried

Grated zest and juice of 1 lemon

2 garlic cloves, minced

2 teaspoons capers, rinsed and chopped

½ teaspoon kosher salt

¼ teaspoon red pepper flakes

1 anchovy fillet, minced

1 large egg, beaten

2 tablespoons extra virgin olive oil

1 recipe Tomato Sauce (page 63)

Mix the breadcrumbs with the water in a medium bowl to hydrate them. Add the chopped squid tentacles, parsley, oregano, lemon zest and juice, garlic, capers, salt, red pepper flakes, anchovy, and egg and mix well.

Working over the bowl, loosely stuff the squid bodies with the filling. Secure the top opening of each one with a toothpick and place on a baking sheet. (*The stuffed squid can be wrapped well and frozen for up to 2 months. Defrost overnight in the fridge and then cook as directed.*)

Heat a large skillet over medium-high heat and swirl in the olive oil. When it glistens, add the squid parcels, leaving a little room between them, and brown on both sides, turning once, about 3 minutes total. Pour the tomato sauce into the pan, bring to a simmer, partially cover, and cook over low heat, turning the parcels over halfway through, until the filling is cooked through and the squid is tender, 13 to 15 minutes.

Serve the squid parcels whole or slice each one on the bias, and spoon some of the sauce over the top.

Recipe continues

VARIATION:

To serve the squid with white wine sauce: Brown the squid bundles in the olive oil and transfer to a warm platter. Add 2 sliced garlic cloves to the pan and cook, stirring, until soft and lightly golden, about 1 minute. Pour in 1 cup (240 ml) white wine to deglaze, scraping up the browned bits on the bottom of the pan, and cook until reduced by half, about 3 minutes. Stir in ½ cup (120 ml) fish or chicken broth and the juice of 1 lemon and simmer until reduced and slightly thickened, about 2 minutes. Whisk in 2 tablespoons butter, return the squid bundles to the pan, and warm through.

ASPETTA + Using squid tentacles: *When you are using only the squid bodies for a recipe, you can grind up the tentacles to make meatballs, or to use as a stuffing base for the squid bodies. If not using the tentacles right away, portion as desired into freezer containers and freeze for up to 6 months.*

GREENS + + +

DELICIOUS
SIDE
DISHES
MADE
from
BELOVED
ITALIAN
PRODUCE

222 Sautéed Escarole

223 Garlicky Broccoli Rabe

226 Utica Greens

228 Greens and Beans

229 Jambot (VEGETABLE STEW)

231 Lemony Pole Beans

232 Stuffed Artichokes

236 Braised Fennel

239 Fennel and Orange Salad

240 Tomato Salad

242 Put-Up Tomatoes

243 Italian "Vinaigrette"

IN THEIR NATIVE COUNTRY, CULTIVATING

a garden was necessary for survival for nineteenth-century southern Italians. The instinct to grow and harvest their own food was rooted deep in the peasant psyche. Wild field greens and roadside herbs not only were free but also supplied important nutrients to the impoverished population. Fresh greens were a gift from the earth, picked in the spring and cooked for their health-giving properties after a cold winter without. In one short story collection, an Italian American housewife describes how she cooked escarole a dozen different ways for her family. A recipe for the most basic version, Sautéed Escarole, is on page 222.

Our Italian immigrant forebears introduced dozens of vegetables to the United States, common for the peasants yet unfamiliar to Americans at the time. These include many that we now consider mainstream, including escarole, endive, dandelion greens, broccoli, broccoli rabe, chicory, and spinach, as well as artichokes and fennel.

Little wooden box gardens arose on the roofs of apartment buildings. They produced familiar produce from Italy: greens, herbs, tomatoes, and peppers. The gardens were practical as well as pleasurable; tall vines provided shade, fed the family, and kept folks moored to the earth. Pole bean plants could reach 6 feet (2 m) tall, and the beans then incorporated into many dishes, such as hearty Lemony Pole Beans. Utica Greens turns any cooked greens into a layered casserole. There was always an abundance of zucchini in the summer, used for the vegetable stew Jambot, among many other dishes. Fennel bulbs melt and caramelize in Braised Fennel, and the vegetables' licoricey crunch shines in the fresh Fennel and Orange Salad. An abundance of summer tomatoes are celebrated in both Tomato Salad and jars of Put-Up Tomatoes for the winter months. No matter how small or unlikely a spot they might have access to, Italian Americans had a reputation for growing something out of practically nothing.

SAUTÉED ESCAROLE

"Sca-*roll*" is a melodious word that rolls off the tongues of older Italian Americans when talking about escarole, a slightly bitter fresh green that softens into a gentle-flavored, toothsome texture when cooked. Escarole is essential for Italian Wedding Soup (page 57), and it is the green of choice in Greens and Beans (page 228). A giant pile of cleaned escarole will collapse into a disproportionately small yield, so bear that in mind when preparing it. There is a beautiful alchemy that happens when the green is combined with olive oil and other flavors in the pan. Escarole has a heartier texture than spinach, with less density than kale or collard greens, and it is perfectly cooked in a little more than 10 minutes.

Makes 4 to 6 servings

1 head escarole (about 1 pound/455 g), cleaned and cut lengthwise into quarters and then crosswise into 2-inch (5 cm) pieces

¼ cup (60 ml) extra virgin olive oil

4 garlic cloves, thinly sliced

½ teaspoon red pepper flakes

1 teaspoon kosher salt

Wash the escarole and drain, leaving some water clinging to the leaves.

Combine the olive oil, garlic, and red pepper flakes in a large deep skillet or pot and cook over medium-low heat, stirring, until the garlic begins to sizzle, about 1 minute. Add just enough of the greens to cover the bottom of the pan, stirring to coat in the oil. As the greens cook and collapse in the pan, add more a handful at a time. Once the last batch wilts, stir in the salt, cover, and cook until the escarole is soft and silky, about 10 minutes.

Remove from the heat and serve.

ASPETTA + Cleaning greens: *Properly cleaning greens to remove all sand and grit is an important part of the eating process. Nowadays produce packaging often boasts the label "previously washed," but that is unreliable, and greens should always be cleaned before using, both to make sure any dirt is removed and for proper hygiene. Float the greens in a large bowl of cold water, lift them out into a colander, and check the water for grit or dirt. Repeat the process if necessary until the water is clean and no grit remains.*

For salads, layer the washed greens on a towel, roll it up, and refrigerate until the greens are chilled and dry. For sautés, leave a little water clinging to the greens to help them cook properly without waterlogging them.

GARLICKY BROCCOLI RABE

Pick up a bunch of broccoli rabe at your local market, and it's likely bound with a wire tie that has a logo of a little boy's face; it's called "Andy Boy," a heritage brand from Salinas Valley, California, that is one of the many Italian American success stories in the food business world. Founded by two immigrant brothers from Messina, Sicily, Andrea and Stefano D'Arrigo, the company is now a fourth-generation family business. Indeed, "Andy Boy" D'Arrigo is the son of Stefano, who passed the reins over to his son John. They cultivate and distribute many of the heritage vegetables that originally came as seeds from Italy with their ancestors. Their broccoli rabe is a direct descendant of the wild mustard plants that grew every spring along the hillsides around Messina.

Many recipes call for blanching broccoli rabe before sautéing it to remove bitterness, which isn't always necessary; see the Variation.

Makes 4 to 6 servings

1 bunch broccoli rabe (about 13 ounces/370 g)

3 tablespoons extra virgin olive oil

2 garlic cloves, sliced

½ teaspoon red pepper flakes

1 anchovy fillet (optional)

½ teaspoon kosher salt

Bring a large pot of salted water to a boil. Trim the ends off the broccoli rabe stalks and peel the lower stalks to remove the fibrous skin. (Cut the stalks in thirds if smaller pieces are desired.) Add the broccoli rabe to the boiling water and blanch for 3 to 5 minutes (homegrown rabe will tenderize more quickly than commercial varieties). Drain.

Meanwhile, heat a large skillet over medium-high heat and swirl in the olive oil. Add the garlic, pepper flakes, and anchovy, if using, and cook, stirring constantly, for about 2 minutes, until the garlic is lightly golden.

Add the drained broccoli rabe to the pan, season with the salt, and toss it in the garlicky oil until coated and tender, 3 to 4 minutes. Serve immediately.

VARIATION:

Alternatively, forgo blanching the broccoli rabe and instead simmer it in 1½ cups (360 ml) chicken broth, homemade (page 179) or store-bought, with the garlic, pepper flakes, and salt. Cover and simmer until tender, about 10 minutes. Drizzle with olive oil and serve.

Once the Italian immigrants were stateside, a garden was considered an essential indication of the good life. At first the "garden" might be nothing more than a backyard tenement patch or windowsill. As people moved out of urban areas, the sight of a green lawn surrounding a home with no food growing in it was anathema to the new arrivals, and when given the chance, they put in a garden of their own. Familiar vegetables from back home were also available to cooks by way of pushcart vendors or curbside stands supplied by enterprising farmers, who would lease small plots of land outside urban centers, which became known as truck gardens. Whole generational family businesses arose from the truck gardens, which eventually grew into the wholesale business and marketing of vegetables and fruits. Andy Boy, Planter's Peanuts, Tropicana, and Gallo winery are just a few modern multinational companies that were founded by early Italian Americans.

Grapes for wine, either grown on their own plots or gathered from growers, were vital. Every Italian American family I knew growing up had a tradition of making their own wine, produced in the cellar with a crate of grapes and a pressing machine, bottled, and stored for family use. Wine was a central part of life in Italian families, considered as much a staple as bread. Most of us remember being served wine as children, first a little thimbleful mixed with twice the amount of water, the equation flip-flopping as we got older. We were encouraged to sip it—it was "good for you." Drinking wine with food at the dinner table was taken for granted.

The gardens fed families year-round with fresh vegetables enjoyed during the summer months and preserved once harvested to ensure they could always have the taste of homegrown produce. Nowadays "putting up" vegetables has become a smart way to use up an overabundance in the garden—as in zucchini, tomatoes, and peppers—without waste, as well as to preserve produce bought at a farmers' market, often personalizing it with add-in flavors such as herbs, alliums, and citrus peel. There's great personal satisfaction in pulling your own Put-Up Tomatoes (page 242) off the shelf in the middle of winter for a sauce, or tossing your own pickled hot peppers (see page 83) with pasta and olive oil for a quick meal.

UTICA GREENS

Some of the most beloved Italian American dishes have come from the long-established community in Utica, New York (see, for example, Utica Riggies, page 101). These days you'll find Utica greens eaten all over central New York, from Albany to Syracuse. A love of wild greens, especially dandelion, came to this country with our forebears, who, like so many Mediterranean populations, were used to growing, picking, and eating them for both thriftiness and health. This recipe for escarole is so chock-full of contrasting flavors and textures that it can stand on its own as lighter main course or an appetizer, as well as a side dish. The escarole can be swapped with dandelion greens, spinach, chard, kale, or any combination of them.

Makes 4 to 6 servings

1½ heads escarole (about 1½ pounds/680 g), washed

4 tablespoons (60 ml) extra virgin olive oil, plus more for serving

1 small onion, chopped

4 ounces (115 g) thinly sliced prosciutto, cut into strips

3 garlic cloves, thinly sliced

3 pickled cherry peppers, sliced

½ cup (50 g) grated Romano cheese

½ cup (50 g) dried breadcrumbs

Bring a large pot of salted water to a rolling boil. Meanwhile, cut the whole head of escarole into quarters and cut the half head in half again. Remove the cores and any bruised outer leaves, then cut crosswise into 2-inch (5 cm) pieces.

Add the escarole to the boiling water and blanch for 2 minutes; drain.

Heat a large broiler-safe skillet over medium-high heat and swirl in 2 tablespoons of the olive oil. Add the onions and prosciutto and cook, stirring, until caramelized, 8 to 10 minutes; add the garlic in the final 2 minutes. Add the peppers and drained greens, stir well, and cook until the flavors have blended and the greens are wilted, 6 to 7 minutes. Remove from the heat.

Preheat the broiler to high. Combine the cheese and breadcrumbs in a small bowl and sprinkle evenly over the greens. Drizzle with the remaining 2 tablespoons olive oil. Broil until golden and bubbly, about 5 minutes. Serve immediately, with a final drizzle of olive oil.

GREENS and BEANS

I grew up eating this humble dish, which we called minestra, even though it wasn't soup. My mother made it with spinach and kidney beans, drizzled with olive oil and scattered with grated cheese and ground black pepper. Historically Italian moms have relied on a version of this dish to feed large families a balanced, nutrient-dense, yet affordable meal. Start early teaching your kids to love beans just as well as meat. Rehydrated and cooked dried beans are both more economical and more delicious than canned, but the convenience of canned beans is undeniable. Keep both types in your pantry. Use this recipe as a road map to make any combination of greens and beans of your choosing. It's essential to clean your greens thoroughly to remove all grit before cooking (see Aspetta, page 222).

Makes 4 to 6 servings

¼ cup (60 ml) extra virgin olive oil, plus more for drizzling

4 garlic cloves, thinly sliced

½ teaspoon red pepper flakes

4 ounces (115 g) tomatoes (1 medium), chopped (optional)

1 teaspoon kosher salt

2 cups (350 g) cooked or canned beans (from one can), such as chickpeas, kidney beans, or cannellini beans

1 large head escarole or Swiss chard (1 pound/455 g), washed and chopped (about 10 cups)

1 cup (240 ml) chicken broth, homemade (page 179) or store-bought, vegetable broth, or water

Grated Romano cheese for serving

Sliced crusty bread, toasted, for serving

Heat a large skillet over medium heat and swirl in the olive oil until it glistens. Add the garlic and pepper flakes and cook, stirring constantly, until sizzling and beginning to turn golden on the edges, no more than 2 minutes. Add the tomatoes, if using, and stir until softened and starting to break down, 2 to 3 minutes. Add the salt and beans, stirring to coat the beans completely in the garlicky oil and heat them through.

Raise the heat to high and add the greens a handful at a time, stirring until they wilt and collapse. Pour in the broth or water and bring to a simmer, partially cover, and cook until the greens are tender and the flavors have melded, 15 to 20 minutes.

Serve the beans and greens in bowls, drizzled with olive oil and sprinkled with cheese, with crusty bread on the side.

JAMBOT (VEGETABLE STEW)

My family called this vegetable stew "jambot," but it's also known as giambotta, ciambotta, or gambot—which is how the names sound phonetically, regardless of the dialect they are written in. There are many different variations in the ingredients used as well, but generally the stew is a mash-up of late-summer vegetables, which can include eggplant, green beans, and tomatoes. Our version was a little different, featuring zucchini and potatoes, which make it a solid side dish, a platform for fried eggs, or an ideal vegetarian frittata filling (see the Variation).

Makes 6 to 8 servings, or enough filling for one 12-inch (30 cm) frittata

¼ cup (60 ml) extra virgin olive oil

1 tablespoon unsalted butter

1 small onion, chopped

2 large or 4 small potatoes (1¼ pounds/565 g), peeled and cut into ¾-inch (2 cm) cubes

Kosher salt

2 medium or 4 small zucchini (14 ounces/400 g), cut into cubes a little smaller than the potatoes

2 teaspoons dried oregano or Italian seasoning

Freshly ground black pepper

Chopped fresh flat-leaf parsley for garnish

Heat a 12-inch (30 cm) skillet over medium-high heat and add the oil and butter. When the butter melts, stir in the onions and cook until they start to soften, about 2 minutes. Add the potatoes and a pinch of salt and cook, stirring often, for 8 to 10 minutes.

Increase the heat to high, add the zucchini, herbs, ¾ teaspoon salt, and pepper to taste and cook until the zucchini and potatoes are just tender, 7 to 9 minutes. Serve garnished with parsley.

VARIATION:

To transform the stew into a vegetable-filled frittata, preheat the broiler (use a broiler-safe pan to make the jambot). When the jambot is cooked, with the heat still on high, pour 2 tablespoons white wine, chicken broth, or water into the pan, scraping up the brown bits from the bottom. Push the vegetables to the sides as you swirl 2 to 3 tablespoons olive oil into the center of the pan and heat until hot. Smooth out the vegetable mixture, pour in 8 large eggs, beaten, and a pinch of salt, and lower the heat to medium-low. Swirl the eggs around the pan, letting them run into the crevices of the vegetable mixture. When the eggs are set on the bottom but the top is still loose and wet, sprinkle on ¼ cup (25 g) grated Romano or Parmesan cheese and place the pan under the broiler for 2 minutes, or until the frittata is slightly golden; it will puff up before it settles back down again.

Remove from the broiler and let the frittata rest for a few minutes so the bottom releases from the pan. Cut into wedges and serve with chopped parsley and more grated cheese on top.

LEMONY POLE BEANS

The earliest childhood memory I have from my Italian grandparents' home in central New York is of playing among the pole bean trellises in their garden. Picking beans was the children's job, and it was such fun hiding in the climbing vines, which grew to at least 6 feet tall; it was like a wondrous jungle to me. Similar food memories can span generations and age. One evocative account from seventeenth-century Italian writer Lodovico Castelvetro describes how "the woman of Venice could gaze unseen at passers-by from behind a screen of green pole beans growing up white trellises set in window-boxes." Pole beans are wide, flat, and long, with a meaty texture when cooked until tender enough to meld with other flavors. Green beans or haricots verts can be substituted, and they don't need to be blanched.

Makes 4 to 6 servings

1 pound (455 g) pole beans, trimmed

2 tablespoons extra virgin olive oil

2 garlic cloves, smashed and peeled

4 to 5 thin lemon slices, any seeds removed

½ teaspoon kosher salt

¼ teaspoon red pepper flakes

2 sprigs fresh thyme or ½ teaspoon dried

Bring a large pot of salted water to a rolling boil. Add the beans and blanch for 3 minutes. Drain, leaving some water clinging to the beans.

Combine the olive oil, garlic, lemon slices, salt, red pepper, and thyme in a medium-large skillet with a tight-fitting lid, stir in the beans, cover, and cook over medium-low heat, undisturbed, for 5 minutes. Then cook, stirring occasionally, until the beans are completely tender, 15 to 20 minutes longer. If the beans seem too dry after 10 minutes or so, add a couple tablespoons of water.

Serve hot or at room temperature.

STUFFED ARTICHOKES

The artichoke season extends from late February, for the smallest ones—the size of a large nut, which are eaten whole—to early spring to early summer for the large, fat, plump ones. Artichokes have been enjoyed from Sicily to Naples and beyond since the 1400s. Our immigrant ancestors tucked the seeds and branches from artichokes, thistles, chicory, and figs, among other vegetables and fruits, in their trunks and suitcases when they boarded ships bound for the United States. These were all plants that were not found in America at the time. Today, 80 percent of the globe artichokes sold in the United States are farmed in California, and they are available year-round. Unlike in Italy, where cooks tend to do most of the "prep work" for anyone who will be eating their food, the American way is to have diners pull off the tender cooked leaves to dip in sauce or eat with the artichoke stuffing, then scrape the leaves between their front teeth to capture each soft bite. You need to excavate a mountain of leaves to reach the (disposable) choke and the prized heart. Stuffed artichokes are an ideal starter to the Easter meal, but they are a special treat all on their own at any time.

Makes 6 servings

1 lemon, halved

6 large globe artichokes (about 14 ounces/400 g each)

¾ cup (80 g) fresh breadcrumbs (page 42)

½ cup (50 g) grated Romano cheese

1 garlic clove, minced

2 tablespoons chopped fresh flat-leaf parsley

1 tablespoon extra virgin olive oil

Freshly ground black pepper

Squeeze the juice of the lemon into a large bowl of cold water and reserve the rinds. Working with one artichoke at a time, trim the bottom and then remove the tough outer leaves. Snip off the thorny tips of the remaining leaves and drop the artichoke into the lemon water to prevent it from discoloring.

Bring 1 inch (2.5 cm) of water to a simmer in a large pot with a tight-fitting lid. Stand the artichokes up in the pot, cover, and simmer for 10 minutes, then transfer the artichokes to a clean work surface; drain the pot and set aside.

Combine the breadcrumbs, cheese, garlic, parsley, and olive oil in a small bowl and season with pepper. Working with one artichoke at a time, pull the leaves slightly open and stuff a little of the filling between the leaves. Arrange the artichokes side by side in the pot.

Recipe continues

Pour 1 inch (2.5 cm) of water into the pot around the
artichokes, add the lemon rinds, cover, and bring to a boil
over high heat, then reduce the heat, cover, and steam until
the bottoms of the artichokes are tender, 35 to 40 minutes;
a knife should insert easily. Make sure the water doesn't boil
away; add more if necessary. Remove from the heat.

Arrange the artichokes on individual plates with enough room
for the nibbled leaves, or place a discard bowl on the side. Serve
immediately.

BRAISED FENNEL

Fennel, also referred to as Florence fennel, is called *finocchio* in Italian. It has green celery-like stems and fronds with a bulbous pale greenish-white base and a sweet, delicate anise flavor that mellows when cooked. I remember seeing it served raw in a fruit bowl at the end of a meal when I was a kid; the old-timers would nibble on raw slices of it while drinking their *digestivi*. This savory dish makes a good appetizer with some crusty bread alongside, or serve it as a side for Boneless Pork Roast (page 147) or other roasted meats.

Makes 4 to 6 servings

1 fennel bulb (about
    8 ounces/230 g), trimmed and
    cut lengthwise into 8 wedges

2 tablespoons extra virgin olive oil,
    plus more for drizzling

4 garlic gloves, smashed and
    peeled

½ cup (120 ml) chicken broth,
    homemade (page 179) or
    store-bought

1 teaspoon kosher salt

½ teaspoon cracked black pepper

1 cup (100 g) grated Parmesan
    cheese

Preheat the oven to 400°F (200°C).

Bring a pot of salted water to a rolling boil, add the fennel, and blanch for 2 minutes; drain.

Generously coat an 8-inch (20 cm) square baking dish or similar size oval baking dish with the olive oil. Arrange the fennel cut side up, side by side, in the pan, and tuck the garlic cloves in among the wedges. Pour in the chicken broth and sprinkle with the salt and pepper.

Cover with foil, transfer to the oven, and cook for about 30 minutes, until the fennel is fork-tender. Remove the fennel from the oven and turn on the broiler.

Uncover the fennel, sprinkle on the Parmesan, drizzle on some olive oil, and broil until golden brown and bubbling, 1 to 2 minutes. Remove from the oven and let cool for about 10 minutes before serving.

FENNEL and ORANGE SALAD

Fennel, which has a long history in Italian cooking, was historically prized for its natural digestive properties thanks to the essential oil called anethole, which is also found in licorice. Both fennel seeds and bulbs were used in ancient potions to freshen breath, calm upset stomachs, and whet the appetite. Fresh fennel is versatile, equally welcome nibbled with your aperitivo, dipped in olive oil and salt, as it is layered into a dinner salad or on a dessert plate with fresh fruit.

This bracing, refreshing salad of fennel and oranges often includes small pitted olives or sliced red onions. Serve after the main dish as a palate cleanser and prelude to dessert. To prepare it in advance, arrange the salad on a platter, cover, and refrigerate. Just before serving, drizzle over the dressing and garnish with the fennel fronds.

Makes 4 to 6 servings

2 large oranges

1 small fennel bulb
(7 ounces/200 g), stalks
and fronds removed, fronds
reserved for garnish, bulb
halved, core removed, and
thinly sliced

1 tablespoon white wine vinegar

Pinch of kosher salt

Pinch of sugar

Pinch of red pepper flakes

2 tablespoons extra virgin olive oil

Using a sharp paring knife, peel the skin and white pith from the oranges. Working over a bowl to catch the juices, remove the orange sections by slicing down the membranes on both sides to release the sections, letting them drop into the bowl. Then squeeze the membranes over the bowl to release all the juice.

Arrange the fennel on a platter and top with the orange sections.

Separate the reserved fennel fronds into small feathers. Whisk together the orange juice, vinegar, salt, sugar, and pepper flakes in a small bowl. Drizzle in the olive oil, whisking, and continue to whisk until the dressing is emulsified.

Drizzle the dressing over the salad, top with the reserved fennel fronds, and serve.

TOMATO SALAD

Made with wedges of peak summer tomatoes, minced garlic, and fresh herbs, this salad creates a savory, juicy sugo for which hunks of crusty bread on the side are mandatory to soak up the juices. For many years in America, fresh tomatoes were thought to be a dangerous food that caused various ills. The Italians arriving between 1880 and 1920 held no such superstition against fresh tomatoes, though, having already been introduced to them in Italy by the ruling Spanish Bourbons.

Makes 4 to 6

4 to 6 ripe medium tomatoes (3 to 5 ounces/85 to 140 g each), peeled (see Aspetta)

1 teaspoon kosher salt

1 small red onion, thinly sliced lengthwise (½ cup/110 g)

¼ cup (15 g) chopped fresh flat-leaf parsley

2 garlic cloves, minced

3 to 4 torn fresh basil leaves

Leaves from 2 sprigs fresh thyme, chopped

Leaves from 1 sprig fresh oregano, chopped

3 tablespoons extra virgin olive oil

Cut out the cores of the tomatoes, slice the tomatoes into thin wedges, and place in a medium bowl, along with all the juices. Stir in the salt. Add the onions, parsley, garlic, basil, thyme, oregano, and olive oil and stir gently until well combined. Adjust the salt to taste. Cover and chill until ready to serve, at least 30 minutes.

Serve the chilled salad in individual bowls.

ASPETTA ✛ Peeling tomatoes easily: *Bring a large pot of water to a boil. Add the tomatoes and blanch for 10 seconds, then pull them out with a slotted spoon and immediately place in a bowl of ice water to cool for a few seconds. Remove from the ice water; the skin should easily peel off using your fingers or a paring knife.*

PUT-UP TOMATOES

If you end up with a surplus of fresh tomatoes or can procure them from a farmers' market, here is a basic formula for shelf-stable preservation. Before commercial canning practices, home-canned or sun-dried were the only way for tomato-growing cooks to preserve the bounty from the short growing season and ensure an off-season supply. This recipe can be scaled up as desired, using multiple jars, depending on the number of tomatoes you are canning.

Makes 1 pint (455 g)

6 ripe San Marzano or Roma tomatoes (2 ounces/60 g each), peeled (see Aspetta, page 240)

2 tablespoons fresh lemon juice

½ teaspoon kosher salt

2 fresh basil leaves

Sterilize a 1-pint (475 ml) canning jar and lid in boiling water.

Place the tomatoes in the sterilized jar, taking care to leave ½ inch (1.25 cm) of headspace. Add the lemon juice, salt, and basil leaves. Screw on the lid until finger tight (it will fully seal during boiling). Turn the jar over a few times to distribute the salt and lemon juice.

Bring a large pot of water, enough to cover the jar by at least 1 inch (2.5 cm), to a boil. Add the jar of tomatoes, and once the water returns to a boil, process the tomatoes for 45 minutes. Carefully remove the jar from the water with a slotted spoon or tongs, and a dry towel in hand, turn upside down, and let cool completely.

When the jar is completely cooled, press down on the center of the lid to make sure it is sealed before storing. (If the jar is not properly sealed, store the tomatoes in the refrigerator and use within 3 weeks.) You can store the shelf-stable tomatoes in a cool place for up to 6 months. Once the jar is opened, store in the refrigerator.

ITALIAN "VINAIGRETTE"

Homemade Italian dressing is far fresher and more flavorful than the bottled type. You can use it for marinating chicken, or as a dip for fresh vegetables, as well as for salads: Pour it over the classic mix of crispy lettuce leaves, sliced red onions, tomatoes, olives, and cubed cheese. Once made, it can be stored in the refrigerator in a container with a tight-fitting lid for up to 1 week or so.

Makes 2 cups (475 ml)

¼ cup (60 ml) white wine vinegar

¼ cup (25 g) grated Parmesan cheese

2 tablespoons fresh lemon juice

1 garlic clove, smashed and peeled

1 large egg yolk

½ teaspoon dried Italian herbs, such as oregano, marjoram, thyme, or a combination

½ teaspoon sugar

½ teaspoon kosher salt

¼ teaspoon freshly ground black pepper

1¼ cups (300 ml) extra virgin olive oil

¼ cup (60 g) finely chopped sweet red pepper

¼ cup (25 g) finely chopped Vidalia or yellow onion

Combine the vinegar, Parmesan, lemon juice, garlic, egg yolk, Italian herbs, sugar, salt, and pepper in the jar of a blender and blend until smooth. With the motor running on the lowest speed, slowly add the oil in a thin stream.

Transfer the vinaigrette to a bowl and stir in the red peppers and onions. Transfer to a sealed container and store in the refrigerator for 5 to 7 days.

STREETS + + +

SANDWICHES *and* SWEETS INSPIRED *by* FESTIVAL FOODS

249   Sausage and Pepper
Hoagies

250   Muffuletta Sandwich

252   Sausage and Broccoli Rabe
Hoagies

255   Stromboli

257   Chicago Beef

260   Steak Sandwich, aka Philly
Cheesesteak

262   Beef Rice Balls (ARANCINI)

265   Lemon Ice

266   Espresso Granita

EVERY DAY WE EAT REGIONAL "FAST FOOD"

specialties that sprouted from Italian American communities all across the country. Of course, the most obvious and wide-ranging example is pizza in all its forms, whether a quick slice from a New York City pizza parlor or a whole pie from a national chain. That same pizza dough can be formed into Stromboli, a clever twist invented by a pizza maker in Philadelphia. Some of our most popular sandwiches also come from our Italian American forebears. Philly Italians contributed a sandwich some folks might not even regard as Italian, the Cheesesteak, known simply as a steak sandwich by the locals. The famous Chicago Beef, topped with Giardiniera, may be more sought after today than ever. Muffuletta, the popular New Orleans Sicilian sandwich that has been sold at Central Market there since 1906, is the same round olive relish–cold cut sandwich today that it has always been. Fried stuffed rice balls, aka Arancini, were originally sold to travelers at the train station in Sicily and are still made in Sicilian American homes today, using multiple versions of stuffing. And Italian bakeries and cafés have served frosty Lemon Ices and Espresso Granita before they ever became street-cart staples. All these classic foods from local Italian street fairs are fun to eat at home too.

SAUSAGE and PEPPER HOAGIES

The scents wafting from street festival vendors frying sausage and peppers on flattop griddles conjure up memories for so many of us. This at-home version takes the sausage meat out of the casings for easier eating. You could also dispense with the rolls and serve the filling over romaine lettuce, dressed with Italian "Vinaigrette" (page 243).

Makes 6 sandwiches

1 pound (455 g) hot Italian sausages (about 4 links), removed from casings

1 pound (455 g) sweet Italian sausages (about 4 links), removed from casings

2 tablespoons extra virgin olive oil, or more if needed

2 sweet bell peppers, red and/or orange, cored, seeded, and cut into ½-inch-wide (1.25 cm) strips

1 large or 2 small onions

1 tablespoon white or red wine vinegar

Kosher salt and freshly ground black pepper

6 hoagie rolls, split open

Basil leaves, arugula, or other fresh herbs, for garnish (optional)

Put the sausage meat in a large skillet, add the oil, and cook over high heat, using a spatula to break up the pieces of meat, until golden brown with some crispy bits, about 10 minutes. Transfer the sausage to a paper towel–lined plate. There should be some oil left behind; if not, drizzle in some more.

Add the peppers and onions to the pan and sauté until softened, about 10 minutes. Return the meat to the pan and add the vinegar, stirring to fully combine the mixture and scraping up the bits on the bottom of the pan. Taste for seasoning and add salt (it may not be needed if the sausage was well seasoned) and black pepper to taste.

Meanwhile, if desired, heat the rolls in a 225°F (115°C) oven for about 10 minutes.

Layer the filling into the rolls, sprinkle with the herbs, if using, and serve.

ASPETTA + Choose your sausages wisely: *The quality of commercial sausage brands varies widely, with some way too salty and others too fennel heavy, so experiment to find the best choice. Of course, nothing compares to fresh-made sausages from a reputable sausage company in your area, like Calabria Pork Store, in the heart of Arthur Avenue in the Bronx, New York.*

MUFFULETTA SANDWICH

In New Orleans, the early Italian settlers in the late 1800s, many of whom worked the docks in the citrus trade, were largely of Sicilian descent, and they comprised about 90 percent of the immigrant population at the time. As in other similar enclaves, it wasn't long before they opened grocery stores, bakeries, and salumerias to support their community. Italian cooking had a big influence on the evolution of Creole cuisine, sharing many similar ingredients. My husband's New Orleans Sicilian family, the Contesanos, ate red beans and rice as regularly as they did spaghetti. To this day, NOLA's Central Market serves a muffuletta sandwich that was invented by a Sicilian in the early 1900s, with an olive relish as its chief condiment.

Makes 6 sandwiches

1 cup (225 g) Giardiniera, homemade (page 87) or store-bought

½ cup (115 g) pitted green Italian olives

Olive oil (optional)

1 round loaf muffuletta bread or 1 large oblong Italian loaf

5 ounces (140 g) sliced prosciutto

8 ounces (225 g) sliced mortadella

4 ounces (115 g) thinly sliced sweet or hot soppressata

8 ounces (225 g) thinly sliced provolone cheese

Finely chop the giardiniera and olives together into a spreadable consistency. If necessary, transfer to a bowl and stir in some olive oil to bind the mixture.

Split open the bread loaf and lay cut side up on a work surface. Spread each half with half the olive mixture. Alternate layers of the meats and cheese on the bottom half of the bread. Top with the other half. Wrap tightly with plastic wrap and refrigerate for at least an hour, and up to overnight, to allow the flavors to blend.

Slice the sandwich into 6 wedges and serve.

FESTIVALS

The carnival-like street festivals held today in Little Italys nationwide, redolent of fried zeppole and sausage and peppers, originated with the newly arrived Italians who celebrated holidays and feast days in the same ways they had practiced in their villages and towns in the Old Country. Honoring a patron saint or the Virgin Mary was a way to hold on to traditional customs, to remember, and to reflect on their Italian heritage and religious practices. Processions of dozens or even hundreds of people would move through the streets, following a holy statue that was hoisted up by the faithful. Attendees would pin money on the statues with prayers for divine intervention for friends or family members in need of help.

In America, the music, dancing, and food brought extended families together for a day of celebration to recapture the aura and feelings of a long-gone era, replicating the details as they'd been celebrated throughout the Mezzogiorno. Celebrants from neighboring Italian immigrant enclaves had a rare opportunity to bond and revel together around a common tradition. Even "church-averse" men who considered churchgoing women's duty (and consequently attended Mass only on special occasions like Christmas, weddings, and funerals) participated in these religious events with the whole family.

Family, food, and wine coalesce today around feast celebrations nationwide. Processions, parades, and food stalls mark these special days that are still dedicated to the various regional saints of Italy but also serve as a wider recognition of culture and history. These days there are still more than four hundred such annual festivals in America, from Midwest communities like Chicago, where the longest-running Labor Day feast has honored Maria SS Lauretana since 1900, to Cleveland, Ohio, where August 15 marks the Feast of the Assumption. After the procession and fireworks, marchers and celebrants there eat a traditional meal of cavatelli with sauce prepared by the parish women. In New Orleans, Louisiana, home of the muffuletta sandwich, Una Fiesta d'Italia celebrates some of the world's greatest music from Italian composers. In the west, San Francisco's Feste della Madonna del Lume has celebrated a Sicilian blessing of the fleet since 1935. On the east coast, in Gloucester, Massachusetts, the summer St. Peter's Fiesta is a five-day event that has honored the city's commercial fishing industry since 1925. The largest festival remains the one in New York City that has been held since 1926, when the once-tenement-lined streets of Little Italy along Mulberry Street erupt into a ten-day fair honoring San Gennaro, the patron saint of Naples.

The home-style Sausage and Pepper Hoagies in this chapter (page 249) rival those from any street vendor. The Stromboli (page 255) can be filled with a multitude of on-hand Italian ingredients. The Chicago Beef (page 257) makes a natural transition to the home kitchen, the meat slow-simmered and topped with the pickled-vegetable condiment Giardiniera (page 87). And the original Italian street sweet Lemon Ice (page 265), a cinch to make at home, is a boon for fans of dessert-ready freezer treats.

SAUSAGE and BROCCOLI RABE HOAGIES

In this hoagie—a sandwich also known outside of Philly as a sub, hero, Italian sandwich, or grinder—savory sausage and bitter broccoli rabe unite over a layer of creamy melted cheese. It's inspired by the Philly-style Italian pork sandwich made of pulled pork and smothered in juicy spinach or broccoli rabe, but sausage is a quicker alternative to the roast pork. If there are any leftovers from your Boneless Pork Roast (page 147), though, cook the broccoli rabe as directed and swap the sausage for sliced pork.

Makes 4 sandwiches

2 tablespoons extra virgin olive oil

1 pound (455 g) sweet Italian sausages (about 4 links), each pierced in a couple of spots with a fork

2 garlic cloves, smashed and peeled

12 ounces (340 g) broccoli rabe, trimmed, washed, and cut into bite-sized pieces

Coarse salt (optional)

4 hoagie rolls, split open

8 slices provolone cheese

Pickled Sweet Jimmy Nardello Peppers (page 83) or store-bought marinated peppers

Heat a large skillet over medium-high heat and swirl in the olive oil. Add the sausages and brown, turning over halfway, until golden and almost cooked through, about 10 minutes.

Push the sausages aside, add the garlic, and stir for 30 seconds. Add the broccoli rabe (with the water still clinging to the leaves), stir everything together, cover, and cook until tender, 8 to 10 minutes. Scrape up any brown bits from the bottom of the pan and season with salt if need be (this will depend on how salty the sausage is). Remove from the heat.

Preheat the broiler. Place the rolls on the broiler pan and line the bottom half of each one with 2 slices of provolone. Broil until the cheese melts, 1 to 3 minutes (keep an eye on it so it doesn't burn). Place a sausage in each roll and top with a heaping spoonful of the greens and pickled peppers.

Serve immediately—or wrap in foil to go.

STROMBOLI

The stromboli is another Philadelphia Italian original, made from filled pizza dough rolled into a spiral and baked. Its name may seem to have come from the volcanic island off the coast of Sicily, but it's more likely that it is from the 1950 Italian American movie *Stromboli*, which became popular in America after the affair between its director, Roberto Rossellini, and star, Ingrid Bergman, became public. It made worldwide headlines at around the same time as the dish showed up at a Philly pizza parlor. The stuffed dough is rolled up into a coil before it is baked; its cousin the calzone is folded over, to make a half-moon shape, and baked like a hand pie. The original filling was salami, cheese, and peppers, but contemporary versions using Buffalo chicken or Philly cheesesteak show, once again, how deeply imprinted Italian American street food is in the American psyche.

Makes 8 stromboli

5 cups (625 g) all-purpose or bread flour, plus more for kneading

1 tablespoon kosher salt

2¼ teaspoons (7 g) active dry yeast (from a ¼-ounce packet)

2 teaspoons sugar

2 cups (475 ml) water

2 tablespoons extra virgin olive oil, plus more for coating and brushing

2 cups (112 g) grated cheese, such as provolone

8 ounces (227 g) thinly sliced salumi, such as soppressata, capicola, or pepperoni

½ cup (113 g) marinated peppers, thinly sliced, such as cherry peppers or peperoncini

In a large bowl, or the bowl of a stand mixer, whisk together the flour, salt, yeast, and sugar, Add the water and olive oil and stir to combine the wet and dry ingredients.

Knead by hand, or fit the mixer with the dough hook and knead on low speed, until the dough is soft and smooth, about 5 minutes (a few more minutes if kneading by hand). Turn the dough out and shape it into a tight ball. The dough will be sticky but workable. Dust flour on your hands and the work surface as needed. Use a bench scraper to assist you. Transfer the dough to a large oiled bowl and turn to coat with oil.

Cover the dough tightly and set aside to rise in a warm spot until almost doubled, 3 to 4 hours.

Divide the dough in half and work with one piece at a time, keeping the other piece covered. On a clean work surface, using a rolling pin, roll out one piece of the dough to a 12-by-6-inch (30 by 15 cm) rectangle. Cut the dough into 4 equal rectangles. Use one-eighth of the filling for each piece of dough, sprinkling on some of the cheese and then laying down the meat and peppers, leaving ¼-inch (0.65 cm) border all around. Starting from a narrow side, roll up each piece of dough into a coil, pinching the edges as you roll to seal them. Place the stromboli seam side down on a parchment-lined baking sheet. Repeat with the second piece of dough and the remaining filling.

Recipe continues

Loosely cover the dough and let rise in a warm spot for 60 to 90 minutes, until risen by one quarter.

Preheat the oven to 425°F (220° C).

Brush the top of each stromboli with olive oil. Bake for 20 to 25 minutes, or until golden on the outside and cooked inside. Let cool, then slice and serve.

VARIATION:

For a vegetarian version, swap in a couple cups of puttanesca sauce (see page 102) or pesto (see page 60) for the meat and layer it with the cheese, peppers, and some cooked greens.

CHICAGO BEEF

An undisputed jewel in the crown of Chicago-born Italian American specialties, this sandwich has been beloved since its creation the early 1900s. Naturally, several stories lay claim to the invention, all of which include details about the stockyards (now defunct) and the butchers responsible. Whereas a Philly cheesesteak uses thinly sliced and fried cheaper cuts of meat, for Chicago beef, large whole cuts of meat are seasoned with spices and braised in broth until tender. The sliced meat is served piled on top of rolls, which serve to stretch the quantity and fill up a lot more bellies. Spicy giardiniera and pickled hot peppers complete the sandwich.

Makes 6 sandwiches

One 3-pound (1.5 kg) boneless chuck roast or top sirloin roast

4 garlic cloves, slivered

1 tablespoon kosher salt

1 teaspoon freshly ground black pepper

2 tablespoons extra virgin olive oil

1 large onion, chopped

2 celery stalks, chopped

4 cups (950 ml) beef broth, homemade or from bouillon cubes, or store-bought

1 teaspoon dried oregano

1 teaspoon red pepper flakes

1 bay leaf

6 Italian rolls, split open

Giardiniera, homemade (page 87) or store-bought

Jarred pickled peperoncini

Preheat the oven to 350°F (175°C).

Using a sharp knife, make small slits all over the meat and insert the garlic slivers into them. Combine the salt and pepper in a small bowl and rub it all over the meat.

Heat a Dutch oven or other large heavy pot over medium heat and swirl in the olive oil. When it glistens, add the meat to the pot and brown on both sides, about 8 minutes total. Remove the beef to a plate.

Add the onions and celery to the pot, stir, and cook until starting to soften, 3 to 4 minutes. Pour in the beef broth, then add the oregano, red pepper flakes, and bay leaf and scrape up the brown bits from the bottom of the pot.

Return the meat to the pot, cover, and transfer to the oven. Cook, basting the meat a few times, until it is tender, 1½ to 2 hours. Remove from the oven and let the meat cool in the braising liquid, then cover and refrigerate for at least several hours, or overnight.

Skim off and discard the congealed fat from the top of the broth. Transfer the meat to a cutting board and cut into thin slices.

Recipe continues

Meanwhile, reheat the braising liquid over low heat. Place the sliced meat back in the liquid to warm through, about 10 minutes.

Preheat the broiler. Toast the rolls, split side up, under the broiler.

Lift the sliced beef onto the rolls, letting the juices dribble onto the bread. Top with giardiniera and pickled peppers and serve.

ASPETTA + Leftover meat: *Any meat and sauce left over from sandwich making can be tossed with macaroni for a quick meal. Shred the meat, return it to the sauce, and refrigerate in a sealed container for up to a week or in the freezer for up to 6 months. Reheat before tossing together with noodles. Top with grated cheese and minced peperoncini.*

STEAK SANDWICH, AKA PHILLY CHEESESTEAK

Some older Philadelphians think of their famous sandwich as just a plain old steak sandwich, the same as it's been since 1930, when Italian immigrant Pasquale Oliveri and his brother Harry first served it at their hot dog stand near South Philly's Italian market. The original recipe was no more than thin-sliced rib-eye steak, fried onions, salt, and pepper; the steak soaks the hoagie rolls with its juices, which is all the sauce the sandwich needs. Generations later, after cheese became a part of it, most of the rest of the world thinks of the sandwich as the Philly cheesesteak. Pat's King of Steaks and Geno's from the early days still remain, reign, and lead other spots in Philadelphia. These days patrons choose their cheese type and a few other condiments. And precious fat-rich rib-eye steak is no longer used, which may account for the eventual addition of other ingredients for flavor. But everything starts with the vigorous sound of chopping and flipping spatulas cutting through the frying beef as it sizzles on the flattop, which you can mimic at home. Beyond that, the rest is personalized. Add your favorite cheese—provolone, or even Cheez Whiz? Onions or not? Peppers? Hot peppers? Giardiniera? Try them all.

Makes 2 large sandwiches (4 servings cut in half)

1 pound (455 g) boneless beef top round

½ onion, chopped

1 tablespoon vegetable oil

1 tablespoon kosher salt

¼ teaspoon freshly ground black pepper

4 slices provolone cheese

2 hoagie rolls, split open

Giardiniera, homemade (page 87) or store-bought (optional)

Sliced pickled hot peppers (optional)

Freeze the beef for a few hours to allow it to firm up and make it easier to slice. When it is slightly firm, thinly slice it against the grain.

Heat a double-burner griddle or cast-iron pan over medium-high heat. Toss the onions with the vegetable oil in a bowl and put them on the griddle. Cook for a few minutes, until the onions start to sweat and become translucent. Push the onions to the back of the griddle.

Arrange the sliced beef on the griddle and season with the salt and pepper. Cook the meat, turning it occasionally, until no pink remains, about 3 minutes. Fold the onions into the beef slices and chop the mixture with the side of a metal spatula, then divide the beef and onions into two mounds. Place 2 slices of cheese over each mound and then put a split hoagie roll upside down on top of each one.

Using a wide spatula, flip each sandwich over onto a plate. Top with giardiniera and/or pickled peppers, if using, and serve.

VARIATION:

If you want the sandwich with Whiz instead of provolone, make this homemade creamy cheese sauce: Bring 1½ cups (360 ml) evaporated milk to a simmer in a medium saucepan over high heat. Reduce the heat, add a scant teaspoon of mustard, and gradually add 1 pound (455 g) shredded mild cheddar cheese (or Velveeta), stirring gently until fully incorporated. Serve immediately, or keep warm over low heat, stirring occasionally, until ready to use. The sauce can be made ahead of time, cooled, transferred to a container with a tight-fitting lid, and stored in the refrigerator for up to a week; reheat, stirring, in a saucepan over low heat, and spoon over the meat just before serving.

BEEF RICE BALLS (ARANCINI)

Arancini (rice balls) are hot and crispy on the outside and soft and creamy inside. They are a historic street food, purchased hot from Sicilian train station trolley vendors while in transit. Today many Sicilian American home cooks make larger versions, from recipes handed down through the generations, as a main course. But arancini are also served as a cocktail snack, an excellent use for leftover risotto. Meat sauce, with melty cheese and peas, is the typical filling, but it's fun to play around with other fillings. Shrimp Rice Balls (page 202), for example, make an excellent addition to a Feast of the Seven Fishes (see page 190) menu.

Makes twenty-four 2-inch (5 cm) balls

4 cups (950 ml) chicken broth, homemade (page 179) or store-bought, or beef broth

2 cups (370 g) Arborio or Carnaroli rice

2 teaspoons kosher salt

Pinch of saffron threads

¾ cup (75 g) finely grated Parmesan cheese

4 tablespoons (55 g) unsalted butter

3 large eggs

¼ cup (60 g) frozen peas, thawed (optional)

4 ounces (115 g) mozzarella cheese, cut into twenty-four ½-inch (1.25 cm) cubes

½ cup (115 g) Meat Sauce (page 49), cooled

1 cup (125 g) all-purpose flour

2 cups (210 g) dried breadcrumbs

2 to 3 cups (475 to 720 ml) extra virgin olive oil for frying (depending on the size of the pan)

Tomato Sauce (page 63) for serving

Bring the broth to a boil in a medium pot. Stir in the rice, salt, and saffron, reduce the heat to low, and simmer, stirring occasionally (especially toward the end), until the rice is tender and most of the liquid has evaporated, 18 to 20 minutes (if the water has evaporated before the rice is tender, add up to 1 cup/240 ml warm water). Stir in the Parmesan and butter, remove from the heat, and let cool.

Beat one of the eggs, stir into the rice until thoroughly combined, and spread the mixture out on a parchment-lined baking sheet, smoothing the top. Let cool completely.

Using a knife, score the rice mixture into 24 sections (to make sure the rice balls are evenly sized). Dip your hands in cool water and scoop up a section of cooked rice. Smooth it out a little in one hand and place a couple of peas, if using, a cube of mozzarella, and a spoonful of meat sauce in the center, then loosely close your hand around the rice mixture to enclose the filling and form a smooth ball, and transfer to a baking sheet. Repeat with the remaining rice and filling, laying the balls side by side on the pan. Cover and refrigerate for at least 20 minutes.

Beat the remaining 2 eggs together in a small bowl. Put the flour and breadcrumbs in two separate shallow bowls. Roll each rice ball in the flour, and then in the eggs to coat, and then roll in the breadcrumbs and return it to the baking pan.

Pour about ¾ inch (2 cm) of oil into a large heavy pot and heat over high heat until it bubbles up when a bit of rice is added; the temperature should be 375°F (190°C). Fry the balls in batches, without crowding the pot, turning them occasionally as they cook, until golden brown and crispy, 5 to 8 minutes. Remove from the oil, drain on a rack or paper towels, and serve immediately, with tomato sauce.

ASPETTA + Make-ahead: *There are several options for preparing and serving these. You can shape them, coat in the egg and flour, and cook, then refrigerate for a couple of days, then reheat the balls in a 400°F (200°C) oven until crisped and warm, less than 10 minutes. Alternatively, the arancini can be formed several days ahead and refrigerated (or frozen, well wrapped, for up to 6 months; thaw in the fridge), then bring them to room temperature, coat in the flour, eggs, and breadcrumbs, and cook them.*

LEMON ICE

Food references abound in stories of Italians in early twentieth-century America. Lemon ice and Tomato Pie (page 69) turn up over and over as treats for children purchased from the numerous Italian bakeries in their neighborhood enclaves. My earliest summer memory with my grandmother (besides picking pole beans) is of our special time together at the caffè, me eating a lemon ice, she an espresso granita topped with whipped cream. An ice is basically a Sicilian granita that's been blended with water to a fine texture before freezing it again.

Makes 6 servings

FOR THE SIMPLE SYRUP

½ cup (115 g) sugar

½ cup (120 ml) water

1 teaspoon grated lemon zest

1 cup (240 ml) fresh lemon juice (from 6 or 7 lemons)

¾ to 1 cup (180 to 240 ml) ice water

Make the simple syrup: Combine the sugar with the water in a small saucepan, stir well, and bring to a simmer, stirring occasionally, then cook, stirring, until the sugar is dissolved; remove from the heat and let cool.

Combine the lemon zest, juice, and 1 cup (240 ml) of the simple syrup (add water if needed to make 1 cup) in an 8-inch (20 cm) square baking pan, stirring well.

Cover the pan and place in the freezer. Every 30 minutes, rake the surface of the mixture with a fork to dislodge and distribute the ice crystals, and continue to freeze until it has a granular texture, 2 to 3 hours total.

After the mixture is frozen, transfer it to a blender or food processor, add ¾ cup (180 ml) of the ice water, and blend or process to a fine texture, adding a little more ice water if necessary. Divide the mixture among six 4-ounce (115 g) freezer-safe cups or small bowls, cover, and freeze for at least 4 hours, and up to 4 days.

When ready to serve, remove the ices from the freezer and let stand for 15 minutes.

ESPRESSO GRANITA

The only real attention required for this granita is the intermittent raking of the ice crystals as they form over a 2- or 3-hour period, something to weave into an afternoon of other household chores. This treat is summertime adult dessert perfection. Each bite offers a contrast of textures and temperatures: cold sweet coffee crystals shrouded in soft clouds of chocolate-curl-topped whipped cream.

Makes 6 servings

2 cups (475 ml) strong brewed espresso, still warm

¼ cup (50 g) sugar

1 cup (240 ml) water

1 cup (240 ml) heavy cream

8 ounces (225 g) bittersweet chocolate, shaved into curls

Pour the warm espresso into a bowl and stir in 3 tablespoons of the sugar until dissolved. Whisk in the water and let cool.

Pour the mixture into a 13-by-9-inch (33 by 23 cm) baking pan and place in the freezer. Every 30 minutes, rake the surface of the mixture with a fork to dislodge and distribute the ice crystals, and continue to freeze until it has a granular texture, 2 to 3 hours.

Combine the cream with the remaining tablespoon of sugar in a bowl and, using a whisk or handheld mixer, beat until soft peaks form, 2 to 4 minutes. Cover and refrigerate until ready to serve.

Scoop about ⅔ cup (100 g) of granita into each of six parfait glasses. Top each with a dollop of whipped cream and some shaved chocolate and serve.

TRADITIONAL
PASTRIES,
CAKES,
and
COOKIES

273 Tiramisu

275 Italian Sponge Cake

276 Nonny's Cannoli

279 Lena Strozzi's Chocolate Roll

282 Cassata Siciliana

284 Orange Olive Oil Cake with Whipped Ricotta Frosting

286 Ricotta Pie

289 Half-Pound Cake

291 Sherbet-Stuffed Frozen Lemons

292 Sweet Wine Taralli

296 Tarallucci (GLAZED LEMON KNOT COOKIES)

299 Biscotti Barricelli

300 Pistachio Drops

301 Chickie's Cherry Cookies

303 Chocolate Toto Cookies

304 Nana's Pizzelles

TALK TO ANY ITALIAN AMERICAN FOOD

lover about desserts, and you'll find that passions run hot! Traditionally, everyday dinners usually end with a piece of fruit, some wine-soaked peaches, or an icy granita. But at Sunday suppers and holidays, Italians let desserts shine.

Nothing captures the Italian American dessert imagination quite like the mighty Cannoli, star of special family meals as well as bakeries and street fairs. Tiramisu, which reigns over menus at establishments ranging from pizza parlors to high-end restaurants around the world, is a simple but impressive dessert to make at home. One of the first Italian desserts I learned at my gateway teenage cooking job was Cassata Siciliana. Every family has their personal favorite cakes, and Lena Strozzi's Chocolate Roll is mine. The do-ahead Sherbet-Stuffed Frozen Lemons go straight from freezer to plate for a creamy yet bracing finish to a meal. No Easter is complete without Ricotta Pie. Biscotti are a must in any Italian home, served alongside an after-dinner espresso or grappa. And Pizzelles are made with an ancient cooking technique, but when the cookies are sandwiched together with whipped cream, they become a modern take on an icebox cake.

The Italian cookie tray is a must at Christmas and at traditional weddings, with multiple varieties stacked on top of each other on platters. Turn to page 295 for techniques for baking and serving cookies at home during the holidays, along with packaging ideas for gifting cookies.

TIRAMISU

While this recipe was invented and popularized in Italy, it's become a beloved dessert on Italian American menus. Cake strips or ladyfingers, mascarpone, cocoa, and coffee are nonnegotiable ingredients, but, naturally, there are competing techniques. A creamy filling of raw egg yolks whipped over simmering water with wine and sugar (i.e., zabaglione) or a custard sauce make the dessert a little more complex tasting. I prefer the nutty, caramel flavor of the Marsala-whipped egg yolks, which in this recipe are then combined with mascarpone. Another, simpler approach is to fold plain whipped cream into mascarpone. The Italian Sponge Cake works beautifully here when cut into shapes and left overnight to dry out before assembling the dessert, but you can use store-bought Italian ladyfingers.

Makes 6 to 8 servings

1 recipe Italian Sponge Cake (page 275), baked in a 13-by-9-inch (33 by 23 cm) baking pan and cooled, or half a 1-pound (455 g) package savoiardi (Italian ladyfingers)

2 cups (475 ml) brewed espresso, chilled

1 tablespoon rum or whiskey (optional)

4 large egg yolks, at room temperature (refrigerate or freeze the whites for another use)

¼ cup (60 ml) dry Marsala wine

¼ cup (50 g) sugar

1 cup (240 g) mascarpone

2 tablespoons milk

Unsweetened cocoa powder for dusting

Chocolate shavings for garnish (optional)

If using the sponge cake, cut the cooled cake into thirty-four 6-by-4-inch (15 by 10 cm) rectangles and place on a baking sheet. Preheat the oven to 200°F (120°C) and turn it off, then transfer the baking sheet of cake to the oven and allow the pieces to dry out for at least several hours, or overnight.

Mix the espresso with the rum or whiskey, if using, in a small bowl (or just pour the espresso into a small bowl).

Set a large heatproof bowl over a saucepan of simmering water, add the egg yolks, Marsala, and sugar, and whisk until thick and foamy, 4 to 5 minutes. Remove from the heat and let cool completely.

In the bowl of a stand mixer fitted with the whisk attachment, or in a large bowl, using a handheld mixer, beat the mascarpone and milk together until smooth and somewhat thinner. Fold in the egg yolk mixture.

One at a time, dip half the cake rectangles or ladyfingers into the espresso, turning once to moisten both sides, and lay side by side in an 8-inch (20 cm) square baking pan. Spread half the mascarpone mixture on top, smoothing it out to cover the cake or ladyfingers completely. Using a small sieve, shake a fine layer of cocoa to cover. Repeat the process with the remaining cake or ladyfingers and mascarpone mixture, and

dust with cocoa. Pour any remaining espresso into the bottom of the pan (pour it around the edges of the tiramisu). Cover and refrigerate for at least 4 to 6 hours, or overnight.

Cut the tiramisu into squares to serve. Any leftovers can be stored in an airtight container in the refrigerator for up to 2 days.

ASPETTA ✛ *The Italian ladyfingers called savoiardi are typically used for tiramisu. Using them, of course, makes a quicker version than one with homemade cake. They are made from a sponge batter of flour, sugar, and whipped eggs or egg whites, with no other leavener. The outsides are crunchy and porous, but the inside is soft and airy, which lets them absorb the soaking liquid used for the dessert.*

ITALIAN SPONGE CAKE

Italian sponge cake, or pan di Spagna, can be used as a component for various desserts, depending on the pan you use. When made jelly-roll style, it can be rolled up with a filling. If cut into rectangular ladyfinger shapes, it's perfect for Tiramisu (page 273). If you bake it in a round pan and slice it horizontally in half, you can use it for a cream-filled cake such as cannoli cake or a layered birthday cake.

Makes one 8-inch-round (20 cm) cake or one 13-by-9-inch (33 by 23 cm) sheet cake

1 cup (120 g) all-purpose flour (or substitute pastry or cake flour for a more delicate crumb)

1 teaspoon baking powder

¼ teaspoon kosher salt

4 large eggs, at room temperature, separated

¾ cup (150 g) sugar

¼ teaspoon cream of tartar

¾ teaspoon vanilla

Preheat the oven to 325°F (165°C). Butter the baking pan, line it with parchment paper, and butter the paper.

Sift together the flour, baking powder, and salt into a small bowl.

Beat the egg yolks and sugar together in a large bowl until light yellow and foamy.

With an electric mixer or by hand, beat the egg whites in another large bowl until foamy. Add the cream of tartar and beat until stiff peaks form, 2 to 5 minutes. Carefully and gently (to avoid deflating the whites) fold the egg whites and vanilla and then the flour mixture into the egg yolks until just combined.

Pour the batter into the prepared pan and smooth the top. Bake until the cake is set and lightly golden on top, 12 to 14 minutes. Cool in the pan for 10 minutes before removing the cake to a rack to cool completely.

The cake can be stored in an airtight container in the refrigerator for up to 2 days before using.

NONNY'S CANNOLI

Cannoli are the undisputed queen of Sicilian and other southern Italian desserts, and arguably the most popular Sicilian dessert here. Big Italian family get-togethers from birthdays to weddings are celebrated with trays of cannoli. Hundreds were made for my Italian grandparents' fiftieth anniversary party to celebrate their May 18, 1918, marriage. This recipe is for traditional cannoli, but they can also be filled with chocolate cream, dipped in chocolate, and garnished with chopped pistachios. You will need to procure metal cannoli rings to make the shells. The fried shells can be kept in an airtight container for a couple of days, but fill them as close to serving time as possible. If the idea of frying puts you off, the batter for the shells can also be cooked in a pizzelle iron, then rolled up around the rings to set (see the Variation below).

Makes
12 to 16 cannoli

FOR THE SHELLS

- 1½ cups (190 g) all-purpose flour
- 1 tablespoon sugar
- ¾ teaspoon ground cinnamon
- ¼ teaspoon kosher salt
- 2 tablespoons cold unsalted butter, cut into small pieces
- ½ cup (120 ml) fortified wine, such as Marsala or port

FOR THE FILLING

- 2 cups (455 g) whole-milk ricotta cheese, drained if not thick
- ¼ cup (25 g) confectioners' sugar
- ½ teaspoon vanilla
- 2 ounces (55 g) semisweet or bittersweet chocolate, roughly chopped (⅓ cup)
- 1 heaping tablespoon chopped candied citrus, lemon, or orange, or a combination
- 2 to 3 tablespoons heavy cream or whole milk, if necessary
- 4 to 6 cups (950 ml to 1.5 L) vegetable oil for deep-frying
- Confectioners' sugar for dusting

SPECIAL EQUIPMENT

- 5-inch (13 cm) cannoli rings

FOR THE SHELLS: Whisk together the flour, sugar, cinnamon, and salt in a medium bowl. Using a pastry cutter or your fingers, work the butter into the dough until it resembles coarse meal. Pour the wine over the top and mix quickly to distribute it evenly and then blend it all into a ball. Cover the dough and refrigerate for at least 30 minutes, or up to overnight.

FOR THE FILLING: Combine the ricotta, confectioners' sugar, and vanilla in a medium bowl and beat by hand or with an electric mixer until smooth. Stir in the chocolate chips and citrus. If the mixture is too thin to pipe, chill it briefly until thickened. Or, if it is too thick (different types of ricotta have different consistencies), stir in a little heavy cream or whole milk. (*The filling can be made in advance and refrigerated for up to 2 days.*)

Cut the dough into 4 equal pieces. Work with one piece at a time, keeping the remaining dough covered as you work. On a lightly floured clean work surface, thinly roll one piece of dough out. Using a cookie cutter (or use an upturned bowl as a guide), cut out three 5-inch (13 cm) disks of dough. If desired,

reroll the scraps to get one more disk (it will be thicker than the others).

Roll up each disk of dough around a cannoli tube; brush one section of the dough with warm water and overlap the edges to seal (the shells will come undone when fried if not firmly "glued"). Repeat with the remaining dough and set aside on a tray. (If you have limited cannoli rings, shape and fry the cannoli in batches).

Line a tray with a towel for draining the fried shells. Fill a deep heavy pot with 3 to 4 inches (7.5 to 10 cm) of oil and heat over medium heat until hot; the oil should sizzle immediately if a small scrap of dough is dropped into it, and the temperature should be 375°F (190°C). Working in batches to avoid crowding, use a slotted metal spoon or tongs to lower the formed shells (on their rings) into the hot oil and fry until golden, 1 to 1½ minutes. Using the tongs or slotted spoon, transfer the fried shells to the lined tray and let cool for a couple of minutes, then carefully loosen the rings, remove them, and let the shells cool completely.

Spoon the ricotta mixture into a pastry bag fitted with a large tip, or transfer to a large resealable bag and snip off a bottom corner. Pressing the top of the bag gently, pipe the filling into both ends of each shell to fill it completely. Dust the top of the cannoli with confectioners' sugar and serve.

These are best eaten fresh, but you can loosely wrap any leftovers and refrigerate for up to a day.

VARIATION:

If you don't have cannoli rings but you do have a pizzelle iron (see page 304), you can cook the shells in the iron. Pour the batter for each shell into the iron and cook it according to the manufacturer's instructions; as soon as it is cooked, roll it up around an oiled 1-inch (2.5 cm) dowel to form a shell and let cool slightly before removing.

LENA STROZZI'S CHOCOLATE ROLL

When Lena Strozzi shared this recipe with my grandmother in 1946, she couldn't have imagined that in the future it would also be prized because it is gluten-free! The cake part of the roll, which gets its structure from whipped egg whites and cocoa powder, bakes for only 20 minutes. If your oven tends to run hot, check it after 15 minutes; it can easily overbake, which means it will crack when rolled. The loopy penciled writing in Mrs. Strozzi's recipe was scant on instructional details, but the ingredient quantities were spot-on; the addition of salt, which enhances all the flavors, something rarely seen in an old-time sweet recipe, is mine. The whole cake and filling can be made in under an hour, and it holds up well if chilled overnight in the refrigerator, making it a strategic yet spectacular presentation for a celebratory meal.

Makes one 12-inch (30 cm) roll; 8 to 10 servings

5 large eggs, at room temperature, separated

½ cup (100 g) sugar

3 tablespoons unsweetened cocoa powder, plus more for garnish

¼ teaspoon kosher salt

12 ounces (340 g) ricotta cheese, drained if not thick

3 tablespoons confectioners' sugar, plus more for garnish

½ teaspoon vanilla

1¼ ounces (45 g) semisweet chocolate, chopped (¼ cup)

2 tablespoons finely chopped candied citron

Preheat the oven to 325°F (165°C). Grease a 13-by-9-inch (33 by 23 cm) straight-sided baking sheet or a baking pan. Line it with parchment or wax paper, leaving an overhang on two opposite sides, and grease the paper.

In the bowl of a stand mixer fitted with the whisk attachment, or in a large bowl, using a handheld mixer, whip the egg whites to stiff peaks, 3 to 5 minutes. If using a stand mixer, transfer the whites to another bowl and set aside; clean the mixer bowl and return it to the mixer stand.

In the mixer bowl or another large bowl, beat the egg yolks until they begin to thicken, about 1 minute. Add the sugar, cocoa powder, and ⅛ teaspoon salt and beat until they are fully incorporated and the color turns to a pale brown, about 2 minutes. Fold in the egg whites until just combined.

Pour the batter into the prepared pan and smooth it evenly. Bake for about 20 minutes, until the cake is just set. Remove from the oven and let cool for about 10 minutes; the cake should still be slightly warm when you fill and roll it so it doesn't crack apart. Lift the cake out of the pan.

Meanwhile, in the clean mixer bowl or another large bowl, whip together the ricotta, confectioners' sugar, vanilla, and the

remaining ⅛ teaspoon salt until smooth and creamy, about 2 minutes. Stir in the chocolate and candied citron.

Spread the mixture evenly over the cake. Loosen the cake from the parchment paper. Starting at one narrow end, lift the paper and begin to roll up the cake, using the paper to help you and slightly tighten the cake as you roll it; end with the seam side down. Transfer the roll to a platter and refrigerate until ready to serve.

Just before serving, sift some confectioners' sugar and cocoa over the top of the roll. Slice into ¾-inch (2 cm) pieces to serve. Store any leftover cake in the refrigerator, loosely tented with foil or plastic wrap, for up to 4 days.

CASSATA SICILIANA

The top trio of Italian American desserts to my mind are cannoli, tiramisu, and Cassata Siciliana. This Americanized Sicilian recipe uses the filling from Nonny's Cannoli (page 276), mixed with dried cherries, layered into a sliced perfect pound cake. A store-bought cake can be substituted if you're short on time.

Makes one 9-by-5-inch (23 by 13 cm) loaf cake

1 recipe Half-Pound Cake (page 289)

1 recipe filling for Nonny's Cannoli (page 276)

½ cup (115 g) dried cherries, chopped

2½ ounces (70 g) unsweetened chocolate, chopped (½ cup)

⅓ cup (80 ml) heavy cream

¼ cup (50 g) sugar

3 tablespoons unsalted butter

Jarred Luxardo or Maraschino cherries (optional)

VARIATION:

For a more free-form version of this cake, don't cut the top off to level it. Build as directed right side up in the loaf pan. You'll have a more rustic (i.e., less professional-looking) domed dessert.

Line a 9-by-5-inch (23 by 13 cm) loaf pan with plastic wrap, leaving an overhang on the two long sides. Using a serrated knife, carefully slice off the dome of the cake to level the top (reserve the trimmings for a snack). Then slice the loaf horizontally into 3 equal slices.

Place the cannoli filling in a large bowl and add the cherries, mixing well.

Place the top slice of the cake upside down in the lined loaf pan and spread it evenly with half of the cannoli filling. Place the second layer upside down on top and spread evenly with the remaining filling. Place the third layer upside down on top. Cover the cake with the plastic wrap overhang and chill thoroughly, about 2 hours.

Place a heatproof bowl over a pot of simmering water. Add the chocolate, cream, sugar, and butter and stir until the chocolate is melted and well combined. Remove from the heat and let cool slightly, to warm.

Remove the cake from the refrigerator and pull back the plastic. Place a rectangular or oval platter on top and turn over the loaf pan to remove the cake. Remove the plastic wrap. Spread the chocolate glaze evenly over the top of the cake and dot with a line of jarred cherries down the center, if desired. Chill the cake until ready to serve. (If making it in advance, tent the cake with foil to keep the glaze from sticking.)

One hour before serving, remove the cake from the refrigerator. To serve, cut the cake into 1-inch (2.5 cm) slices. Store any leftovers tightly covered in the refrigerator for up to 4 days.

ORANGE OLIVE OIL CAKE with WHIPPED RICOTTA FROSTING

A note on the handwritten recipe card for this cake in my family files says it's "From Mrs. Reggia, 1940." I wonder how her friends in the 1940s interpreted the last line of the recipe: "Beat well & bake in layers in a moderate oven." But while there are scant details, the bones of the recipe work beautifully. Citrus and dried fruit in many forms are often featured in early Italian dessert recipes, since back in southern Italy and Sicily, sugar was scarce and expensive but citrus was plentiful. Rehydrated raisins enhance both the sweetness and texture of this cake. It cries out for a creamy counterpoint, so here it's topped with ricotta whipped with confectioners' sugar and vanilla until smooth.

Makes one 8-inch (20 cm) layer cake; 8 servings

1 orange, scrubbed, cut into small pieces (including rind), and seeds removed

½ cup (115 g) raisins, soaked in hot water until plump and drained

1 cup (200 g) sugar

½ cup (120 ml) extra virgin olive oil

2 large eggs

2 cups (240 g) all-purpose flour

1 cup (240 ml) buttermilk

1 teaspoon baking soda

Large pinch of kosher salt

FOR THE FROSTING

12 ounces (340 g) ricotta cheese, drained if not thick

½ cup (65 g) confectioners' sugar

1 teaspoon vanilla

1 tablespoon raw sugar (optional)

Preheat the oven to 350°F (175°C). Brush two 8-inch (20 cm) round cake pans with olive oil.

Pulse together the orange and raisins in a food processor until finely minced.

In the bowl of a stand mixer fitted with the paddle attachment, or in a large bowl, using a handheld mixer, beat together the sugar and olive oil on high speed. Reduce the speed to medium and beat in the eggs and then the raisin-orange mixture. Add half the flour and half the buttermilk, the baking soda, and salt and mix to combine. Beat in the remaining flour and buttermilk until the batter is smooth.

Divide the batter evenly between the prepared pans. Bake for 25 to 30 minutes, or until a toothpick inserted into the thickest part of a cake comes out clean. Remove from the oven and let cool in the pans for 15 to 20 minutes.

Invert the cake layers onto a rack and let stand for 1 hour, or until completely cooled.

Make the frosting: Combine the ricotta, confectioners' sugar, and vanilla in a food processor and process until completely smooth and thickened, 3 to 4 minutes.

Using a serrated knife, slice the top off one of the cake layers to level it. Place it cut side down on a serving platter and spread half of the frosting over it. Top with the second layer and spread the remaining frosting over the top. (Leave the sides unadorned.) Refrigerate until ready to serve.

If desired, sprinkle the raw sugar over the top of the cake, and cut into slices to serve. Store any leftover cake in the refrigerator, loosely tented with foil or plastic wrap, for up to 4 days.

RICOTTA PIE

No Easter celebration is complete without a ricotta pie. Italian American bakeries make and sell dozens, yet it's very easy to make at home. I usually make a couple and gift one. The two main ingredients, eggs and wheat berries, symbolize rebirth and renewal. The grains offer a toothsome textural chew suspended in the creamy, citrusy egg filling. Hulled wheat berries are easily found at health food stores, but farro or spelt can be substituted. The grains must be soaked, cooked, and drained before using them in the filling. But you can omit them if you want, letting the dough itself represent wheat.

Makes one 9-inch (23 cm) lattice-topped pie

¼ cup (57 g) hulled wheat berries, spelt, or farro

4 large egg whites

Pinch of cream of tartar

2 cups (455 g) ricotta cheese, drained if not thick

⅓ cup (40 g) confectioners' sugar

½ teaspoon vanilla

½ teaspoon grated orange zest

½ teaspoon ground cinnamon

1 recipe Pasta Frolla (recipe follows)

Whole milk, cream, or beaten egg for brushing the top of the crust

1 to 2 tablespoons granulated sugar

Bring 4 cups (950 ml) salted water to a boil in a medium saucepan. Add the wheat berries, spelt, or farro and boil until tender, about 1 hour. Drain and let cool.

Preheat the oven to 375°F (190°C).

In the bowl of a stand mixer fitted with the whisk attachment, or in a large bowl, with a handheld mixer, whip the egg whites with the cream of tartar to stiff peaks, 4 to 5 minutes. Transfer the whites to another bowl if using a stand mixer, and place the bowl of whites in the fridge. Clean the mixer bowl and reattach it to the mixer stand.

Combine the ricotta, sugar, and vanilla in the mixer bowl or another large bowl and whip until smooth and creamy, about 2 minutes. Stir in the wheat berries, orange zest, and cinnamon.

On a lightly floured surface, roll out one disk of Pasta Frolla dough into an 11-inch (28 cm) round and fit it into a 9-inch (23 cm) pie plate. Trim the edges flush with the edges of the plate. Roll out the second disk of dough and cut it into 10 equal strips.

Fold the reserved egg whites into the ricotta mixture and pour it into the pie shell. Weave the dough strips over the top of the filling to form a lattice pattern. Trim the ends of the strips flush with the edges of the bottom crust. Using a fork, crimp the strips and the bottom crust together around the entire

edge. Lightly brush some milk, cream, or beaten egg over the lattice strips and edge of the bottom crust, then sprinkle a light dusting of sugar over the top.

Bake for 30 to 40 minutes, or until the edges of the pie are golden brown and the center is set. Remove from the oven and let cool slightly before serving.

The pie can be stored in the refrigerator, loosely tented with foil or plastic wrap, for up to 4 days.

PASTA FROLLA

This sweet pastry is an all-around recipe for multiple Italian desserts. It's a very workable dough for any level of baker, as it mixes quickly, firms up beautifully after 30 minutes of chilling, and rolls out easily. The olive oil lends it a unique flavor, and the sugar-salt balance is just right without being too sweet. It has a cookie-like crispness rather than the flakiness of a French pâte brisée. The recipe can be made by hand or in a food processor.

Makes two 9-inch (23 cm) piecrusts

2 cups (240 g) all-purpose flour

½ cup (100 g) sugar

¾ teaspoon kosher salt

½ teaspoon baking powder

4 large egg yolks, beaten (reserve the whites for another use)

¼ cup (60 ml) olive oil

¼ cup (60 ml) cold water

1 teaspoon vanilla or other extract

In a large bowl, whisk together the flour, sugar, salt, and baking powder. Drizzle over the beaten egg yolks, olive oil, water, and vanilla and stir to combine, then mix the dough together by squeezing it with your hands into a ball. Or, if using a food processor, pulse together the flour, sugar, salt, and baking powder, then add the egg yolks, olive oil, water, and extract and pulse several times, just until the dough comes together in a ball.

Turn the dough out, divide it into two pieces, shape each one into a disk, and wrap each one in plastic wrap. Chill for 30 minutes before using. (*The dough can be frozen for up to 6 months. Defrost at room temperature for 1 hour before using.*)

VARIATION:

To make a crostata, an open-faced tart, with this dough, roll it out into a rough 10-inch (25 cm) circle and place it on a parchment-lined baking sheet. Spread a thick layer of your favorite jam or marmalade all over the dough (and top with thin sliced plums or peaches, if you like), leaving a border all around. Fold the edges of the dough over toward the center to form a free-form round. Bake in a 350°F (175°C) oven for 25 to 30 minutes, until the crust is golden brown. Serve with sweetened whipped ricotta.

HALF-POUND CAKE

Experienced bakers know that equal weights of butter, sugar, eggs, and flour blended with a touch of vanilla will yield a perfect classic pound cake. This recipe calls for *half-pound* measures of each to achieve the gold standard of pound cakes; a golden domed rectangle with a vertical crevice on top and a delicate crumb that's just moist enough. The butter and eggs must be at room temperature. Using cup measures is less accurate than measuring by weight, so use a scale if you have one. Slice the cake and top with fresh berries and whipped cream, glaze with your icing of choice, or serve plain with coffee; this recipe is also the base for the Cassata Siciliana (page 282).

Makes one 9-by-5-inch (23 by 13 cm) loaf cake

8 ounces (2 sticks/225 g) unsalted butter, at room temperature

8 ounces (1¼ cups/225 g) sugar

8 ounces (225 g) eggs (4 to 5 large eggs), at room temperature

8 ounces (1½ cups/225 g) all-purpose flour

½ teaspoon kosher salt

½ teaspoon vanilla

Preheat the oven to 325°F (165°C). Butter a 9-by-5-inch (23 by 13 cm) loaf pan.

In the bowl of a stand mixer fitted with the paddle attachment, or in a large bowl, using a hand mixer, beat the butter and sugar until light and fluffy, 2 to 3 minutes. Add the eggs one at a time, beating until each one is fully incorporated, about 30 seconds, before adding the next. Slowly add the flour and salt, and then the vanilla, beating until just combined; don't overmix.

Add the batter to the prepared loaf pan and smooth the top. Bake for about 1 hour and 10 minutes: When the first delicious scents start wafting from the oven (after about 1 hour), start testing at 5-minute intervals by inserting a toothpick into the thickest part of the cake; it should come out clean.

Remove the cake from the oven and let cool in the pan for 15 minutes, then invert the cake onto a wire rack, turn it right side up, and let cool completely.

ASPETTA + Room-temperature ingredients: *Bringing the eggs and butter to room temperature ensures uniform results in a cake like this. When the components are mixed, the batter will fully emulsify and trap air that will expand during baking for an even, fluffy texture.*

SHERBET-STUFFED FROZEN LEMONS

Italian American food is all about evolution. Think of this beautiful presentation as Lemon Ice 2.0. It's an unusual, festive, make-ahead dessert for a bracingly refreshing finish to any summer meal. Or serve these citrus charmers after any seafood meal, especially at the holidays. They pair beautifully with the Tarallucci (page 296) for a double dose of lemon. If you make these on a rainy day to stock the freezer, you will always have something special to pull out for a sweet treat.

Makes 6 servings

6 large lemons (about 6½ ounces/185 g each)

1 recipe Lemon Ice (page 265), prepared and frozen

4 ounces (115 g) mascarpone cheese

Cut off the top third of each lemon and set aside. Slice a thin disk off the bottom of each one so they will stand up without falling over. Carefully juice the lemons without breaking the skin (use the juice for the Lemon Ice recipe). Using a bird's beak knife, grapefruit spoon, or small sharp spoon, scrape all the pulp and membranes from the lemons and reserved tops (use for the Lemon Ice or freeze for future use). Rinse the lemon shells and tops in water and smooth out the insides with your finger.

Place the lemon shells and tops on a tray and freeze them completely. (If not using them right away, once they are frozen, place in a resealable freezer bag and freeze until ready to fill.)

Place the lemon ice and mascarpone in a food processor or blender and blend until completely combined and smooth. If the sherbet is too soft, freeze it for a bit before filling the lemons. Mound a scoop of sherbet into each lemon shell and crown with a lemon top. Freeze for at least a couple of hours, until the sherbet has completely firmed up. (*The stuffed lemons can be stored in a resealable freezer container for up to 6 months.*)

Serve in parfait glasses or dessert bowls.

SWEET WINE TARALLI

Historically, taralli were savory cookies, originating in Puglia and reputedly devised by starving peasants who found a way to transform leftover bread scraps into something edible—crunchy baked bread bits eaten soaked in seawater! Eventually taralli became popular throughout the south, most notably those from Neapolitan seaside street vendors. Styles varied from region to region but were often served with wine. My grandmother's old recipe files contain more than six slightly different versions, all attributed to various relatives. My father loved this one, from his aunt Carolina Scala, the best. The icing is optional.

Makes 2½ dozen cookies

3 cups (375 g) all-purpose flour

2 teaspoons baking powder

1 teaspoon kosher salt

½ cup (100 g) sugar

1 large egg

½ cup (120 ml) extra virgin olive oil

½ cup (120 ml) Marsala wine

FOR THE GLAZE (OPTIONAL)

1 cup (125 g) confectioners' sugar

2 tablespoons milk, plus more if necessary

1 tablespoon fresh lemon juice

Preheat the oven to 375°F (190°C). Line two baking sheets with parchment paper or silicone baking mats.

Whisk together the flour, baking powder, and salt in a large bowl.

Beat together the sugar and egg in a small bowl until well combined. Stir in the olive oil and wine. Make a well in the center of the dry mixture and slowly stir in the wet mixture until the dough thickens and the well collapses. Finish by kneading the dough a few times in the bowl until smooth, slightly soft, and easy to handle without sticking.

Scoop out the dough into thirty-six 1-inch (2.5 cm) balls and put on a tray. On a clean work surface, roll each ball into a 6-inch-long (15 cm), ½-inch-diameter (1.25 cm) "cigar" shape. Form each one into a loop, press the ends of the dough together with your fingers to seal, and place the cookies side by side on the lined baking sheets.

Place the pans side by side on one oven rack or on separate racks (switching the top one for the bottom halfway through if using two racks) and bake the taralli for 15 to 20 minutes, until golden on the bottom. Remove from the oven and cool the cookies completely on a wire rack.

To make the optional glaze, whisk together the confectioners' sugar, milk, and lemon juice in a bowl until the mixture is the consistency of thick whipping cream; add more milk if necessary. Dip the top of each cookie into the glaze and transfer to a wire rack to dry.

Handwritten recipe cards:

Card 1 (top):
2 eggs
1¾ cup sugar
1 cup white wine
¼ oil
5 cups flour
4 tsp bk powd)

(Pencil)
Blend eggs + sugar
add oil and wine
add sifted flour + bkpd
Knead and Roll
Bake @ 375° 20 mm

Card 2 (middle):
Aunt Mame Wine Taralli
1 cup sugar
4 eggs
1 cup of oil o butter melted
1 " of sherry wine
4 Tsps. Bke Powd — (6-7 cups flour)
Flour - as much as it takes to handle
dough medium soft - Roll and
Bake @ 375° 20 mm -

Card 3 (lower left):
Taralli
12 eggs
1½ cup sugar
6 tsp baking powder
¼ lb. butter
enough flour to roll - Roll an bake

Ice 1 cup egg white + powd sugar

Card 4 (bottom):
Easter Taralli (Boiled)
10 eggs
¾ cup sugar
1 tab lard
wine glass   8 cups flour
place in boiling water
+ top - cut

ASPETTA ✛ Boil before baking: *Some taralli recipes direct you to boil them before baking, like the way a bagel is cooked. That step will assure a glossy sheen on the outside of the taralli, which is desirable for savory versions that are eaten naked like crackers or chips with an aperitivo. I've tried the recipe both ways and find the boiling step unnecessary.*

THE ITALIAN COOKIE TRAY

Like the American tradition of gifting holiday cookie boxes, Italian cookie trays are ubiquitous at holiday times, especially Christmas, but also for all the gatherings surrounding the rituals of the Catholic Church, including baptisms, confirmations, weddings, and funerals. Platters of various sizes are stacked with pyramids of cookies in multiple shapes, sizes, flavors, and colors.

Southern Italy, especially around Naples, has dozens of different specialized versions of small cookies, and many treasured recipes traveled to the New World with the arriving families. Today Italian bakeries across the United States stock multiple popular varieties, but, unfortunately, when you get them home, they often all taste the same. Within families nowadays, folks seem to be known for a few chosen specialties accumulated over the generations. In extended groups of family and friends, everyone makes an abundance of one or two favorite cookies and swaps with each other (or brings them to a party) to make trays with a full variety. It's important that the cookies on the tray have a range of flavors and color tones, for building an interesting grouping.

"Traying," or making cookies for your personal tray, requires some forethought and decisions when constructing it. For serving at home, choose one of your favorite flat platters or trays and line it with an attractive doily, food-safe paper, or cloth. You want to end up with a pyramid-shaped mound, so the bottom layer must be one of your sturdiest cookies, like Taralli (page 292) or Biscotti (page 299). Continue to layer with other solid choices, like Pistachio Drops (page 300) or Chickie's Cherry Cookies (page 301); be mindful to contrast colors and shapes for a pleasing look. End with the most delicate cookies or filled varieties on top. Or consider an additional side-car tray for the fragile ones.

If you don't have an old-fashioned army of Italian bakers in the family, consider creating a tray with a combination of your most beloved homemade recipes along with a few reliable store-bought types. You want a combination of dropped, rolled, filled, and bar-style cookies. The classic rainbow cookies, made with three different-colored almond cake layers, filled with jam, and topped with chocolate, are labor-intensive, and tricky for the home baker, but many bakeries make good ones. Same with struffoli; I leave those tiny mounds of fried dough doused in honey syrup to the professionals.

To give an Italian cookie tray as a gift, line a basket or tin with a special cloth. Fill it with the cookies, separating the layers with pieces of colorful baking parchment. Set the container on top of a large sheet of cellophane wrap, gather the edges together at the top, and tie and seal with a festive ribbon or simple piece of twine. Hang a handwritten label with the names of the cookies on it.

TARALLUCCI
(GLAZED LEMON KNOT COOKIES)

These looped wedding cookies from southern Italy allegedly originally symbolized tying the knot. The dough, flavored with citrus, is forgiving and easy to shape, and the lemon flavor is echoed in the glazed topping. The baked cookies, glazed or unglazed, keep well for several days in a sealed container. Or make a batch ahead, cool, refrigerate or freeze, and glaze before serving.

Makes 42 cookies

3 to 3½ cups (375 to 450 g)
   all-purpose flour

2 teaspoons baking powder

1 teaspoon kosher salt

3 large eggs

½ cup (100 g) sugar

½ cup (120 ml) extra virgin olive oil

3 tablespoons heavy cream

Grated zest of 1 medium lemon

2 tablespoons fresh lemon juice

1 teaspoon vanilla

FOR THE GLAZE

2 cups (250 g) confectioners'
   sugar

Grated zest of 2 medium lemons

3 tablespoons fresh lemon juice

1 tablespoon heavy cream

Pinch of coarse salt

Preheat the oven to 350°F (175°C). Line two baking sheets with parchment paper or silicone baking mats.

Whisk together 3 cups (375 g) flour, the baking powder, and salt in a medium bowl.

In the bowl of a stand mixer fitted with the whisk attachment, or in a large bowl, with a handheld mixer, whip the eggs on high speed until frothy, about 3 minutes. Reduce the speed to medium and slowly pour in the sugar, then continue beating until the mixture thickens and forms a ribbon when the beater is lifted, about 2 minutes. Mix in the oil, cream, lemon zest and juice, and vanilla until completely combined. On low speed, blend in the flour mixture until a dough that is soft and slightly tacky forms, 3 to 4 minutes; add a little more flour if needed.

Scoop out the dough into twenty-one 2-inch (5 cm) balls. On a clean work surface, roll each ball into a 10-inch-long (25 cm), ½-inch-diameter (1.25 cm) cigar shape. Cut each one in half, form each piece into a knot, and place the cookies side by side on the lined baking sheets.

Put the pans side by side on one oven rack or on separate racks (switching the top one for the bottom halfway through) and bake for 18 to 20 minutes, until the cookies are golden on the bottom. Remove from the oven and cool the cookies on a wire rack.

To make the glaze, whisk together the confectioners' sugar, lemon zest and juice, heavy cream, and salt in a bowl. Dip the top of each cooled cookie into the glaze and let dry.

BISCOTTI BARRICELLI

This is a classic version of biscotti from the Barricelli family, generations of Italian American bakers that began with Giuseppe in the 1900s. His panetteria in Williamsburg, Brooklyn, was named after his hometown of Nola, Italy. Today his great-grandson John (my friend and the sole man in our Martha Stewart TV kitchen) continues the family trade at his SoNo bakeries in Connecticut. Note that other nuts, such as hazelnuts or macadamias, can be substituted for the almonds.

Makes 30 cookies

- 2½ cups (315 g) all-purpose flour
- 2 tablespoons coarse yellow cornmeal
- 2 teaspoons baking powder
- ¾ cup (150 g) sugar, plus more for sprinkling
- 8 tablespoons (1 stick/115 g) salted butter, at room temperature
- 1 teaspoon kosher salt
- 2 large eggs, at room temperature
- 1 tablespoon anise seeds
- 1 cup (140 g) whole almonds, coarsely chopped
- 1 egg, beaten, for egg wash

Preheat the oven to 350°F (175°C). Line a baking sheet with parchment paper or a silicone baking mat.

Whisk together the flour, cornmeal, and baking powder in a medium bowl.

In the bowl of a stand mixer fitted with the paddle attachment, or in a large bowl, with a handheld mixer, beat the sugar, butter, and salt until light and fluffy, 2 to 3 minutes. Add the eggs and beat until blended. With the mixer on low speed, add the dry ingredients and beat until well combined. Fold in the anise seeds and almonds.

Turn the dough out onto a lightly floured surface and divide it in half. With floured hands, gently roll each half into a log about 17 inches (43 cm) long and 2 inches (5 cm) wide. Using two spatulas, carefully transfer the logs to the prepared baking sheet, leaving space between them. Press down on the top of each one with your palms to flatten. Brush with the egg wash and sprinkle with sugar.

Bake, rotating the pan two-thirds of the way through, for about 20 minutes, until the logs are a light golden brown and spring back when you press on the thickest point.

Remove the logs from the oven (leave the oven on) and let cool for 10 minutes. Using two spatulas, carefully transfer one log at a time to a cutting board. Using a serrated knife and sawing motion, cut the logs on the diagonal into ¾-inch (2 cm) slices. Return the slices to the baking sheet, laying each one on its side, and bake for about 12 minutes, until the biscotti are completely dried and browned on the edges. Cool the biscotti for 10 minutes on the baking sheet and then transfer to a wire rack to cool completely. Store for up to a month.

PISTACHIO DROPS

The original family recipe for this cookie calls for commercial pistachio pudding, no doubt added during the post–World War I rise in food manufacturing when convenience items became all the rage. But it's a difficult product to find today, so this recipe gives pistachio extract as an option. Just as in Chickie's Cherry Cookies (opposite), the food coloring is optional, but a little will enhance the beautiful natural green tone of the cookie inside the nutty coating.

Makes 64 cookies

3 ½ cups (440 g) all-purpose flour

2 teaspoons baking powder

1 teaspoon kosher salt

1 cup (130 g) shelled pistachios, finely chopped

8 tablespoons (1 stick/115 g) unsalted butter, at room temperature

1 cup (200 g) granulated sugar

2 large eggs, at room temperature

½ cup (120 ml) milk

¾ teaspoon pistachio or vanilla extract

A couple drops of green food coloring (optional)

Whisk together the flour, baking powder, salt, and ½ cup (65 g) of the pistachios in a medium bowl.

In the bowl of a stand mixer fitted with the paddle attachment, or in a large bowl, with a handheld mixer, cream together the butter and sugar until fluffy, 3 to 4 minutes. Add the eggs one at a time, beating to fully incorporate the first one before adding the second one, then blend until thoroughly combined. Slowly pour in the flour mixture to combine, then continue mixing, adding the milk, pistachio extract, and food coloring (if using), halfway through, until the dough is thoroughly blended. Cover the dough and chill for 30 minutes.

Preheat the oven to 350°F (175°C). Line two baking sheets with parchment or silicone baking mats.

Pour the remaining pistachios into a small bowl. Scoop out 1-inch (2.5 cm) balls of the dough onto a tray (alternatively, each piece can be formed into an oblong shape) and roll each one in the chopped pistachios. Arrange the cookies 1 inch (2.5 cm) apart on the lined baking sheets.

Put the pans side by side on one oven rack or on separate racks (switching the top one for the bottom halfway through if using two racks) and bake for 12 to 14 minutes, until the bottoms are golden brown. Remove from the oven and cool on a wire rack.

Store the cookies in an airtight container for up to 1 week.

CHICKIE'S CHERRY COOKIES

Family friend Chickie, so the story goes, like so many Italian brides, learned to cook from her husband's mother. The slice-and-bake method is my make-ahead addition to her recipe. These contribute a contrasting shape (and pretty pink color) to the other drop cookies on our cookie tray. During the holiday cooking bustle, it's always wise to have a couple logs of frozen cookie dough on hand. See the Variations below for the original shaping method.

Makes 48 cookies

3 cups (360 g) all-purpose flour

2 teaspoons baking powder

½ teaspoon kosher salt

8 tablespoons (1 stick/115 g) unsalted butter, at room temperature

1 cup (100 g) sugar, plus more for glazing

½ cup (100 g) jarred Luxardo or Maraschino cherries, finely chopped, plus 2 tablespoons juice from the jar

2 large eggs

1 teaspoon almond or vanilla extract

A couple drops of red food coloring (optional)

1 egg white, beaten, for glazing

Whisk together the flour, baking powder, and salt in a medium bowl.

In the bowl of a stand mixer fitted with the paddle attachment, or in a large bowl, with a handheld mixer, beat together the butter, sugar, and cherries for 2 to 3 minutes. Add the eggs one at a time, beating to fully incorporate the first one before adding the second one, then blend until fully combined.

Slowly pour in the flour mixture, beating on low speed to combine and then continue to beat, adding the almond or vanilla extract, cherry juice, and, if desired, the food coloring (to achieve a pink color) halfway through, until the dough is well mixed. Cover and chill until firm, about 2 hours.

Divide the dough in half and form into two 11-inch-long (28 cm) logs, about 1½ inches (4 cm) in diameter (I use a paper towel tube slit lengthwise to form the logs). Wrap the logs tightly in plastic wrap, twist the ends to seal, and chill until firm, at least 2 hours. (*The dough can be refrigerated for up to 1 week or frozen for up to 2 months; defrost in the refrigerator before moving on.*)

Preheat the oven to 350°F (175°C). Line two baking sheets with parchment paper or silicone baking mats.

Recipe continues

Unwrap the dough logs and brush them all over with the beaten egg white to coat. Spread some sugar on a small baking sheet and roll the logs in the sugar to coat. Cut the logs into ¼-inch (0.65 cm) slices and place the cookies 1 inch (2.5 cm) apart on the lined baking sheets.

Put the pans side by side on one oven rack or on separate racks (switching the top one for the bottom halfway through if using two racks) and bake for 10 to 13 minutes, until the cookies are golden on the bottom. Remove from the oven and cool on a wire rack.

Store the cookies in an airtight container for up to 1 week.

VARIATIONS:

These can be made as drop cookies: After the dough chills, scoop out 1-inch (2.5 cm) balls of dough onto the baking sheets and bake as directed.

Make a thumbprint version by pressing your thumb into the center of each drop cookie halfway through baking. For an attractive display, add a cherry to the center of each one just before serving.

ASPETTA ✦ Fat for cookie baking: *Lard or Crisco is called for in most of the original versions of Italian American cookie recipes. Lard was originally used, and then replaced with Crisco vegetable shortening, which was inexpensive and shelf-stable, when it arrived on the scene in the early part of the twentieth century. Crisco gives a similar flakiness to a cookie as lard but without the "gamey" flavor. Cookies made with butter bake differently; it improves the flavor, but they will spread out more, and the edges will tend toward a golden crisp.*

CHOCOLATE TOTO COOKIES

Regulars on the Ferlo family cookie tray and ubiquitous in Italian American homes at Christmas, these are alternately called tetu or tutu, meaning "one for you and one for me." And they are sometimes referred to as Italian meatball cookies. Indeed, they bake into round brown cake-like morsels. The cookies originated in Sicily, where they're traditionally made on All Saints' Day, November 1. Over the decades, old-time recipes have used first lard, and then Crisco, and now I like to use olive oil or coconut oil. For a crinkly white exterior, the cookies are rolled in confectioners' sugar before baking.

Makes 40 cookies

3 cups (375 g) all-purpose flour

½ cup (50 g) unsweetened cocoa powder

1 tablespoon baking powder

½ teaspoon kosher salt

½ teaspoon ground cinnamon

¼ teaspoon ground allspice

⅛ teaspoon ground cloves

2 large eggs

¾ cup (150 g) sugar

½ cup (120 ml) whole milk

¼ cup (60 ml) olive oil or coconut oil

½ teaspoon grated orange zest

¼ cup (60 ml) fresh orange juice

½ teaspoon vanilla

½ cup (115 g) chocolate chips

1 cup (125 g) confectioners' sugar

Whisk together the flour, cocoa, baking powder, salt, cinnamon, allspice, and cloves in a medium bowl.

In the bowl of a stand mixer fitted with the paddle attachment, or in a large bowl, with a handheld mixer, beat together the eggs and sugar until frothy, 3 to 4 minutes. Beat in the milk, oil, orange zest and juice, and vanilla. Reduce the speed and slowly add the flour mixture, beating until it is completely combined. Stir in the chocolate chips. Cover the dough and chill until it is firm.

Preheat the oven to 350°F (175°C). Line two baking sheets with parchment paper or silicone mats. Pour the confectioners' sugar into a bowl.

Scoop out the dough into 1-inch (2.5 cm) balls and place them on a tray or baking sheet. Roll each dough ball in the confectioners' sugar to thickly coat and place them side by side on the lined baking sheets, leaving 1 inch (2.5 cm) between them.

Place the pans side by side on one oven rack or on separate racks (switching the top one for the bottom halfway through if using two racks) and bake the cookies for 8 to 10 minutes, until slightly firm. Remove from the oven and cool the cookies completely on a wire rack.

Store the cookies in an airtight container for up to 1 week.

NANA'S PIZZELLES

This cookie from the Abruzzo region in Italy is reputed to be the oldest cookie in history. You will need a pizzelle iron to make these. In the Old Country, a cookie iron, emblazoned with the couple's initials, was a fashionable wedding gift. These cookies make a wonderful addition to a cookie tray. They are very versatile: crispy, citrusy, and not too sweet eaten on their own, but also delicious topped with sweetened ricotta and raspberries, slathered with hazelnut spread, or turned into an ice cream sandwich.

Don't despair when cooking your first one—it takes a few tries to get the hang of it. The familiar scent of a golden baked cookie indicates that it's ready to come out of the iron. And this batter is very forgiving: once the cookies are cooled, any wonky edges will break off for a clean circle (although the imperfect ones look charmingly homemade).

Makes 16 cookies

1¾ cups (220 g) all-purpose flour

2 teaspoons baking powder

¾ teaspoon kosher salt

3 large eggs, beaten

¾ cup (150 g) sugar

8 tablespoons (1 stick/115 g) butter, melted and cooled

1½ teaspoons vanilla

1½ teaspoons pure anise extract

1½ teaspoons pure orange extract

1½ teaspoons lemon extract

SPECIAL EQUIPMENT

Pizzelle iron

Whisk together the flour, baking powder, and salt in a small bowl.

Beat the eggs and sugar together in a medium bowl until smooth and fluffy, about 1 minute. Stir in the cooled melted butter and all the extracts. Fold in the flour mixture until well combined.

Preheat the pizzelle iron. For each pizzelle, place a rounded tablespoon of batter in the center of the iron. Close it and press down lightly. Cook until most of the cookie is golden, 60 to 90 seconds (depending on the type of iron). Transfer to a wire rack to cool.

Store the pizzelles in an airtight container, layered between pieces of parchment paper, for up to 2 weeks or freeze for 2 months.

ASPETTA ✛ Pizzelle irons: *These irons vary in size and heat level. Nowadays most are nonstick and indicate readiness with a light that turns on when the cookie is done; each cookie usually take a little over a minute to bake. Units with 2 to 4 cookie sections within them are worthwhile if you make pizzelles often. But if you are a once-a-year pizzelle maker, single-cookie irons are compact and easy to store.*

Recipe continues

VARIATION:

For a quickly made icebox-style cake, whip 1 quart (950 ml) heavy cream with ⅓ cup (65 g) sugar. Fold in some chopped candied citrus fruit and/or chocolate bits, if desired. Spread each pizzelle with a layer of cream and sandwich them one next to the other, vertically, on a serving platter. Loosely cover and refrigerate for 4 hours (so the pizzelles can absorb some of the cream and soften). Dust with cocoa powder or confectioners' sugar before slicing and serving.